A Penny a Copy

A Penny a Copy

 Readings from The Catholic Worker

Edited by THOMAS C. CORNELL *and* JAMES H. FOREST

The Macmillan Company, New York
Collier-Macmillan Ltd., London

TO PETER, TO DOROTHY
and to all those who came

Library of Congress Catalog Card Number: 68–18870

FIRST PRINTING

The Macmillan Company, New York
Collier-Macmillan Canada Ltd., Toronto, Ontario

Printed in the United States of America

Contents

1445487

PART IV · RADICALS IN ACTION 1956–

Preface

DOROTHY DAY wrote, in the Postscript to her book *The Long Loneliness*, of the beginnings of the Catholic Worker movement:

> We were just sitting there when Peter Maurin came in.
> We were just sitting there when lines of people began to form, saying, "We need bread." We could not say, "Go, be thou filled." If there were six small loaves and a few fishes, we had to divide them. There was always bread.
> We were just sitting there talking and people moved in on us. Let those who can take it, take it. Some moved out and that made room for more. And somehow the walls expanded.
> We were just sitting there and someone said, "Let's all go live on a farm."
> It was as casual as that, I often think. It just came about. It just happened . . .
> It all happened while we sat there talking, and it is still going on.

These pages represent articles printed in *The Catholic Worker*, the organ of the Catholic Worker movement, over the years since 1933, when the first issue of the CW was sold on Union Square, during a Communist Party rally on May Day, for a penny a copy. The price of the paper has remained the same to this day.

Much has changed since that year deep in the Depression. But much has remained substantially the same. World War II did not end the Depression, not for at least one fifth of the United States population. And most of the rest of the world would envy the living standards of the American Depression.

Indeed, it is still going on. The jacket of this volume pictures a slum neighborhood, a street of tenements and storefronts near the Williamsburg Bridge in Manhattan's Lower East Side. The type face for the title and the look of the slum have the flavor of the early thirties, when the story of *The Catholic Worker* begins. But that slum is still there, more crowded and decayed than ever. It is still going on. And the Bowery. The Third Avenue El came down in 1955. A new coat of paint was put on the building housing the Amata Opera house, and the Bouwerie Lane Theatre, valiantly sandblasted, threatened to change the image of the Bowery. The pensioners in the $1.10 hotels hardly took notice, and the drunks in the One Mile House certainly did not. But popular wisdom had it that the Depression was over, that we had entered into an age of affluence. It is true, some of us had. Some of us. Those who had could afford to forget, for a while at least.

In 1957 the Communist Party, surfacing after the McCarthy era, held a national convention in a catering establishment, the Chateau Gardens, around the corner from the Catholic Worker house of hospitality on Chrystie Street. They were quite an attraction at the time. The press came in large numbers, along with the FBI men with prurient cameras. A reporter from the *Times* happened around the corner and came upon the CW soupline. He followed into the office and expressed shocked astonishment that there should be a soupline in New York in 1957! It was explained very gently to him that there are still a great many poor people on inadequate pensions, no pensions, people who have slipped through the loose net of social security altogether, people who are unable to be pigeonholed into the categories for the indigent and disabled that Holy Mother City has established. There are a great many who do not fit, or cannot be made to fit, and these come.

Michael Harrington in his book *The Other America* drew attention to the invisibility of the poor. We do not have to see them as we commute from the suburbs to downtown air-conditioned offices. We do not see them. Therefore they do not exist, at least to our consciousness. And so, after seven years of reporting, our friend from the *Times* was able to be astonished. Harrington's book did much to stimulate the "war on poverty." The great battle never really began. The infant was starved in its cradle to feed the monstrous war in Southeast Asia.

Some would like to consign this volume to the racks as a memento of the thirties. Let it be a thorn in the side of our parents. But that cannot be. For it is still going on, and to tell the truth the misery is deeper and the frustration more bitter, the apocalypse closer and each present moment more acute. Wars and rumors of war, race war, class war. Wars of liberation and wars to liberate the liberated. And as always the same victims. The people. The vast majority of the people, poor and hungry, sick unto death of liberators, whose cry is "Peace and Bread." The Body of Christ bleeding from a billion wounds. And still the Catholic Worker movement, poor among the poor, a quiet leaven, a bowl of soup, an oddly dated monthly, still a penny a copy, bringing news that is so old it looks like new.

Faithful readers of *The Catholic Worker* will wonder why various outstanding articles of the past are not found here. We cannot apologize for the unforgivable slight we are giving to several who contributed so splendidly over the years, but we have had to discipline ourselves to select for this slim volume only what seemed to us to retain the power of its first days, in order to present a unified and balanced work. Some will look for articles by great French and Latin American intellectuals and revolutionaries, but we have selected only material that was written expressly and solely for *The Catholic Worker*, so you will not find Emmanuel Mounier on World War II, or Dom Luigi Sturzo on the Spanish Civil War, though *The Catholic Worker* was their sole platform in America. We hope the book catches some of the pervasive atmosphere of the Catholic Worker, the feel and smell of the recurring spring, working its way into the streets and dank slum apartments of our Lower East Side.

Special thanks are extended to Marjorie Hughes, who typed the manuscript and who once sat at the feet of Peter Maurin, and to our editor, Elizabeth Bartelme, herself a graduate of the Catholic Worker community.

Thomas C. Cornell
James H. Forest

Introduction

THE CATHOLIC WORKER movement has proved exceedingly important. It seems quite certain that future historians will judge it to be the most important social movement within the Church in this country during the second third of the present century. Its influence has been equally great in the areas of thought and action. Many, many people have been deeply affected personally: seminarians, priests, and nuns, intellectuals and the uneducated, students, white-collar and blue-collar workers, the young and the not-so-young. The movement reoriented their thought and motivated them to give themselves to forms of social action that were, for them, wholly novel.

Dorothy Day is the principal contributor to the present anthology. This of course is natural and inevitable, for she, along with Peter Maurin, gave the movement its special character. However, the Catholic Worker has always encouraged individuality. As Peter said in one of his inimitable essays: "The Communist Party / has a party line. / The Catholic Worker / has no party line." The almost thirty writers with signed articles in the present volume illustrate this fact. They do not repeat a stereotyped creed. They speak as individuals.

In spite of individual differences, there are certain principles which everyone participating in the movement is likely to accept, for they pertain to its essence. The first is a literal acceptance of the

New Testament as a practical guide to social action. "The Catholic Manifesto is The Sermon on the Mount," declared an editorial of January, 1935. Next there is the belief that one must accept the obligation of doing something personally, immediately, about the ills that plague society. To quote Peter again: "The Catholic Worker believes / in the gentle personalism / of traditional Catholicism. / The Catholic Worker believes / in the personal obligation / of looking after / the needs of our brother."

The most visible manifestation of this "gentle personalism" has been the direct service of the abandoned poor in the inner-city slums. The striking thing about what goes on in these houses of hospitality is not the mere fact that a great many of the poor are fed and clothed and given lodging. After all, a good many social agencies do more or less the same thing. What is rather unique is the spirit of the activity. One helps the poor man personally and sees him as a person—not as a "case," but as a person. The obituaries of Maurice O'Connell, Dick Conors, and George Clements in the present volume are illuminating in this respect. They are written about primarily as human beings. They were indeed people who had had very special experiences in life, but this did not alter the fact that they were fundamentally like everybody else, men with some likable and some irritating qualities. This vivid consciousness that we all share a common humanity, that we are all members of the Mystical Body, gives Catholic Worker activity among the poor a very, very special quality.

In its opposition to war, the activity of the Catholic Worker movement has been outstanding. During World War II it sponsored the Association of Catholic Conscientious Objectors, the only group in the country that provided opportunity for Catholic conscientious objectors to carry out their required Civilian Public Service under Catholic auspices. More recently, the Catholic Peace Fellowship, directly inspired and assisted by the Catholic Worker group, has become the most active Catholic peace society. The present volume contains clear statements about the Catholic Worker's position on war. See particularly Dorothy's mordant "We Go on Record" from the September, 1945, issue.

With its caustic irony it is certainly one of the most vivid condemnations of the Hiroshima and Nagasaki murders ever published.

The principle of "gentle personalism" has guided the anti-war activities of the Catholic Worker group just as it has guided their work among the poor. The group's attitude toward conscientious objection illustrates this. By refusing service the objector does something personal. He uses his reason and free will and makes a choice. In addition to conscientious objection, the Catholic Worker group has made other personalistic protests. See Dorothy's "Life Behind Bars" from the February, 1957, issue. She was one of a group that refused to participate in a compulsory air-raid drill and as a result she was jailed. At present, as is well known, young men inspired by the Catholic Worker have been protesting the Vietnam War by burning their draft cards, and have dissented in other dramatic ways.

The Catholic Worker group traditionally has shown a great interest in economic justice. Often this interest takes the form of support for the workers in a particular labor dispute. See, for example, "Picket Lines and the Cardinal," from the April, 1949, issue. The group's concern for social justice, however, far transcends such specific cases; it extends to a criticism of capitalism itself as it now exists. Such criticism is a constantly recurring theme. The attitude of the group is shown very dramatically in the letter "This Money Is Not Ours" from the September, 1960, issue; the letter returned to the City of New York a check for $3,579.39, which represented interest on money awarded to the Catholic Worker but still unpaid. The explanation for the refusal was "We do not believe in the profit system, and so we cannot take profit or interest on our money." Not every reader will agree with such a radical rejection of the modern economic system, but few will fail to agree with many or most of the criticisms of the workings of capitalism that appear in the pages of *The Catholic Worker*.

In many ways the Catholic Worker group has done pioneer work. In the recent past, with the talk of a "war on poverty," the

misery of the poor in inner-city ghettos has been gradually penetrating the public consciousness, but in the mid-1930s the Catholic Worker movement was calling attention to this misery in the
most vivid language possible. The Peace Corps and parallel proj-
ects testify to a new realization of the need of personal service to
one's neighbor. It is not enough to give money or vote for social
legislation; one must do something in person. This is an old story
with the Catholic Worker group. It is merely the principle of
"gentle personalism." During World War II conscientious objection was not nearly so widely accepted as a principle as it now is,
but it is a principle that the Catholic Worker group supported as
solidly then as now. Dorothy Day was jailed for refusing to participate in an air-raid drill over a decade ago. In those days civil
disobedience was as novel a technique as it is now familiar. The
Catholic Worker group seems consistently to have been ahead of
the times.

The present volume tells the story of the Catholic Worker
movement since its beginning in 1933. It has been a fruitful
thirty-five years. Let us hope that the next thirty-five years will be
at least equally fruitful.

Paul Hanly Furfey

February 26, 1968

PART I

Depression Years
1933–1939

To Our Readers

DOROTHY DAY

FOR THOSE who are sitting on park benches in the warm spring sunlight.

For those who are huddling in shelters trying to escape the rain.

For those who are walking the streets in the all but futile search for work.

For those who think that there is no hope for the future, no recognition of their plight—this little paper is addressed.

It is printed to call their attention to the fact that the Catholic Church has a social program—to let them know that there are men of God who are working not only for their spiritual, but for their material welfare.

FILLING A NEED

It's time there was a Catholic paper printed for the unemployed.

The fundamental aim of most radical sheets is the conversion of its readers to radicalism and atheism.

Is it not possible to be radical and not atheist?

Is it not possible to protest, to expose, to complain, to point out abuses and demand reforms without desiring the overthrow of religion?

In an attempt to popularize and make known the encyclicals of the Popes in regard to social justice and the program put forth by the Church for the "reconstruction of the social order," this news sheet, *The Catholic Worker*, is started.

It is not as yet known whether it will be a monthly, a fortnightly or a weekly. It all depends on the funds collected for the printing and distribution. Those who can subscribe, and those who can donate, are asked to do so.

This first number of *The Catholic Worker* was planned, written and edited in the kitchen of a tenement on Fifteenth Street, on subway platforms, on the "L," the ferry. There is no editorial office, no overhead in the way of telephone or electricity, no salaries paid.

The money for the printing of the first issue was raised by begging small contributions from friends. A colored priest in Newark sent us ten dollars and the prayers of his congregation. A colored sister in New Jersey, garbed also in holy poverty, sent us a dollar. Another kindly and generous friend sent twenty-five. The rest of it the editors squeezed out of their own earnings, and at that they were using money necessary to pay milk bills, gas bills, electric light bills.

By accepting delay the utilities did not know that they were furthering the cause of social justice. They were, for the time being, unwitting cooperators.

Next month someone may donate us an office. Who knows?

It is cheering to remember that Jesus Christ wandered this earth with no place to lay His head. *The foxes have holes and the birds of the air their nests, but the Son of Man has no place to lay His head.* And when we consider our fly-by-night existence, our uncertainty, we remember (with pride at sharing the honor), that the disciples supped by the seashore and wandered through corn fields picking the ears from the stalks wherewith to make their frugal meals.

For Gentle Sabotage, Style, and Economy, Dine by Candle Light

FASHION ITEM: "Nowadays a note of elegance is introduced by the presence of candles on the dinner table."

This should be of comfort to the workingman whose electricity has been turned off for non-payment of bills or deposit.

"Dine by candle light" is the slogan adopted by the men who have been thrown out of work by the Brooklyn Edison Electric Company, and they are soliciting the help of other customers and urging their ultimate advantage by advocating this little act of peaceful sabotage.

But as a matter of fact, candles are expensive and it is only hostesses with ambitions toward elegance, and ladies of fading charm who wish a softer light over their dining room tables and drawing rooms, who can afford candles.

It is much more practical, though it doesn't make so good a slogan, to dine by kerosene lamp. You can buy a lamp in any little hardware store and kerosene is cheap.

If you dine by candle light (or kerosene lamp) one night a week, and if a few million follow your example, the electric light company suffers severely. Of course, it is a shame to inflict suffering, but then, the poor consumer does a lot of suffering too when it comes to paying the bill.

Mary Is Fifteen

DOROTHY DAY

Children to take care of, meals to prepare, clothes to wash, boards over the bathtub to sleep on and two dollars a week—
—Mary's job.

IT IS NOT YET six-thirty in the morning and Mary is sleeping soundly, arms up, fists clenched gently like those of a baby. It is fortunate that Mary is still a little girl for the bed she is sleeping on is not very long. As a matter of fact, it is not a bed at all, but a bathtub, in the extra bathroom, and a rather short bathtub at that with table leaves stretched out over the top of it and blankets spread out on that. The Ferguson home was short on beds, but long on blankets. Of course it might have been possible to have bought another bed, but the apartment was small and what should have been the maid's room was already crowded with the children's cribs and there was no use messing up the living room by having a girl sleeping there.

So little Mary slept on the tub.

Mrs. Ferguson was a voluble woman and always had excuses for everything. Sleeping on hard boards was very good for the spine she used to say too. We do have to put up with so much in this time of depression.

For instance, she was putting up with Mary. What she would have liked, of course, would be a larger apartment with a spare room for a regular maid and she would have liked to have been able to pay a maid forty or fifty a month, the wages maids used to get. But she had to put up with little Mary and pay her two a week and sleep her on a board. It was the best she could do.

And of course, Mary had to put up with her. She was one of a family of six children. ("Why will poor people have so many children?" Mrs. Ferguson always frowned.) And by working out and being a mother's helper, Mary was supporting herself, and the two dollars she earned at least paid the milk bill at home.

Six o'clock. Mary didn't need an alarm clock. Young Junior acted the part perfectly well. Every morning he started his carolling, "Mary, Mary!" And Mary had to get up quick and take him and his little sister out to the kitchen before Mrs. Ferguson and her husband were awakened. They liked to sleep until eight. And even then their sleep was disturbed. It was impossible to keep the children quiet. They liked to make noise in the morning.

There was breakfast to prepare. Cereal, orange juice and milk and toast and a soft-boiled egg for each. It was good there was enough food always for breakfast. Usually there wasn't enough for lunch or for supper. Mrs. Ferguson cooked those meals and she watched the food carefully and complained bitterly over Mary's large appetite. "Really, people eat twice as much as they need to. And I do like to keep the food bills down."

By the time Mrs. Ferguson and her husband were up there was another breakfast to get, and then there were other little things to do for the children. And after breakfast dishes to wash, the floor to mop up—Mrs. Ferguson was a rigid housekeeper. And the tub of clothes. But if it were a nice day— "You can leave the clothes until you get back, Mary, and do them then. Take the children out now to the park."

Clothes changed, faces washed, and all the paraphernalia of a morning in the park. Leggings, rubbers, sweaters, coats, pull-down hats, shovels, pails, skates, bicycles—she was always laden down.

Her own coat was not very warm, and she used to think longingly of Mrs. Ferguson's second-best raccoon coat which she had once secretly tried on. "The nerve!" Mrs. Ferguson would have said had she known.

Two hours out in the wintry sun and then in to lunch, and the long task of making the children eat their lunch. "Now Bobby, don't put your plate on the top of your head!"

"Mary, you must be more careful! How many times have I told you? Don't keep saying don't to them. If you would read those books I gave you on the treatment of children you'd be learning something and fitting yourself for something better than just a mother's helper job. You might even be a kindergarten teacher some day."

After lunch, changing the children, washing them again, putting them away for their naps. Mary's eyes were pretty heavy too, just at this time of the day. Even the boards set up on the top of the bathtub beckoned invitingly. But there were too many things to do. Dishes again, and the floor around the children's table to be washed up, the table and even the little chairs themselves to be scrubbed. And then the clothes, neglected in the morning, to be washed.

Mrs. Ferguson always forgot that she had shooed Mary out with the children. "If only you had more system and got them done first thing in the morning! If you only moved a little faster!"

And so the day went. At three-thirty the children were up again. There were vegetables to be prepared for supper. Errands to be run. "And you might as well take Junior with you, he's such a nuisance around the house." Supper for the children, dishes, dinner for the grownups and sometimes company. Children to be put to bed, more dishes to be washed. And then sometimes interminable evenings when the children cried and fussed and Mary was kept running.

Oh, it was a long day, a hard day, and life with a succession of such days seemed too hard to be borne.

And this, unfortunately, is not a "story" but an account of facts. Of course, another sad little story could be written about the harassed mother who was used always to having help and what a difficult time she was having to adjust herself, and how she was put upon by the inefficient little girl she had taken in, and how the girl ruined more than she helped things, and how she neglected the children, and how she demanded afternoons off just when other plans had been made—and so on and so on —but somehow the condition of the mistress does not seem to us so moving as that of the little maid.

One could tell sad stories, too, of the bosses and how they are having to cut down on trips to Europe and doing with one car instead of three, and taking their kids out of expensive schools and putting them in public schools—and oh, the weight of responsibility on their shoulders! But that, too, does not seem so sad as the plight of the worker, who has had nothing in the past, nothing in the present, and to all intents and purposes, nothing to look forward to in the future of the present social system.

 Easy Essays

PETER MAURIN

WHAT THE CATHOLIC WORKER BELIEVES

The Catholic Worker believes
in the gentle personalism
of traditional Catholicism.
The Catholic Worker believes
in the personal obligation
of looking after
the needs of our brother.
The Catholic Worker believes
in the daily practice
of the Works of Mercy.
The Catholic Worker believes
in Houses of Hospitality
for the immediate relief
of those who are in need.
The Catholic Worker believes
in the establishment
of Farming Communes
where each one works
according to his ability

and gets
according to his need.
The Catholic Worker believes
in creating a new society
within the shell of the old
with the philosophy of the new,
which is not a new philosophy
but a very old philosophy,
a philosophy so old
that it looks like new.

No Party Line

The Catholic Worker
is a free-lance movement,
not a partisan movement.
Some of the Bishops
agree with our policies
and some don't.
We are criticized
by many Catholics
for some of our policies
and especially
our Spanish policy.
The Communist Party
has a party line.
The Catholic Worker
has no party line.
There is no party line
in the Catholic Church.

God and Mammon

Christ says:
"The dollar you have
is the dollar you give
to the poor

for My sake."
The banker says:
"The dollar you have
is the dollar
you lend me
for your sake."
Christ says:
"You cannot
serve two masters,
God and Mammon."
"You cannot,
and all our education
is to try to find out
how we can
serve two masters,
God and Mammon,"
says Robert Louis Stevenson.

IRISH CULTURE

After the fall
of the Roman Empire
the scholars
scattered all over
the Roman Empire,
looked for a refuge
and found a refuge
in Ireland,
where the Roman Empire
did not reach
and where the Teutonic barbarians
did not go.
In Ireland,
the scholars formulated
an intellectual synthesis
and a technique of action.
Having formulated

that intellectual synthesis
and that technique of action,
the scholars decided to lay
the foundations of medieval Europe.

In order to lay the foundations
of medieval Europe,
the Irish Scholars
established *Salons de Culture*
in all the cities of Europe,
as far as Constantinople,
where people could look for thought
so they could have light.
And it was
in the so-called Dark Ages
which were not so dark,
when the Irish
were the light.
But we are now living
in a real Dark Age,
and one of the reasons why
the modern age
is so dark,
is because
too few Irish
have the light.

The Irish Scholars established
free guest houses
all over Europe
to exemplify
Christian charity.
This made
pagan Teutonic rulers
tell pagan Teutonic people:
"The Irish are good people

busy doing good."
And when the Irish
were good people
busy doing good,
they did not bother
about empires.
That is why we never heard
about an Irish Empire.
We heard about
all kinds of empires,
including the British Empire,
but never about
an Irish Empire,
because the Irish
did not bother about empires
when they were busy
doing good.

The Irish Scholars established
agricultural centers
all over Europe
where they combined
cult—
that is to say liturgy,
with culture—
that is to say literature,
with cultivation—
that is to say agriculture.
And the word America
was for the first time
printed on a map
in a town in east France
called Saint-Die
where an Irish scholar
by the name of Deodad
founded an agricultural center.

What was done
by Irish missionaries
after the fall
of the Roman Empire
can be done today
during and after the fall
of modern empires.

FEEDING THE POOR

In the first centuries
of Christianity
the hungry were fed
at a personal sacrifice,
the naked were clothed
at a personal sacrifice,
the homeless were sheltered
at a personal sacrifice.
And because the poor
were fed, clothed and sheltered
at a personal sacrifice,
the pagans used to say
about the Christians
"See how they love each other."
In our own day
the poor are no longer
fed, clothed and sheltered
at a personal sacrifice
but at the expense
of the taxpayers.
And because the poor
are no longer
fed, clothed and sheltered
at a personal sacrifice
the pagans say about the
Christians
"See how they pass the buck."

Blowing the Dynamite

Writing about the Catholic Church,
a radical writer says:
"Rome will have to do more
than to play a waiting game;
she will have to use
some of the dynamite
inherent in her message."
To blow the dynamite
of a message
is the only way
to make the message dynamic.
If the Catholic Church
is not today
the dominant social dynamic force,
it is because Catholic scholars
have failed to blow the dynamite
of the Church.
Catholic scholars
have taken the dynamite
of the Church,
have wrapped it up
in nice phraseology,
placed it in an hermetic container
and sat on the lid.
It is about time
to blow the lid off
so the Catholic Church
may again become
the dominant social dynamic force.

Out of the Temple

Christ drove the money changers
out of the Temple.
But today nobody dares

to drive the money lenders
out of the Temple.
And nobody dares
to drive the money lenders
out of the Temple
because the money lenders
have taken a mortgage
on the Temple.
When church builders build churches
with money borrowed from money lenders
they increase the prestige
of the money lenders.
But increasing the prestige
of the money lenders
does not increase the prestige
of the Church.
Which makes Archbishop McNicholas say:
"We have been guilty
of encouraging tyranny
in the financial world
until it has become
a veritable octopus
strangling the life
of our people."

THE CASE FOR UTOPIA

The world would be better off
If people tried to become better.
And people would become better
if they stopped trying to become
better off.
For when everybody tries to
become better off,
nobody is better off.
But when everybody tries to
become better,

everybody is better off.
Everybody would be rich
if nobody tried to become richer.
And nobody would be poor
if everybody tried to be poorest.
And everybody would be
what he ought to be
if everybody tried to be
what he wants the other fellow to be.

Why Not Be a Beggar?

God wants us to be
our brother's keeper.
To feed the hungry,
to clothe the naked,
to shelter the homeless,
to instruct the ignorant,
at a personal sacrifice,
is what God
wants us to do.
What we give to the poor
for Christ's sake
is what we carry with us
when we die.
As Jean Jacques Rousseau
says:
"When man dies
he carries
in his clutched hands
only that
which he has given away."

People who are in need
and are not afraid to beg
give to people not in need
the occasion to do good

for goodness' sake.
Modern society
calls the beggar
bum and panhandler
and gives him the bum's rush.
The Greeks used to say
that people in need
are the ambassadors of the gods.
We read in the Gospel:
"As long as you did it
to one of the least
of my brothers,
you did it to me."
While modern society
calls the beggars
bums and panhandlers,
they are in fact
the Ambassadors of God.
To be God's Ambassador
is something
to be proud of.

 ## Shoes Needed

(*First appeal for clothing*)

ONE OF OUR FRIENDS brought in some men's shirts and two pairs
of shoes, all of which were immediately given to other friends
who were in need.

We ask any of our readers who have winter coats or men's
or women's shoes to send them in to the office. Men's shoes are
more necessary than anything else.

Editorial—And Now a Note of Melancholy

LATE FALL IS HERE. A haze hangs over the city. Fogs rise from the river, and the melancholy note of the river boats is heard at night. The leaves are dropping from the fig tree in the back yard. There is the smell of chestnuts in the air, and if you buy the chestnuts, most of them are wormy. It is better to make popcorn over the fire at night. For we have fires now. The kettle sings on the range in the kitchen (the range cost eight dollars second-hand and doesn't burn much coal), and visitors to *The Catholic Worker* office are drinking much tea and coffee. The stove in the front office has burst in its exuberance and has to be mended with stove clay and a piece of tin.

And there is also the smell of grapes in the air—rich luscious Concord grapes. If this editorial has a melancholy note, it is not because chestnuts are wormy or because the stove has cracked, but because all our Italian neighbors are too poor this year to buy grapes and make wine. Grapes that used to be one dollar a box are now one dollar fifty. And the Italian fathers who love their wine and have it in lieu of fresh vegetables and fruits all during the long winter, are still out of jobs or on four-day-a-month work relief and this year there is no pleasant smell of fermenting grapes, no disorderly heaps of mash dumped in the gutters.

And Mr. Rubino and Mr. Scaratino and Mr. Liguori will not rent a wine press together this year, and the children will not hang over them with breathless interest in the mysterious basement while they manipulate the press rented for the house.

And, what is worse, Mr. Rubino will not be dropping into the office of *The Catholic Worker*, when he sees our light late at night, to console us for our long hours by the gift of a milk bottle of wine.

For the long hard winter is before us. Evictions are increasing, people come in to ask us to collect winter clothes and to help them find apartments where relief checks will be accepted.

We must work, and we must pray, and we meditate as we write this that it would be so much easier for all our Italian friends to work and pray, to have courage to fight and also to be patient, if they could make as usual their fragrant and cheering grape wine.

NOVEMBER 1933

 Day After Day

DOROTHY DAY

A DEER GETS TRAPPED on a hillside and every effort is brought to bear to rescue him from his predicament. The newspapers carry daily features.

Mrs. A., with her four children and unemployed husband living on $1.50 a week, is trapped by economic circumstance and everyone is so indifferent that it took three or four afternoons of Mike Gunn's time to see to it that the Home Relief came to the rescue. Though Mike has enough to do with his Labor Guild over in Brooklyn, he was doing his bit as part of the Fifteenth Street Neighborhood Council.

Three little pigs are crowded into a too-small cage, the case is brought into court, the judge's findings in the case being that pigs should not be crowded the way subway riders are. And a family of eight children, mother and father are crowded in three rooms and the consensus of opinion is that they're lucky to have that and why don't they practice birth control anyway.

One of the Home Relief workers came in the other day and

was voicing just such sentiments. She was absolutely unacquainted with Catholic teaching on birth control and abortion, and we forced her to listen to a lecture on the subject which, though it may not have convinced her, at least served the purpose of toning down her propaganda among unemployed families, we hope.

A scavenger hunt is the latest game of "Society." An hilarious pastime, The New York Times society reporter calls it, and describes in two and one-half columns the asinine procedure of several hundred society and literary figures, guests at a party at the Waldorf Astoria, surging forth on a chase through the highways and byways of Manhattan Island. "The scavenger hunt of last night brought an enthusiastic response even from persons whose appetites for diversion are ordinarily jaded." The hunt was a search through the city streets for a "ridiculously heterogeneous list of articles."

Any morning before and after Mass and straight on through the day there is a "scavenger hunt" going on up and down Fifteenth Street outside the windows of The Catholic Worker and through all the streets of the city. People going through garbage and ash cans to see what they can find in the way of a heterogeneous list of articles. The Times does not state what these things were but probably the list was made up of something delightfully and quaintly absurd, such as old shoes, bits of string, cardboard packing boxes, wire, old furniture, clothing and food.

If the several hundred guests at the Waldorf had to scavenge night after night and morning after morning, the hunt would not have such an enthusiastic response.

Teresa, aged seven, member of the Fifteenth Street Neighborhood Council, took part in her first eviction the other day. She had a cold and was staying home from school in order to keep out in the air, it being a balmy day, so she had her chance to help.

The Friday before, a Home Relief worker from Twenty-second Street came to the office to get aid for a woman and child who were being evicted from a decrepit flat in one or the tenements of William Horn (on Union Square). There were five stalwart friends of The Catholic Worker in the office at the time.

Understanding that the eviction was at three in the afternoon, we sallied forth, but when we got there, the landlord's agent had called off his men, expecting us to do the job of putting the woman out, and thus saving him eighteen dollars.

We refused to move the woman's furniture until it had been brought down by the marshal. We explained to the agent that often a landlord who was unwilling to accept a Home Relief voucher offered to move the family himself, paying five dollars to a neighborhood truckman rather than eighteen to the marshal. This agent, standing sneering and scoffing by the door, refused to do anything.

"You have no sympathy for landlords, have you?" he wanted to know.

We assured him that our sympathy was rather with the weaker party. All right then, he would call the marshal! The eviction would be the following Monday then, at three o'clock.

It was hard to understand his unwillingness to have the poor woman moved. It was as though he delighted in the idea of heaping humiliation on her.

Monday came, and the relief worker hastened around to the office, to tell us that the marshal was about to arrive, though it was only one, not three in the afternoon. Only Harry Crimmins, Teresa, Dorothy Weston and I were in the office, so leaving Dorothy to mind the office, the three of us sallied out.

Several police and huskies were standing at the door of the tenement to greet what they thought was going to be a delegation of Communists, only to meet instead seven-year-old Teresa, Harry Crimmins and me. They dissolved into thin air. (It is a wonder they wouldn't stay and help us.)

Teresa carried toys, pieces of the baby's crib, parlor ornaments and dishes, and Harry Crimmins and I managed the rest. The Mission Helpers of the Sacred Heart, a community of nuns who run a day nursery and do visiting work in the neighborhood, promised to keep an eye on our evicted friend—she is a Protestant— taking charge of her two-year-old child while she works as a dishwasher for seven a week.

This is only one of the dozen eviction cases we have had in

the last month. We have moved Jews, Protestants and Catholics. A German livery stable man loaned us his horse and wagon to move a Jewish neighbor. Jews, Protestants and Catholics have helped us by contributing clothes, furniture and their services.

We call our readers' attention to the petition published in this issue against evictions which we urge you to clip out, attach to a sheet of paper and send back filled with the signatures of men, women and children who protest against this injustice.

Letter from Jacques Maritain

DEAR PETER MAURIN:

How can I tell you how moved I was at finding the package you had left for me when I entered my cabin. I don't know what's in it (I'm leaving the pleasure of opening it to my wife), but I know it is the gift of fraternal charity and friendship. Will you also thank Margaret, *The Catholic Worker* cook, for me with all my heart, and tell her that she pleased me very much.

Tell Dorothy Day, too, how very happy I was to visit her, and how touched at the reception given me by your friends. I wish I could have said all that was in my heart—never was I more vexed by inability to speak fluent English. It seemed as if I had found again in *The Catholic Worker* a little of the atmosphere of Péguy's office in the Rue de la Sorbonne. And so much good will, such courage, such generosity! It is thus, with meager means and great love, that the future for which we long is prepared.

I'm of the impression that I didn't make myself quite clear on the subject of the Pluralist State, when I replied to your explanation of it. I want to make it quite clear that such a state, with its "federation" of diverse juridical structures, would be not merely a simple collection, but would have a real moral unity of orientation. It would deserve the name of Christian because it would tend in a positive fashion, across these diverse structures, toward an integral Christian ideal. Instead of being polarized by a materialistic conception of the world and of life, like the Capitalist and the Communist state, it would be polarized through the knowledge of the spiritual dignity of the human person and on the love which is due to him.

Thank Dorothy Day again, and Ade Bethune, and Margaret. And be assured of my gratitude to you, dear Peter.

Why did you run away after you left the package on board? I had hoped to see you again on board the *Aquitania.*

Let us pray for each other.

Cordially yours in Christ Jesus,
JACQUES MARITAIN

JANUARY 1935

 Editorial—Mid-Winter

IT IS A COLD NIGHT and we are writing in the kitchen where there are no drafts. Barbara, our cooperative apartment baby, sits on her mother's lap by the table and she, too, is writing an editorial though she is only five months old. In her zeal she tries first to eat the pencil her fond mother has given her, and then the paper.

On the wall there are three pictures which attract her attention. She calls out to them, trying to crow. There is a Polish Madonna, a Negro Madonna, and a picture of a Madonna and a worker by Ade Bethune. She likes that best of all.

Teresa is drawing pictures too, and when she shows them to the baby, Barbara laughs and makes bubbles. The black cat lies in restful abandon in front of the stove.

It is one of those rare evenings when there are no visitors, when the work of the day seems to be over, though it is only seven-thirty. It is a good time to sit and write editorials. An editorial, for instance, on charity. St. Saviour's High School and Cathedral High School sent down so many baskets of food, including hams and canned goods, potatoes and all the trimmings for Christmas dinners, that the office was piled high for at least three hours until they were all distributed.

It is true it did not take long to distribute them, there is such need around here.

There were toys too, dolls for the girls, and other toys for the boys, all beautifully wrapped and beribboned.

Bundles of clothes came in, including many overcoats, and they went out as fast as they came in. They came in response to the story of the man who had to accept a woman's woolen sweater in lieu of underwear or overcoat. I hope they keep on coming in.

I'd like to have everyone see the poor worn feet, clad in shoes that are falling apart, which find their way to *The Catholic Worker* office. A man came in this rainy morning and when he took off one dilapidated rag of footwear, his sock had huge holes in the heel and was soaking wet at that. We made him put on a dry sock before trying on the pair of shoes we found for him, and he changed diffidently, there under the eye of the Blessed Virgin on the bookcase, looking down from her shrine of Christmas greens. But his poor, red feet were clean. Most of the men and women who come in from the lodging houses and from the streets manage cleanliness, what with the public baths. I heard of one man who washed his underwear in the public baths, and sat there as long as he could in that steam-laden, enervating atmosphere until it was not quite too wet to put on. For the rest, it could dry on his skin. Not a pleasant thought in bitter weather.

Our prayer for the new year is that "the members might be mutually careful one for another. And if one member suffers anything, all the members suffer with it; or if one member glory, all the members rejoice with it."

It would seem, however, that the glory comes only through suffering this present day when we look upon the Mystical Body reviled and assaulted in Mexico, Spain, Russia, not to speak of the physical suffering of the poor all over the world.

The only immediate remedy is the practice of the corporal and spiritual works of mercy. When asked what is the program of *The Catholic Worker* by those who are interested in political action, legislation, lobbying, class war, we reply: It is the program set forth by Christ in the Gospels. The Catholic Manifesto is The Sermon on the Mount. And when we bring *The Catholic Worker* into the streets and public squares, and when we picket the Mexican consulate, it is to practice the spiritual works of mercy—to instruct the ignorant and to comfort the afflicted.

Unless the Lord build the house, they labor in vain that build it. There is no use looking for a revival in business, a return of prosperity, until the hearts and minds of men be changed. If we wish for a program, let us look into our own hearts. The beginning is there.

MARCH 1935

 ## Christ and the Patriot

PAUL HANLY FURFEY

THE *"Patriot"*: I love peace as well as any man, but I am a realist. A strong system of national defence is our best assurance of peace. National defence is the patriotic duty of every American citizen. The R.O.T.C. affords the Catholic college student a fine opportunity to fulfill this patriotic duty.

Christ: All that take the sword shall perish by the sword.

The "Patriot": Yet we must be practical! There are, of course, some nations whom we can trust. Canada is a good neighbor. We shall never have a war with her. But unfortunately not all nations are like that. Japan and Russia are casting jealous eyes at us. Our basic policies conflict. We must arm to defend ourselves against such nations.

Christ: You have heard that it hath been said, Thou shalt love thy neighbor and hate thy enemy. But I say to you, love your enemies, do good to them that hate you; and pray for them that persecute and calumniate you.

The "Patriot": A noble doctrine! We must always keep before us the ideal of international good will. At the same time we must realize that it is merely common sense to be on our guard. We shall not start a war, but if some other nation starts one, then we must be in a position to defend our territory.

Christ: To him that striketh thee on the one cheek, offer also the other. Of him that taketh away thy goods, ask them not again.

The "Patriot": But national defense is not merely a question of defending our material rights. It is a question of life and death. Only a strong system of national defence will guarantee our personal security.

Christ: Be not afraid of them who kill the body, and after that have no more that they can do.

The "Patriot": But there is such a thing as a just war. Under certain circumstances a nation has a right to declare war. In the Old Testament war is approved under certain circumstances.

Christ: You have heard that it hath been said, an eye for an eye, and a tooth for a tooth. But I say to you not to resist evil.

Lord Jesus Christ, Lover of Peace, kindle in our poor hearts the flame of Thy heroic love, that we may see Thy beloved image in all men, our enemies as well as our friends, that we may rather suffer injury than protect our rights by violence, for Thy sweet sake Who died for all men. Amen.

☙❧ Catholics Have No United Front with William R. Hearst

IN REGARDING YOUR RECENT congratulations to the Catholic press, and your editorial compliments to Catholics on their militant fight against Communists, may we inform you that Catholics do not fight Communists, but Communism. Catholics do not fight Communism because they wish to support a vicious Capitalism or because Communism objects to the jingoistic Nationalism with which you fill your sorry sheets. Catholics do not subscribe to the class war which you are doing your best to advance. No do Catholics support the anti-peace movement you foster. In other words, Catholics are not working alongside you, so your compliments are lost. All these things are just as un-Catholic as is Communism itself. Which makes your papers and other media of propaganda un-Catholic, too.

The Catholic fight on Communism is one based on philosophies, not on economics. And by the same token your brand of Americanism, your bourgeois Capitalism, your class war, your militaristic attitude come in for the same condemnation as does the philosophy of Marx and Engels.

The difference is that the followers of Marx are honest enough to hold to a doctrine which they believe is right. You, like all Fascists, are a perfect pragmatist. Utility takes the place of morality for you. And unlike some pragmatists, the utility is not for the common good. It is utility for Hearst.

Please, Mr. Hearst, Catholics have a tough enough time trying to be understood. Do not complicate the issues more. Stay on your own side of the fence; do your own dirty work; work up the passions of one mob against the other; do your best to stir up world conflagrations; rant and rave about "my country, right or wrong"; support exploitation of labor; support everything that is evil in the world today, as you do; but please, please, do not try

28

to convince the world that Catholics have any share in your
sordid adventures.

MAY 1936

 ## Why I Like the Communist

DONALD POWELL

FLOCKS AND FLOCKS of bunk appears in the Catholic press against
Communism. Some Catholic papers appear bent on rivaling the
imbecilic inveighings of William Randolph Hearst. No convert
to the metaphysics of Communism, I purpose here and now
raising my sword in defence of the Communist and telling why
I like him.

One of the characteristics of the Communist that I like is his
spirit of self-sacrifice. Plato, centuries ago, had the notion that a
government was best administered by guardians. These men
would be specially trained in statecraft, would lead frugal lives
and would get their rewards, not in money, but in honors and the
knowledge that they were serving the common good. In short, he
would train Jesuits not for the Church, but for the State. Europe
was governed by such administrators, directly and indirectly, for a
thousand years. The antithesis of this type of government is rule
by the plutocrat, or by his agents. The plutocrat is in politics
solely for money. Croker of Tammany Hall bluntly asserted that
he was in politics to line his pockets. The Tammanyites of 1936
know no better philosophy of government. Between the Stalin
and the Croker attitude toward politics, I have a vast and unholy
preference for Stalin's. Gladly would I hire him to inculcate some
elementary Christian principles into the boys at Tammany Hall.
Odd isn't it, that Al Smith, who believes that a public office is a

public trust (à la Stalin) and whose whole career in public office was an exemplification of that belief, seems to get more kick out of spanking Stalin than his brother Sachems?

Another thing I like about the Communist is his intellectual honesty. He says he is a materialist and bases his life and his State on his belief. He says he believes in class warfare and forthwith goes out and fights.

To red baiters and Communist haters, I want to point out that mistaken as I think the Communist is, and happy as I am to swap sock for sock with him, he is no slick and slimy hypocrite. You know and I know just where he stands.

But consider, for the moment, the Capitalist; the Calvinist, plutocrat, bourgeois Capitalist. He says he believes in God, that, in fact, he is a Christian. He says he is a dualist and that he and all his brothers possess both body and soul. Then he bases his whole life and his whole society upon materialism, and not, by any means, upon a materialism which is softened by a spirit of self-sacrifice for the common good. He Tammanyizes business. For all his profession of faith, he has not even that sense of stewardship which characterizes Stalin. When, therefore, Catholics argue against Communism because it asserts that man is matter, they leave me quite cold. When the Capitalist stops thinking of the worker as a machine, a commodity, then I shall be prepared to grant that he, too, is not a materialist.

No Capitalist wants class warfare. He shouts and fumes against the arraying of class against class. So he forms an American Liberty League, or a National Manufacturers Association or a U.S. Chamber of Commerce, all organizations whose sole purpose is the shedding of sweetness and light to the worker. Or he orders in a few thugs, politely known as strikebreakers or spies, to have tea with his employees, in order that they may learn what a swell guy he is. Furthermore, when he buys a gross of machine-guns and a thousand tear-gas bombs, it is just because he wants to play soldier or maybe cops and robbers. If, in the process, he happens to murder a few workers, it is all just good clean fun.

Another thing I like about the Communist is his candid refusal to make a little tin god out of private property. He believes that the right to private property is an acquired rather than a natural right. In this, I can get support for him from Catholic ethicians. I cannot go along with him in his assumption that the right to private property has ceased to serve the individual and common good. Yet, here again, he is honest. But the Capitalist, while mouthing about the divine right to private property, does his level best to corral everything in sight, thereby depriving everyone else of their natural rights. His whole tradition is that of the hog in the trough. No ethical case can be made out for private property which endangers the common good. What the Capitalist does is to use the institution of private property to destroy his fellows. When he so acts, he is rat-like. Hans Zinsser in *Rats, Lice and History* says pleasantly, "Man and rats are merely, so far, the most successful animals of prey." So, while I cannot get up much enthusiasm for the bee brigade in which the Communist wants to regiment me, I can get up still less for the rat culture of Capitalism.

From what has been written, it will have been gathered that the major difference between the Communist and the Capitalist is that the one is two-fisted and the other is two-faced. The Catholic press can take its pick. But so long as it fails to grasp the only distinction between the two, I shall continue to blow these Bronx cheers in its direction.

Moreover, I shall also continue to heave my raspberries at both the Communist and the Capitalist. Man was not meant for Stalin's Sissy State. Man was not meant for the Rat State. For if he is not a sissy, neither is he a bully. In fine, man is neither a son of a bee, nor the son of a rat. He is the son of God.

On the Coffee Line

ONE OF THE SERVERS

HAVING SPENT most of the night in heated discussion and neglecting the time, I was in no mood to crawl out at 5:30 this morning to do a turn on the breadline. But the quickest way to forget sleepiness is to roll out, wet my face and turn on the radio in the store—this I did.

It is hard to cut a mountain of bread and prepare it for serving. I say hard because it seems hours before the job is complete. The eyes of the men outside peering in keep saying—it's cold out here, or, he's about ready now. The bread is all set (this is about 6:15) and Scotty has the first of a hundred gallons of steaming coffee ready to serve as we open the door.

On a cold morning such as this I can imagine the stream of hope that flows through the long line right down Mott Street and around the corner on Canal. Cups are taken and the three-hour session of feeding our friends is under way. I can watch the faces and see thanks written between the lines denoting age and fatigue and worry.

Ade Bethune's drawings always arrest the attention of the men for a moment. No matter how anxious they are about reaching the coffeepot there is always time to cast eyes along the wall, and admiration for Christ the Worker momentarily makes them forget their hunger. Many are old faces who come every morning. One is called the "Cardinal" because of his purple knitted cap, so worn and shy of edges it looks like a skull cap. He always has a kindly word. As usual my Japanese friend comes early. He too always has a greeting.

Now today there are three youngsters with unkempt hair, wrinkled clothes and looking very tired. Knocking around the country with exposure to night air with no place to wash or get cleaned is new to them. In spite of their youth and strength the condition is more obvious. The oldsters are more used to it. Every morning there are several who carry shopping bags or bundles with their last few belongings. They place them under the table so as to better handle a hot cup and a huge chunk of bread.

One of the regular bundle-toters had a new coat this morning. All winter he has had a dirty trench coat heavy with the dirt of many nights' sleeping out and smoke from many a fire. His new coat must have belonged to some stylish young boy with extreme taste. In spite of this he looked better, the coat was warmer and he had a more confident air.

I am relieved now to go to Mass which means I must pass a whole block of hungry, waiting men. It seems a long walk some mornings, especially when it is cold or wet. I receive greetings from those who have come to know us. I wish many more would pass them during their long days to give them a chance to share and realize their troubles. The line is broken at the corner so to enable pedestrians to pass. The line running west on Canal Street extends for about two hundred feet. It is really impossible, then, to forget them at Mass.

On returning it is easy to recognize the familiar hats, coats, shoes and other misfitting clothing of the regular comers. Faces are mostly turned out facing the street. I know many of these men have no one for miles around here who knows them, yet every one of them feels that each passerby recognizes them. From the rear one can notice the long hair under the caps and hats of most men. All, after being out for hours in the cold, are hunched against the weather and have their hands in their pockets. Across the street three are at a fire made of cardboard boxes. The huge flames will soon die away. There is one Negro and two aged white men. None talk but just stare at the flames, absorbing the heat and probably seeing better days gone by.

I can recognize one of my regular friends. He is a midwesterner with an attractive drawl. He lives his nights in subway trains. The newspapers in his pockets he has picked up from trains, and generally he gives them to us. A small gift indeed, but a gift given out of real appreciation. He is tanned because of two warm days sitting in the park facing the new spring sun and catching up on much-needed sleep.

There is the usual complexity of disposition. Some are almost bitter. The hunger of some makes them a little too eager and they irritate those around them. Many are indifferent because they have accepted their condition as fate. Some even sing in keeping with the radio. Some whistle. Others engage in conversation. There are enough coming daily to understand there is no disciplinary measure used; kind treatment has effected a self-discipline. Some just stare and seem to be counting those in front of them.

Here comes the little Irishman who will ask for the softest kind of bread. He has no teeth and cannot chew the crusts of the rye bread. He appreciates our remembering this and he knows we will have some kind of soft bread ready.

They continue to come. When I am busy putting peanut butter on bread and can't see their faces, I can recognize the arms that reach for bread. One gets to know all the familiar marks of the garments. The hands of some tremble from age, sickness or drink. It is near closing time and the line thins out. They must go out now into a world seemingly full of people whose hearts are as hard and cold as the pavements they must walk all day in quest of their needs. Walk they must for if they sit in the park (when it is warm) on Chrystie Street, the police will shoo them off. Then there is the worry of the next meal or that night's sleeping arrangements. Here starts their long weary trek as to Calvary. They meet no Veronica on their way to relieve the tiredness nor is there a Simon of Cyrene to relieve the burden of the cross. It is awful to think this will start again tomorrow.

Editorial—CW Stand on the Use of Force

DOROTHY DAY

DEAR FATHER:

You are one of many priests and laymen who have written to us of *The Catholic Worker* these past two years on the stand we have taken in the Spanish conflict. Many times we have been misquoted, or sentences from articles or public speeches have been taken from their context and distorted, and our friends have written us with pain that our attitude should seem to be at variance with that of Catholic leaders.

I am writting this letter to explain as best I can the points which we are trying to bring out in *The Catholic Worker*. I am writing it with prayer because it is so hard to write of things of the spirit—it is so hard to explain. If we had made ourselves clear before, we should not have to keep restating our position. But perhaps conflict is good in that it brings about clarification of thought.

We all know that there is a frightful persecution of religion in Spain. Churches have been destroyed and desecrated, priests and nuns have been tortured and murdered in great numbers.

In the light of this fact it is inconceivably difficult to write as we do. It is folly—it seems madness—to say as we do—"we are opposed to the use of force as a means of settling personal, national, or international disputes." As a newspaper trying to affect public opinion, we take this stand. We feel that if the press and the public throughout the world do not speak in terms of the counsels of perfection, who else will?

We pray those martyrs of Spain to help us, to pray for us, to guide us in the stand we take. We speak in their name. Their blood cries out against a spirit of hatred and savagery which aims toward a peace founded upon victory, at the price of resentment

35

and hatred enduring for years to come. Do you suppose they died, saying grimly: "All right—we accept martyrdom—we will not lift the sword to defend ourselves but the lay troops will avenge us!" This would be martyrdom wasted. Blood spilled in vain. Or rather did they say with St. Stephen, "Father, forgive them," and pray with love for their conversion. And did they not rather pray, when the light of Christ burst upon them, that love would overcome hatred, that men *dying* for faith, rather than *killing* for their faith, would save the world?

Truly this is the folly of the cross! But when we say "Saviour of the World, save Russia," we do not expect a glittering army to overcome the heresy.

As long as men trust to the use of force—only a superior, a more savage and brutal force will overcome the enemy. We use his own weapons, and we must make sure our own force is more savage, more bestial than his own. As long as we are trusting to force—we are praying for a victory by force.

We are neglecting the one means—prayer and the sacraments —by which whole armies can be overcome. "The King is not saved by a great army," David said. "Proceed as sheep and not wolves," St. John Chrysostom said.

St. Peter drew the sword and our Lord rebuked him. They asked our Lord to prove His Divinity and come down from the cross. But He suffered the "failure" of the cross. His apostles kept asking for a temporal Kingdom. Even with Christ Himself to guide and enlighten them they did not see the primacy of the spiritual. Only when the Holy Ghost descended on them did they see.

Today the whole world has turned to the use of force.

While we take this stand we are not condemning those who have seized arms and engaged in war.

Who of us as individuals if he were in Spain today, could tell what he would do? Or in China? From the human natural standpoint men are doing good to defend their faith, their country. But from the standpoint of the Supernatural—there is the "better way"—the way of the Saints—the way of love.

Who of those who are combating *The Catholic Worker* stand would despise the Christian way—the way of Christ? Not one.

Yet again and again it is said that Christianity is not possible —that it cannot be practiced.

Today the whole world is in the midst of a revolution. We are living through it now—all of us. History will record this time as a time of world revolution. And frankly, we are calling for Saints. The Holy Father in his call for Catholic Action, for the lay apostolate, is calling for Saints. We must prepare now for martyrdom—otherwise we will not be ready. Who of us if he were attacked now would not react quickly and humanly against such attack? Would we love our brother who strikes us? Of all at *The Catholic Worker* how many would not instinctively defend himself with any forceful means in his power? We must prepare. We must prepare now. There must be a disarmament of the heart.

Yes, wars will go on. We are living in a world where even "Nature itself travaileth and groaneth" due to the Fall. But we cannot sit back and say "human nature being what it is, you cannot get a man to overcome his adversary by love."

We are afraid of the word love and yet love is stronger than death, stronger than hatred.

If we do not, as the press, emphasize the law of love, we betray our trust, our vocation. We must stand opposed to the use of force.

St. Paul, burning with zeal, persecuted the church. But he was converted.

Again and again in the history of the church, the conquered overcome the conquerors.

We are not talking of passive resistance. Love and prayer are not passive, but a most active glowing force.

And we ask with grief who are they amongst us who pray with faith and with love, and so powerfully that they can move the mountains of hatred that stand in our path. The soul needs exercise as well as the body and if we do not exercise our soul in prayer now, we will be puny and ineffectual in the trials that await us.

We are not praying for victory for Franco in Spain, a victory won with the aid of Mussolini's son who gets a thrill out of bombing; with the aid of Mussolini who is opposing the Holy Father in his pronouncements on "racism"; with the aid of Hitler who persecutes the church in Germany. Nor are we praying for victory for the loyalists whose Anarchist, Communist and anti-God leaders are trying to destroy religion.

We are praying for the Spanish people—all of them our brothers in Christ—all of them Temples of the Holy Ghost, all of them members or potential members of the Mystical Body of Christ.

And we add daily to this prayer for peace: "Lord, teach us to pray." "Lord, I believe; help Thou my unbelief." "Lord, take away my heart of stone and give me a heart of flesh."

This editorial is not intended to be a complete statement of *The Catholic Worker's* stand on the Spanish war. Neither does it purport to be anything dogmatic, merely an expression of the sincere convictions of *The Catholic Worker* staff.

 ## Editorial—To the Workers

An Appeal to Workers to Sacrifice for Peace

WE ADDRESS this appeal to the workers of America, you whose sweat and labor is the lifeblood of our country, you whose blood must flow if the United States engages in another imperialist war, you whose fellow workers are now dying for Capitalist gain and imperialist ambition in Europe.

Appeals are being made to your selfishness; you are told that prosperity will accompany a war boom, that if the United States shall sell to warring nations or other nations to be transferred to warring countries, the long-awaited lift from unemployment and depression is at hand. Those who tell you this speak the truth. They know how long you have suffered, they know the agonizing years have taken toll. And, depending on your despair, they would make you party to blood profits they hope to make in a war that is the result of their actions in the past.

Firmly believing in the essential integrity of the American worker, and his sense of brotherhood with the workers of the world, we address another appeal; an appeal to your idealism, to your desire for justice, to your Charity. No matter how the legislative tide turns, no matter what laws are passed abridging the neutrality of the United States, you hold it in your power to keep our country aloof from the European war. This is our appeal, then, that you use your power as workers to refuse to manufacture or transport articles of war that are intended for foreign nations, warring or neutral. That you serve notice on your employers, in organized fashion, that you will have no part of such blood money, and that you will strike if necessary to maintain your position.

Is this asking a tremendous sacrifice? We know it is. And yet, it is necessary sometimes for workers to make overwhelming sacrifices. You have made them in order that your right to organize, to strike, to picket, to get a fair share of the profits of industry be recognized. Hundreds of workers have suffered imprisonment, injury and death, at the hands of those very people who make war, in order that they and their work might be accorded the dignity that belongs to them. You do not think their sacrifices were in vain. You honor and revere the memory of labor's martyrs. Sacrifice has been labor's lot; it still is. Sacrifice is always the lot of the noble, and only sacrifice can keep noble what sacrifice has ennobled.

Have you the courage necessary? You, the steel workers, the seamen, the rubber workers, the cotton workers, the chemical workers? Can you, the steel workers, insist that the industry that is partly yours by virtue of your work engage only in peaceful pursuits, that the industry devote itself to the positive program of making only those materials calculated to build a better society, not wreck the one we have? You can if you have the capacity for sacrifice that we think you have.

Can you, the seamen, employ the same courage that carried you through the tumultuous years of organization, the strikes, the long hardships of picket lines in the dead of winter? You can, you can use the rights you have won through the suffering and deaths of your fellow seamen, to enforce a policy of real neutrality for the United States. You have the capacity for sacrifice, we have seen it; will you use it now in order that warmongers do not get the materials they need to kill your fellows in Europe? There's something greater than mere money bonuses to fight for. Don't let those who talk unctuously of neutrality by force of arms fool you into supplying guns and gas to kill and maim your fellow workers.

We address all workers in the same vein. It is yours to say whether the United States shall dip its hands in the blood of European workers. You can say NO! You can close the plants if necessary. You can proclaim to the world that at long last the workers are refusing to be the pawns of Capitalist and imperialist gain; that they have searched for truth and have found it; that you know now that workers' security lies in truth and justice, so truth and justice will be your aims. Actually, whether you know it or not, you, the workers, hold in your hands the power to tip the scales in favor of peace or crime. Are you afraid of your power? We are waiting for your answer.

PART II

A World At War
1940–1945

Aims and Purposes

DOROTHY DAY

FOR THE SAKE of new readers, for the sake of men on our bread-lines, for the sake of the employed and unemployed, the organized and unorganized workers, and also for the sake of ourselves, we must reiterate again and again what are our aims and purposes.

Together with the Works of Mercy, feeding, clothing and sheltering our brothers, we must indoctrinate. We must "give reason for the faith that is in us." Otherwise we are scattered members of the Body of Christ, we are not "all members one of another." Otherwise our religion is an opiate, for ourselves alone, for our comfort or for our individual safety or indifferent custom.

We cannot live alone. We cannot go to Heaven alone. Otherwise, as Péguy said, God will say to us, "Where are the others?" (This is in one sense only as, of course, we believe that we must be what we would have the other fellow be. We must look to ourselves, our own lives first.)

If we do not keep indoctrinating, we lose the vision. And if we lose the vision, we become merely philanthropists, doling out palliatives.

The vision is this. We are working for "a new heaven and a new *earth,* wherein justice dwelleth." We are trying to say with action, "Thy will be done on *earth* as it is in heaven." We are working for a Christian social order.

We believe in the brotherhood of man and the Fatherhood of God. This teaching, the doctrine of the Mystical Body of Christ,

43

involves today the issue of unions (where men call each other brothers); it involves the racial question; it involves cooperatives, credit unions, crafts; it involves Houses of Hospitality and Farming Communes. It is with all these means that we can live as though we believed indeed that we are all members one of another, knowing that when "the health of one member suffers, the health of the whole body is lowered."

This work of ours toward a new heaven and a new earth shows a correlation between the material and the spiritual, and, of course, recognizes the primacy of the spiritual. Food for the body is not enough. There must be food for the soul. Hence the leaders of the work, and as many as we can induce to join us, must go daily to Mass, to receive food for the soul. And as our perceptions are quickened, and as we pray that our faith be increased, we will see Christ in each other, and we will not lose faith in those around us, no matter how stumbling their progress is. It is easier to have faith that God will support each House of Hospitality and Farming Commune and supply our needs in the way of food and money to pay bills, than it is to keep a strong, hearty, living faith in each individual around us—to see Christ in him. If we lose faith, if we stop the work of indoctrinating, we are in a way denying Christ again.

We must practice the presence of God. He said that when two or three are gathered together, there He is in the midst of them. He is with us in our kitchens, at our tables, on our breadlines, with our visitors, on our farms. When we pray for our material needs, it brings us close to His humanity. He, too, needed food and shelter. He, too, warmed His hands at a fire and lay down in a boat to sleep.

When we have spiritual reading at meals, when we have the rosary at night, when we have study groups, forums, when we go out to distribute literature at meetings, or sell it on the street corners, Christ is there with us. What we do is very little. But it is like the little boy with a few loaves and fishes. Christ took that little and increased it. He will do the rest. What we do is so little we may seem to be constantly failing. But so did He fail.

He met with apparent failure on the Cross. But unless the seed fall into the earth and die, there is no harvest.

And why must we see results? Our work is to sow. Another generation will be reaping the harvest.

When we write in these terms, we are writing not only for our fellow workers in thirty other Houses, to other groups of Catholic Workers who are meeting for discussion, but to every reader of the paper. We hold with the motto of the National Maritime Union, that every member is an organizer. We are upholding the ideal of personal responsibility. You can work as you are bumming around the country on freights, if you are working in a factory or a field or a shipyard or a filling station. You do not depend on any organization which means only paper figures, which means only the labor of the few. We are not speaking of mass action, pressure groups (fearful potential for evil as well as good). We are addressing each individual reader of *The Catholic Worker.*

The work grows with each month, the circulation increases, letters come in from all over the world, articles are written about the movement in many countries.

Statesmen watch the work, scholars study it, workers feel its attraction, those who are in need flock to us and stay to participate. It is a new way of life. But though we grow in numbers and reach far-off corners of the earth, essentially the work depends on each one of us, on our way of life, the little works we do.

"Where are the others?" God will say. Let us not deny Him in those about us. Even here, right now, we can have that new earth, wherein justice dwelleth!

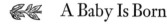 # A Baby Is Born

DOROTHY DAY

IT IS JANUARY 9, 1941, and *The New York Times* this morning is filled with news of total war and total defense. Every day four-column headlines of the costs of war: "1942 Budget $17,485,528,-049. Funds for British to Be Sought Later."

Wonder what that $49 tacked on at the end of the $17,485,-528,000 is for? Fifty dollars, we know, will pay for a baby, if you are poor, at any hospital in the city. A flat rate of fifty dollars, ward care, the ministrations of any doctor that happens to be on hand, and ten days' hospitalization.

At Bellevue Hospital, if you are poor, if you are a resident of the great City of the New York, it doesn't cost a cent.

William, our new baby down here at Mott Street, is hereby headlined on our front page, as the biggest news of the month, the gayest news, the most beautiful news, the most tragic news, and indeed more worthy of a place in a headline than the seventeen billion, four hundred and eighty-five million, five hundred and twenty-eight thousand and forty-nine dollars headlined in *The New York Times* this morning. William himself is worth more than that sum, more indeed than all the money in the world. He is indeed but dust, the Lord knoweth it, but he is also little less than the angels. He is a creature of body and soul, a son of God and (by his baptism down at Transfiguration Church last Sunday at 2 P.M.) a temple of the Holy Ghost. For his sake our Lord God came down from Heaven, was begotten by the Holy Ghost, born of the Virgin Mary, was made man, lived with us for thirty-three years, and suffered and laid down His life. For William's sake as well as for the sake of each one of us.

And this tiny creature who little realizes his dignity as a member of the Mystical Body of Christ, lies upstairs from me now as

46

I write, swaddled in a blanket and reposing in a laundry basket. He is rosy and calm and satisfied, a look of infinite peace and complacency upon that tiny countenance. He little knows what is in the world, what horrors beset us on every side.

We had awaited his arrival, the week before Christmas, breathlessly. Every night before we went to bed we asked the young mother, "How do you feel?" and asked each other (us women on the two top floors of St. Joseph's House on Mott Street), "Is there taxi money?" in case it would be too late to call an ambulance.

And then, one morning at five, I heard rapid footsteps in the room above, the voice of the ambulance interne in the hall, "I'll be waiting downstairs." And I realized that the great moment had arrived.

It was still dark out, but it was indubitably morning. Lights were on in the kitchens of surrounding tenements. Fish peddlers, taxi drivers, truckmen, longshoremen, were up and on their way to work. The business of life was beginning. And I thought, "How cheerful to begin to have a baby at this time of the morning!" Not at 2 A.M., for instance, a dreary time of low vitality, when people sink beneath their woes and courage flags. Five o'clock is a cheerful hour.

Down in our little back yard (where we had the Christmas tree this year), down in that cavernous pit with tenements looming five and seven stories up around, we could hear them dragging out the ash cans, bringing in the coffee cans for the line.

Peter Clark and his crew were on hand, cutting pumpernickel (none of this already sliced, pasty, puffy white bread for us) getting out the cups, preparing the coffee for our eight hundred or so breakfast guests.

Out in front the line was forming already and two or three fires in the gutters brought out in sharp relief the haggard faces of the men, the tragedy of their rags. The bright flames, the blue-black sky, the grey buildings all about, everything sharp and clear, and this morning a white ambulance drawn up in front of the door.

This is not the story of the tragedy of the mother. We are not going into details about that. But I could not help thinking that while I was glad the morning was beginning, it was a miserable shame that the departure of the young woman for her ordeal should be witnessed by a long, silent waiting line of men. They surveyed her, a slight figure, bundled on that cruelly cold morning (and pain and fear make the blood run cold), come running down from the dark, silent house to get into the ambulance.

Not one man, not a dear husband, not a protector on whom she could lean for comfort and strength. There was no Joseph on this winter morning. But there were hundreds of men, silent, waiting and wondering perhaps as they watched the ambulance, whether it was life or death that had called it out.

"This is worse than war," one woman friend said a few days before, contemplating the siutation. And we agreed, wondering if anything indeed could be more desperate and sad than a woman left to have her child alone.

There you have the tragedy of the refugee, there you have the misery of homelessness, the uncertainty as to food and clothing and shelter (and this woman had known hunger). And there, too, you have the pain and agony of the flesh. No soldier with his guts spilled out on the battlefield, lying for hours impaled upon barbed wire, suffers physically more than a woman in childbirth. Physically, I say, because does not the soldier in his horror and pain wonder what has brought him to this pass— what is being accomplished by the gigantic agony of war? With the woman the suffering brought forth life. In war, death. And despite shame and fear and uncertainty, as in this case, still there cannot but be joy over a child born into the world.

So it is with joy that we announce the newcomer to our House of Hospitality on Mott Street, knowing that our readers who have suffered with us in the past will be glad to rejoice with us now.

For us most truly this has been a season of happiness. "For unto us a son is born, unto us a child is given." Christ Himself came so truly to us this Christmas Day in this baby boy, just as in the persons of the hungry men. "For inasmuch as ye have done it unto one of the least of these my brethren, ye have done it unto me."

Letter to Fellow Workers

BEN JOE LABRAY

DEAR FELLOW WORKERS:

We crept into the Soo in a ghostly fog at dawn today after a perfectly calm trip over Lake Superior. We are now nearly half-way over Lake Huron and it is calm and warm. Too warm for November 13, but it may wind up in rain and do nothing worse.

When the Union ships got their increase in July of this year, the phony Lake Carriers' Association, a ship owners' company union, broke out with the news that all who shipped before August 1 would be given a $25-a-month bonus if they finished the season and laid up the ship. Those who already had the first half of the season in would get theirs dating back to the spring fitout. It was a master stroke on the part of the ship owners. It held the crews on and greatly discouraged organization by the NMU, which was going forward very successfully.

Well, the boys stuck on and the company, the engineers and mates and stewards took full advantage of the situation. No one who had already sailed five months would want to get off now as he'd be throwing $125 away. So the abuse began. The fighting began and the trouble. The stewards began cutting down on the grub and competing with other cooks of the other ships of the line, knowing no one would dare squawk as they might get fired and lose their bonus. Fights of all kinds, and on this rust pot they all seem to hate each other's guts. Everyone afraid to talk to the other.

The other day Shorty, the deck watch on my watch, had a cup of coffee and when finished poured the remains in the sink. The steward growled and one word got louder than the next. A battle started and while they were wrestling near the door, the steward's wife walked up and slapped Shorty so hard he nearly went over the side.

Their nerves are all on edge and they all say they'll never fall

49

for that bonus stuff again. I take advantage of each beef to talk on the glories of a free union where nobody worries, gets fired or hungry and the wages are always ahead of the Lake Carriers, etc. etc. Say I: "Let freedom ring"—down with the Lake Carriers' Association! Day before yesterday the steward on a steel trust ship hung himself in his stateroom. Another "bonus jittered" case, I suppose.

A clear, sunny, calm trip all the way here! Passing Detroit this P.M. it was like summer. We are now running along slow speed heading into Lorain, to anchor and await orders. It's warm out and the stars are blazing and the lighthouse blinks right ahead and the fog horn is howling its mournful, weird, eerie and blood-curdling moan as though to rebuke us for throwing off the lad into the seething maelstrom near here last trip.

The ship continues to be hungry and at six tonight when I came off watch I ran into a dish of half-cooked baked beans, etc. This guy is a prize belly robber. If we were living in a land without laws and without Christianity we'd all bump each other off in no time. Without restraint the race wouldn't last three generations. It's bad enough if one is a Christian or trying to be one.

I just had to cease writing awhile to put out a fire. I miscued with a cigarette butt and my partner's dungarees caught fire. He's sleeping blissfully right under me. He's a Hungarian and says I write more than anyone he ever saw. He's a patient soul— my orange fell off the nail this morning and bounced off his dome. He didn't say a word—just retrieved it, peeled it and ate it. If only all problems could be solved as easy as that. A little thing like that aboard ship could cause a murder.

I see by the papers that King, Ramsay and Connor have been paroled out on the west coast. Everyone of *The Catholic Worker* crowd that wrote in to the Governor and talked the case to their friends and got them to write had something to do with getting them out. Visiting the prisoner is one of the works of mercy. When you start doing something for people it is like praying for them.

Work is prayer, St. Benedict says. Let's ask them to pray for Wallace, the fink that committed the murder for which the other three were framed. That'll get a laugh! And yet, that's what

Christianity means. Forgiving your brother. Or let's scrap Christianity, forget about Christmas and join the Communist party. They've got more love in them than many a Christian. Love Hitler? Pray for Stalin? That's what Christianity means. No wonder Christians are persecuted.

Please excuse the sermon. It's Christmas and I feel I'll be off the lakes this month with plenty of money to last through the winter on, and I'll be walking the streets, looking in all the lighted windows and basking in the warmth of the holiday.

But come to think of it, there's that appeal of yours. Why should I think of the morrow. True, I'm not exactly a lily of the field but with the help of God I'll get by. So enclosed is a hundred and fifty, no more and no better than that dollar some young woman sent in from scrubbing floors with the thermometer up to a hundred.

Yours for the green revolution,

BEN JOE

 Our Country Passes from Undeclared War to Declared War; We Continue Our Christian Pacifist Stand

In Addition to the Weapon of Starvation of Its Enemy, Our Country Is Now Using the Weapons of Army, Navy and Air Force—In a Month of Great Feasts, a Time of Joy in Christian Life, the World Plunges Itself Still Deeper into the Horror of War

DOROTHY DAY

DEAR FELLOW WORKERS IN CHRIST:

Lord God, merciful God, our Father, shall we keep silent, or shall we speak? And if we speak, what shall we say?

I am sitting here in the church on Mott Street writing this in your presence. Out on the streets it is quiet, but you are there too, in the Chinese, in the Italians, these neighbors we love. We love them because they are our brothers, as Christ is our Brother and God our Father.

But we have forgotten so much. We have all forgotten. And how can we know unless you tell us. "For whoever calls upon the name of the Lord shall be saved." How then are they to call upon Him in whom they have not believed? But how are they to believe Him whom they have not heard? And how are they to hear, if no one preaches? And how are men to preach unless they be sent? As it is written, "How beautiful are the feet of those who preach the gospel of peace." (*Romans* X)

Seventy-five thousand *Catholic Workers* go out every month. What shall we print? We can print still what the Holy Father is saying, when he speaks of total war, of mitigating the horrors of war, when he speaks of cities of refuge, of feeding Europe. . . .

We will print the words of Christ who is with us always, even to the end of the world. "Love your enemies, do good to those who hate you, and pray for those who persecute and calumniate you, so that you may be children of your Father in heaven, who makes His sun to rise on the good and the evil, and sends rain on the just and unjust."

We are at war, a declared war, with Japan, Germany and Italy. But still we can repeat Christ's word, each day, holding them close in our hearts, each month printing them in the paper. In times past, Europe has been a battlefield. But let us remember St. Francis, who spoke of peace and we will remind our readers of him, too, so they will not forget.

In *The Catholic Worker* we will quote our Pope, our saints, our priests. We will go on printing the articles which remind us today that we are *all* "called to be saints," that we are other Christs, reminding us of the priesthood of the laity.

We are still pacifists. Our manifesto is the Sermon on the Mount, which means that we will try to be peacemakers. Speaking for many of our conscientious objectors, we will not participate in armed warfare or in making munitions, or by buying government bonds to prosecute the war, or in urging others to these efforts.

But neither will we be carping in our criticism. We love our country and we love our President. We have been the only country in the world where men of all nations have taken refuge from oppression. We recognize that while in the order of intention we have tried to stand for peace, for love of our brother, in the order of execution we have failed as Americans in living up to our principles.

We will try daily, hourly, to pray for an end to the war, such an end, to quote Father Orchard, "as would manifest to all the world, that it was brought about by divine action, rather than by military might or diplomatic negotiation, which men and nations would then only attribute to their power or sagacity."

"Despite all calls to prayer," Father Orchard concludes, "there is at present all too little indication anywhere that the tragedy of humanity and the desperate need of the world have moved the faithful, still less stirred the thoughtless masses, to turn to prayer as the only hope for mankind this dreadful hour.

"We shall never pray until we feel more deeply, and we shall never feel deeply enough until we envisage what is actually happening in the world, and understand what is possible in the will of God; and that means until sufficient numbers realize that we have brought things to a pass which is beyond human power to help or save.

"Those who do feel and see, however inadequately, should not hesitate to begin to pray, or fail to persevere, however dark the prospects remain.

"Let them urge others to do likewise; and then, first small groups, and then the Church as a whole, and at last the world, may turn and cry for forgiveness, mercy and deliverance for all.

"Then we may be sure God will answer, and effectually; for the Lord's hand is not shortened that it cannot save, nor His ear heavy that it cannot hear."

Let us add, that unless we combine this prayer with alms-giving, in giving to the least of God's children, and fasting in order that we may help feed the hungry, and penance in recognition of our share in the guilt, our prayer may become empty words.

Our works of mercy may take us into the midst of war. As editor of *The Catholic Worker*, I would urge our friends and associates to care for the sick and the wounded, to the growing of food for the hungry, to the continuance of all our works of mercy in our houses and on our farms. We understand, of course, that there is and that there will be great differences of opinion even among our own groups as to how much collaboration we can have with the government in times like these. There are differences more profound and there will be many continuing to work with us from necessity, or from choice, who do not agree with us as to our position on war, conscientious objection, etc. But we beg that there will be mutual charity and forbearance among us all.

This letter, sent to all our Houses of Hospitality and to all our farms, and being printed in the January issue of the paper, is to state our position in this most difficult time.

Because of our refusal to assist in the prosecution of war and our insistence that our collaboration be one for peace, we may find ourselves in difficulties. But we trust in the generosity and understanding of our government and our friends, to permit us to continue, to use our paper to "preach Christ crucified."

May the Blessed Mary, Mother of love, of faith, of knowledge and of hope, pray for us.

Herbs of the Field

GRAHAM CAREY

GOD PUT MAN in a garden to dress and keep it. Man has been expelled from the original Paradise, but plants are still a most necessary part of that natural world which is made for his physical support. Plants are made for him to use, not to abuse. This means he must know what they are, know the truth about them. And it means he must desire their goodness and use them for what they are good for.

These strengths or virtues of the plants are for food and medicine, clothing and the fulfillment of other needs. The truth about plants is known, their goodness desired and their beauty is appreciated. When plants were thought of as herbs these abstractions were all in their proper relations.

Herbs were good, true and beautiful because they were what they were, and man was more or less as he ought to be. But man became less rather than more what he ought to be, less disinterested and less intelligent, that is to say, less human. He divided plants up into classes.

The plants of the botanist are things to be known about. The botanist, as such, cares not for goodness or beauty, but only to get his categories accurately lined up with the facts. To him plants are particularly examples of his categories, or as he calls them, specimens.

The plants of the commercial farmer are things to be profited from, things that can be marketed with financial advantage. As such the commercial farmer cares not for truth or beauty, but only to grow crops which will help him to meet his payroll and show a profit. To do this he specializes in those plants which produce most cheaply the greatest quantities of the substance he wants. He ignores all other plants as out of place in his scheme and calls them weeds. Weeds are plants that interfere with the profits to be derived from crops.

The plants of the gardener are things to be enjoyed for their beauty. The gardener as such, cares not for truth or goodness but grows only those plants which are thought of as pretty or attractive. All other plants, because they interfere with his aesthetic scheme, he considers as weeds. The plants he propagates are called flowers.

As all natural plants are extremely beautiful it is curious to see how the distinction between flowers and weeds was worked out in practice. What seems to have happened is this: Familiar plants were chosen as flowers, familiar either because they were cultivated for use, as the larkspur, dahlia or sunflower; or familiar from their symbolism as the rose or lily. Brightly colored plants were chosen, especially those with showy blossoms. Strongly scented plants were chosen.

Now neither familiarity, nor size, nor bright colors and strong and sweet scents have anything directly to do with their beauty. This is at once evident when we see that the gardener in increasing size and bright color actually decreased beauty. Beauty is the resplendence of order, but as we see on examining the "improved" varieties of flowers, order has been distinctly diminished and beauty with it.

So modern man, who has divided his own life into pigeonholes and thus maimed its unity, has treated plants in the same way. In pursuing the thrill of knowledge cut off from use he has made of plants specimens. In pursuing profit rather than use he has turned plants into crops and weeds. In pursuing a romantic retreat from the world his pride and his greed have made, he has turned plants into flowers and weeds.

But neither specimens, nor crops, nor flowers, nor weeds are really plants. They are only plants under certain aspects—the aspects of classification, profit, thrill or the aspect of interference with profit and thrill.

There is nothing wrong with this except in the separation. Life is an organic whole. We are right to separate its parts if we are careful to reassemble them. If we distinguish without reuniting them we have killed the life.

But God placed man in a garden that he might be happy. He did not put him in a botanical laboratory plus a grain factory plus a flowery dream spot. He put him in a garden where he could be instructed by knowledge, served by goodness and refreshed by beauty all in the same operation.

The old word herb, though today it has acquired a rather romantic flavor, reflected the normal holistic attitude to plants. Even the "sweet, pot and medicinal herbs" of the modern seed catalogue are not too dim a survival of the older attitude. Herbs are merely plants looked at from a holistic point of view, as things to be known, used and enjoyed all at once, as things which have survived the intense sifting and combing processes of recent centuries.

If the over-specialization of modern industrialism and of world trade with its attendant evils (which in this year of 1942 we really ought to be beginning to be aware of) are ever to be undone, we must return to the holistic view of life, and also of plants. We must learn the virtues of the plants we have, and use them for food, medicine and clothing, rather than sell ourselves in slavery to money, power, and armed violence, in order to enjoy the properties of exotics. We believe that the exotic plant is superior to the native, not because we have tried the native and found it wanting, but because those who are our economic masters, and wish to remain so, tell us that it is superior. In our complete ignorance we believe them and do as we are told. We even engage in suicidal wars in order to defend access to plants that we consider vital to our happiness and well being, without even attempting to find out whether these plants are vital or not. If we investigate we discover that the claim of the trader is not true. But few investigate and we continue to believe the falsehood.

It is perfect example of truth making free and falsehood making slaves. We believe a lie—that we cannot live in decency and comfort without a vast system of overseas trade—and we therefore sell ourselves and our children into slavery and death to defend that vast system against those who would either overthrow it or rob us of it.

So the lovely word herb is one of the keys to the understanding of this problem.

Man can live today, as he has lived in the past, in his own garden. He has lived in it well in the past and today he can live in it even better. But he can only do so if he will relearn the past and lost knowledge of plants, find out how many uses there are for how many plants which today we call weeds in mere ignorance of their virtues.

SEPTEMBER 1942

Editorial—We Are Defeated!

CHRIST SAID:

"What doth it profit a man if he gain the whole world and suffer the loss of his own soul?"

"Woe to Pharisees. For they bind heavy and insupportable burdens and lay them on man's shoulders; but with a finger of their own they will not move them."

"For I was hungry, and you gave me not to eat; I was thirsty, and you gave me not drink. Amen, I say to you, as long as you did it not to one of these least, neither did you do it to me."

If we do not continue to protest the hunger in Europe, the dreadful starvation that is surely wiping out the whole population of Greece, and if we did not continue to cry out against the sinful blockade of Europe imposed by Great Britain and consented to by us, the very stones would cry out for us.

While we use such means as mass starvation of women and children, the old and infirm, we are already defeated. God is not with us, so we have lost the war already. As long as we use such means, and not only against our enemies but against our friends and allies, no victory is possible. God and Gideon and three hundred saved the day for the Israelites. If we turn to Him and follow His law and beg His aid, He will most certainly bring true peace.

 ## Excerpt from Day After Day

DOROTHY DAY

HERE IS A STORY that began March 19, the feast of our patron, St. Joseph. Every now and then someone came in and said, "Did St. Joseph send you a present yet?" And then later in the day the telephone call came, from a lawyer, saying that someone had just died and left us around five hundred dollars in a will.

We were overjoyed. St. Joseph had behaved as we expected him to do on his feast day. We were broke and that five hundred dollars could have gone to the printer, to the coffee man, to the bread man or for an installment on the farm mortgage.

We went around beaming for days. Only twice before had we been willed anything. An auto worker in Hamtramck had willed us five dollars, and a Finn miner in Minnesota had told his mother when he was dying to send us five dollars. And here was another legacy!

And then this situation arose. We were unincorporated and we did not wish to be incorporated. Nor did we intend to be, either for five hundred or five thousand dollars. It is hard for our friends and readers to get the point of this. It is difficult to explain, too. It is one of those ephemeral things, felt rather than understood, even on our part.

The way we feel about it is this. No one asked us to do this work. The mayor of the city did not come along and ask us to run a bread line or a hospice to supplement the municipal lodging house. Nor did the Bishop or Cardinal ask that we help out the Catholic Charities in their endeavor to help the poor. No one asked us to start an agency or an institution of any kind. On our responsibility, because we are our brother's keeper, because of a sense of personal responsibility, we began to try to see Christ in each one that came to us. If a man was hungry, there was always something in the icebox. If he needed a bed—and we were crowded—there was always a quarter around to buy a bed on the Bowery. If he needed clothes, there were our friends to be appealed to, after we had taken the extra coat out of the closet first, of course. It might be someone else's coat but that was all right too.

Our Houses of Hospitality are scarcely the kind of houses that Peter Maurin has envisioned in his plan for a new social order. He recognizes that himself, and thinks in terms of the future to accomplish true centers of Catholic Action and rural centers such as he speaks of in his column this month.

Our houses grew up around us. Our bread lines came about by accident, our round-table discussions are unplanned, spontaneous affairs. The smaller the house, the smaller the group, the better. If we could get it down to *Christian families*, we would be content. Ever to become smaller—that is the aim. And to talk about incorporating is somehow to miss the point of the whole movement.

So all right, St. Joseph, if you have brought about clarification of thought by your little joke on your feast day, all right, we are grateful to you. Meanwhile there is that printing bill of $1100 that needs to be paid. We are only hinting to you about this, because St. Francis de Sales is the special patron of writers and journalists. Maybe we had better ask him.

A Letter to Christ's Poor

JOHN COGLEY

GOD WAS NO LESS a God because he came into the world destitute. Nor was he less a king.

Neither are you less a man because you have been stripped of respectability. Neither are you less a child of the king because you share his destitution. You are still made to the image and likeness of God though you are beaten and scarred. A man is a man for all that. The whole creation of God trembles before your dignity for all that.

We are keenly conscious of the injustices of the world. Religion does not soft-pedal injustice. We know that hopelessness and discouragement often overtake you and that the faith in your hearts can turn to ashes. A stupid, respectable world lets you eat its garbage and bed in its gutters; and a stupid, respectable world lets its God be born in a beast's hut. If you remember the birth of Christ, faith can brighten for you who are among the world's outcasts. Religion is a fire, a roaring flame, a thundering passion that can drive the lowliest of men to the very heights. Don't let it die within you.

It demands courage to cling to faith when all the world has crumbled around us. It calls for strength to cling to the old beliefs, to keep the old truths in mind. And yet religion is not for the coward or the weak. Religion is a mighty battle for the strong.

When a man has been knocked around, as some of you have, it calls for fortitude to throw back your head and sing a song to the sun, a paean of thanksgiving to God for your very being. That is for strong warriors of the spirit. Spiritual strength is the stuff of saints.

Religion is a warrior's battle, a mighty fortification to be seized, a city to be taken by storm. The Holy Ghost comes like a tempest of wind.

If on Christmas eve your home is the streets, your bed is a gutter, your clothes are rags—remember the stable. You are little kings, and an animal's hovel enthroned the King of kings.

If on Christmas day you receive your Lord in Holy Communion, you are host to the Lord of the world, and angels shall tremble before the temple that is your body. Though a world passes by, all heaven will stand still.

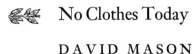 ## No Clothes Today

DAVID MASON

IT IS EARLY Sunday morning. There is a penetrating October chill in the air. This is the kind of morning that makes you feel fine if you've had a good breakfast, or anticipate one, and are well dressed. But the man who hobbles into our courtyard hasn't had breakfast, good or bad, and he is far from well dressed. In fact, he is scarcely dressed at all. His left shoe is missing. So are his socks, shirt and coat. His torn undershirt and beltless trousers are filthy.

He mumbles his plea for help through chattering teeth and quivering blue lips. No need to ask how he got that way. It's an old story. He was drunk last night, and some wretch relieved him of the missing garments, or else he tossed them off in a drunken fit. Either way, it is an everyday occurrence. It is not hard to see in him the "man who fell among thieves," and he has come to us with faith that we will help him. Can we refuse because "it's his own fault"? Yes, if the Good Samaritan looked into that phase of the case before he "bound up his wounds."

Fortunately, we have some clothes that fit him, even a pair of shoes. There is a razor for him to shave with, but first he must have a cup of coffee to steady his shaking hands.

An extreme case, certainly, but there are more extreme cases than you might imagine. Yes, it may often be their own fault, but who are we to judge? So long as we have anything to give, it is our duty in Christian charity to give it.

So long as we have anything. There's the rub. Too frequently, these days, we have nothing, or next to nothing, in the way of old clothing that can be worn by men who come to us in dire need. Some days we have to put a little sign on the door which reads:

NO CLOTHES TODAY
I'M SORRY TO SAY

 Cologne: A Cross for the World

GORDON ZAHN

AT FIRST the story seemed too good to be true. The Cologne cathedral was "structurally intact" in spite of the thoroughgoing obliteration bombings that wiped most of the city off the face of the earth. Some of the papers we read went so far as to refer to its escape as miraculous. Miracle or not, we heaved a great sigh of relief and thanked God for the accuracy of our bombardiers and turned to the other news of that day—including the report that Dortmund had been added to the list of "dead" German cities in one powerful blow by Allied air power.

Relief and reverent gratitude were the first reactions. But, strangely, this was not to be all. This news item did not drop so easily from our interest. Instead it grew and took on new aspects, so that every now and then we found Cologne—or rather, the memory of Cologne—forcing itself into our thoughts. Maybe it was the poignant little report about the children who were terror-stricken whenever they heard the sound of a plane, or any sound resembling that of a plane. Perhaps it was the impact of a vision of hundreds of thousands of people spending most of their waking hours in rat holes under a shaking city. Sometimes we found ourselves asking, "Why?" Sometimes we felt a chilling realization of Cologne's future meaning to the world when our consciences struggled with persistently probing, challenging thoughts. God! How they must hate us.

But always we could comfort ourselves by recalling that picture of the cathedral, the prize of the ages, preserved. True, the historic Rathshaus, the quaint Gothic houses and shops lining countless ancient streets—these things that most of us will know only by description—were gone. Perhaps we caught ourselves questioning this, too. After all, these objectives were not too military in their individual importance (except in so far as they housed and served civilians engaged in the same "total war effort" we praise so highly in our own civilians), these objectives were not too strategic in their value (in fact, the destruction of the city meant merely another headache to its eventual reconstruction authority and served to add new and precious spirit to a dying and desperate nation). There must have been some reason for mercilessly saturating Cologne with exploding death; that much is evident upon looking at the honeycombs of ruin that once were homes. Reason would almost tempt us to doubt the assurances from on high that "terror bombing" is not, and has never been, an Allied policy. And anyway, we were told, the cathedral was saved—or, rather, remains "structurally intact"; that should be cause enough for joy.

I do not know how many decades have passed since the completion of that structure; nor could I tell you how many generations it took to build that structure. These facts could be easily obtained at any public library. But they would prove nothing except that the building was quite old and took quite a while to finish. The name of the master planner (if any one man were responsible for the magnificent architecture) is also immaterial, although it probably is available. Such things are always available in history books or encyclopedias. But they are not always important.

The important item in this case is the fact that men—generations of men—were sufficiently inspired to undertake, plan, dream and build, and *pray*, until they had created an edifice suitable to the honoring of their God, worthy of expressing a faith that enabled them to challenge a span of years beyond their individual lifetimes. To those of us who felt joy in hearing that their work still stands, it didn't matter too much (if it occurred to us at all to remember the fact) that these men who built were of the barbarian, war-creating strain of mankind, the Teutonic monster whose sole aim on earth (we are told by all the better minds of our day) is to crush the innocent and destroy the righteous. We probably forgot also that these very men whose lives were dedicated to the work our men so considerately spared lived in some of those very same dwellings, walked the very same streets that did not fare so well.

The importance of the cathedral lay not in the fact that it was built, but, rather, in *why* it was built. Just so, we must not place our emphasis on the fact that it stands; instead, we must consider *what it stands for*.

Whoever had the desire to undertake so great an effort must have had a mighty faith; and the men who struggled to achieve his goal shared that same faith. No tyrant could have driven men to create so enduring a monument to life. These men of faith were content to add their part to a work they would never see in its completed glory because they knew that what they were expressing could never die. And so they toiled and died, and their sons and their descendants followed the same pattern of life until finally the cathedral stood, not as a mound of stone honoring some departed hero but as a work of faith to house the presence of a living God—a God whose message was eternal love and who poured forth His love in agony, who in that agony suffered even this day when man would reject Him, when man would return ten Colognes for the evil of one Coventry in His Name.

For remember we must that their present-day descendants who also worshipped in the cathedral, lived in the ancient dwellings and walked the ancient streets—these "hateful barbarians," these "murdering, plundering" brothers in the Mystical Body of Christ to our gallant, crusading defenders who flew above their city and so artfully and accurately snuffed out its life, share with us the heritage of Calvary's sorrow and glory and carry the obligation to forgive us these trespasses as we might have forgiven them for trespassing against us.

The miracle of faith that built the cathedral marked the contribution of its builders to the ages. This generation has scarred its monuments into the face of the earth in a never-increasing crescendo from blockbusters to townbusters—and eventually, we may suppose, to worldbusters. Where they left a miracle of construction, we have accomplished a miracle of destruction. The two have met at Cologne. The cathedral that towers over a sea of rubble and ruin is, as the papers say, structurally intact. It is for us now to determine whether it is still intact in the spirit that gave it substance—if the faith of the Christians of today is strong enough to overcome the fury of the prides and hatreds and vengeance they have created and bring all men to their knees in an international prayer for forgiveness.

If we fail in this, if we refuse to accept the cross of responsibility for a peace based on justice, forgiveness and love, we shall have lost our chance to bring about the kind of world toward which these men of ages past were building. And then, perhaps, it might have been just as well had some bombardier done by accident what we will have done by intentional neglect—reduce the Cologne cathedral structure to what it actually is, a pile of old stones.

We Go On Record—

DOROTHY DAY

Mr. Truman was jubilant. President Truman. True man; what a strange name, come to think of it. We refer to Jesus Christ as true God and true Man. Truman is a true man of his time in that he was jubilant. He was not a son of God, brother of Christ, brother of the Japanese, jubilating as he did. He went from table to table on the cruiser which was bringing him home from the Big Three conference, telling the great news; "jubilant" the newspapers said. *Jubilate Deo.* We have killed 318,000 Japanese.

That is, we hope we have killed them, the Associated Press, on page one, column one of the *Herald Tribune*, says. The effect is hoped for, not known. It is to be hoped they are vaporized, our Japanese brothers, scattered, men, women and babies, to the four winds, over the seven seas. Perhaps we will breathe their dust into our nostrils, feel them in the fog of New York on our faces, feel them in the rain on the hills of Easton.

Jubilate Deo. President Truman was jubilant. We have created. We have created destruction. We have created a new element, called Pluto. Nature had nothing to do with it.

"A cavern below Columbia was the bomb's cradle," born not that men might live, but that men might be killed. Brought into being in a cavern, and then tried in a desert place, in the midst of tempest and lightning, tried out, and then again on the eve of the Feast of the Transfiguration of our Lord Jesus Christ, on a far off island in the eastern hemisphere, tried out again, this "new weapon which conceivably might wipe out mankind, and perhaps the planet itself."

"Dropped on a town, one bomb would be equivalent to a severe earthquake and would utterly destroy the place. A scientific brain trust has solved the problem of how to confine and release almost unlimited energy. It is impossible yet to measure its effects."

"We have spent two billion on the greatest scientific gamble in history and won," said President Truman jubilantly.

("UNRRA meets today facing a crisis on funds. It is close to scraping the bottom of its financial barrel, will open its third council session tomorrow, hoping to get enough new funds to carry it through the winter.")

(Germany is told of Hard Winter by Eisenhower.)

(Pall of Apathy Shrouds Bitter, Hungry Vienna)

The papers list the scientists (the murderers) who are credited with perfecting this new weapon. One outstanding authority "who earlier had developed a powerful electrical bombardment machine called the cyclotron, was Professor O. E. Lawrence, a Nobel prize winner of the University of California. In the heat of the race to unlock the atom, he built the world's most powerful atom smashing gun, a machine whose electrical projectiles carried charges equivalent to 25,000,000 volts. But such machines were found in the end to be unnecessary. The atom of Uranium-235 was smashed with surprising ease. Science discovered that not sledgehammer blows, but subtle taps from slow traveling neutrons managed more on a tuning technique were all that were needed to disintegrate the Uranium-235 atom."

(Remember the tales we used to hear, that one note of a violin, if that note could be discovered, could collapse the Empire State Building. Remember too, that God's voice was heard not in the great and strong wind, not in the earthquake, not in the fire, but "in the whistling of a gentle air.")

Scientists, army officers, great universities (Notre Dame included), and captains of industry—all are given credit lines in the press for their work of preparing the bomb—and other bombs, the President assures us, are in production now.

Great Britain controls the supply of uranium ore, in Canada and Rhodesia. We are making the bombs. This new great force will be used for good, the scientists assured us. And then they wiped out a city of 318,000. This was good. The President was jubilant.

Today's paper with its columns of description of the new era, the atomic era, which this colossal slaughter of the innocents has ushered in, is filled with stories covering every conceivable phase of the new discovery. Pictures of the towns and the industrial plants where the parts are made are spread across the pages. In the forefront of the town of Oak Ridge, Tennessee, is a chapel, a large comfortable-looking chapel benignly settled beside the plant. And the scientists making the first tests in the desert prayed, one newspaper account said.

Yes, God is still in the picture. God is not mocked. Today, the day of this so great news, God made a madman dance and talk, who had not spoken for twenty years. God sent a typhoon to damage the carrier *Hornet*. God permitted a fog to obscure vision and a bomber crashed into the Empire State Building. God permits these things. We have to remember it. We are held in God's hands, all of us, and President Truman too, and these scientists who have created death, but will use it for good. He, God, holds our life and our happiness, our sanity and our health; our lives are in His hands.

He is our Creator. Creator.

. . . And I think, as I think on these things, that while here in the western hemisphere, we went in for precision bombing (what chance of *precision* bombing now?), while we went in for obliteration bombing, Russia was very careful not to bomb cities, to wipe out civilian populations. Perhaps she was thinking of the poor, of the workers, as brothers.

I remember, too, that many stories have come out of Russia of her pride in scientific discoveries and of how eagerly and pride-fully they were trying to discover the secret of life—how to create life (not death).

Exalted pride, yes, but I wonder which will be easier to forgive?

And as I write, Pigsie, who works in Secaucus, New Jersey, feeding hogs, and cleaning out the excrement of hogs, who comes in once a month to find beauty and surcease and glamor and glory in the drink of the Bowery, trying to drive the hell and the smell out of his nostrils and his life, sleeps on our doorstep, in this best and most advanced and progressive of all possible worlds. And as I write, our cat, Rainbow, slinks by with a shrill rat in her jaws, out of the kitchen closet here at Mott Street. Here in this greatest of cities which covered the cavern where this stupendous discovery was made, which institutes an era of unbelievable richness and power and glory for man. . . .

Everyone says, "I wonder what the Pope thinks of it?" How everyone turns to the Vatican for judgment, even though they do not seem to listen to the voice there! But our Lord Himself has already pronounced judgment on the atomic bomb. When James and John (John the beloved) wished to call down fire from heaven on their enemies, Jesus said;

"You know not of what spirit you are. The Son of Man came not to destroy souls but to save." He said also, "What you do unto the least of these my brethren, you do unto me."

PART III

People and Problems
1946–1955

Pie-Eyed

Notes on a National Crisis

STANLEY VISHNEWSKI

IT ALL STARTED with Tommy—Tommy was definitely to blame for everything that happened. And yet were one directly to accuse Tommy of being the cause of it all, one would be quickly disarmed by the innocence of Tommy's demeanor and no doubt would wonder how it was possible for one so sweet and innocent to have been the instigator of one of the greatest intellectual squabbles of the ages.

It all started with Tommy—I know that I am repeating myself, but it all started when Tommy refused an extra piece of pie for dinner. His action was certainly harmless, and in fact was even meritorious, but little did Tommy dream of the far-reaching effects that were to follow as a result.

"No, Ma'am." Tommy was all politeness in refusing the second helping of pie that Mrs. Piet generously offered him.

"No second piece of pie!" Mrs. Piet could scarcely believe the evidence of her ears and for a moment thought that she had misunderstood Tommy. But it was true. Tommy actually pushed the piece of pie to one side.

"No, Ma'am, no second piece of pie." And Tom looked longingly and lovingly at the piece of pie.

"What is the matter, Tommy?" Mrs. Piet's feelings were easily injured. "Don't you like it?"

"I do, and that precisely is the reason why I am offering it up. I wish to mortify myself."

"Mortify yourself!" Mrs. Piet uttered the words out loud as she looked long and searchingly at Tommy.

"That is just what Tommy said," Mrs. Piet told the members of her sewing circle that same evening. "The poor boy actually refused a second helping of pie."

"I don't blame him," was the thought that ran through Mrs. Teip's head. Mrs. Teip was rather scornful of Mrs. Piet's culinary abilities, but wisely she kept her thoughts to herself.

"The poor child—why he will starve himself to death." Mrs. Sniff commented.

"This sort of nonsense must stop!" Mrs. Feethink exclaimed. "The Church is ruining the health of our children with medieval notions of fasting and mortifications."

"Imagine the child not eating!" Mrs. Goan indignantly exclaimed.

Mrs. Piet just sat back in her rocking chair and rocked and rocked and rocked.

(Overheard in a subway:)
Did you hear the tragic news?
No, what happened?
A child committed suicide . . .
You don't say!
He was bad and he was refused a second helping of pie and so he got mad and so he killed himself and it's so tragic . . .

"I never refuse a second helping of pie," Mr. Gout said as he poured himself a cup of coffee.

"Neither do I," replied Mr. Pur. "I see nothing wrong in a piece of pie."

"Sure. Eating pie isn't sinful. I can't see why they're making such a fuss over pie eating."

The meeting of the Woman's League for Improved Social Relations Between Man and Wife buzzed with indignation. Numerous comments could be overheard:

"I think that it is a perfect crime to deprive children of their toys and pies in the name of a misguided asceticism."

"Children should be free to express themselves. It is up to a child to determine whether or not he should have a second helping of pie. Parents must not interfere."

The excitement died down as the speaker of the evening mounted the platform.

"Women of America," she began. "We have called this meeting together to discuss a grave problem which is threatening to destroy our beloved nation. Statistics prove that the rise of juvenile delinquency is due to the fact that children will do anything to get hold of a piece of pie. Our children have not been taught the truism that you can't have your pie and eat it. Frankly speaking, I believe that the Communists are in back of this."

"It would be terrible," Mrs. Athos said at the conclusion of the talk, "if we couldn't get pie for breakfast."

"The question of pie is nothing but a red herring to divide the working class," the local Communist paper screeched in a fighting editorial. "The C.P. in its traditional historic fight against the bourgeois imperialistic fascistic oligarchy has always championed the rights of the workers to have all the pie they wanted. It is the Communists who want their pie now and not in some future sky."

The American Committee for Babies Delivered on Schedule came out boldly: "It is not a question of pies. It is a question of children who eat pies. The solution is not to do away with pies but to do away with children who demand pies."

The entire nation was becoming pie conscious. Brother was turning against brother, and many families were ruined over the question of how many and how often. *I Sigh for Pie* became the latest song hit. Pie-shaped hats were the craze among the girls. The vegetarians passed a resolution condemning the use of meat pies. Sober pedants came to blows over the problem of the contents of the Babylonian lunch pails. One group held that pie eating was a mainstay of the ancient Babylonians while the other school of thought derided the idea as preposterous.

The sudden interest of the nation in pie was ably exploited by Senator Filler, who addressed a joint session of Congress:

"It is my opinion as a good American that un-American interests are at work in this country doing their utmost to undermine a great American institution which you and I know and revere as that supreme accomplishment of the American housewife—I refer to the pie." (*Applause.*) "Already it has been brought to my attention that a group of people called themselves the Ascetics are working night and day to have the people stop eating pies. And there is no end to where they will stop. First it will be the pies, then it will be cosmetics, then the radio, then the movies and then where will our great culture be? I ask Congress to pass a law outlawing Asceticism and Penance as unconstitutional and un-American."

Senator Filler's remarks to Congress had a sobering effect on the nation at large. Laws making the eating of pies compulsory were passed. Special bureaus were created to stir up people's interest in eating bigger and better pies. Pie-eating contests became the vogue, and it was said that a man could be elected to public office on the strength of his pie-eating record.

Principal speaker at the Pastry Workers' Annual Banquet, Deapdissh C. Rust, Congressional candidate of the Proprietary Party, tartly excoriated opponents and violators of the Pie law. "I will not mince my words," he said. "I charge that these unprincipled wretches are plotting to drive a subversive wedge between the upper crust and the lower crust of our social structure, thereby shortening the life of our nation."

Special agents were assigned to each restaurant to see that the patrons did not leave their pies. The jails soon became filled with offenders who violated the Pie-Eating Enactment. Secret restaurants opened up where a person could eat a meal in peace without being disturbed by the thought of having to eat a piece of pie. The nation was fast becoming pie conscious.

Tommy, the innocent cause of it all, sat down to dinner at Mrs. Piet's and with great gusto ate a second helping of pie. "No, thank you," Tom politely said as he refused the chocolate which Mrs. Piet offered him. "I'd like to give it up as an act of mortification."

 # Will They Go Again?

JACK ENGLISH

MANY FORMER GI's are today hesitant sheep wandering with both ears cocked for the clear, confident voice of their shepherds.

They are wondering about the justice of their varied activities in the past war, not that they have a "guilt complex" for they know that sin is not *ex post facto*, but because the promised era of peace and justice grows more improbable and because they believe that once again they will be called upon to make a decision and this will have to be made in the light of a whole mass of war experiences.

Many of us were interested in pacificism before World War II. *Interested* but not convinced. Our interest was not lost during the conflict but rather it deepened as the war seemed to conflict more and more with the qualifications necessary to wage it justly. Sometimes we consulted our chaplains on the subject, sometimes we wrote to friends but more often we just sweated the whole thing out in anguish by ourselves. Usually the whole question of a decision was pigeonholed for we were in the army and that was a *fait accompli*. When we got out of the service we would study and investigate. We would talk to our priest friends. This much we promised ourselves. There would be some definite word from the theologians on this subject for after all it was one in which millions of people were involved.

There would be answers for the flyers who were told at briefings that if the target was overcast to dump the bombs any place over the city. And there would be answers for the Ranger who made his way out of the prison camp near Berlin and walked to freedom in Paris. He had to leave a whole trail of dead men and women and children behind him to make his escape final. Should he have remained in the camp and sat out the war or should he obey orders and make the attempt to make his way back home when the opportunity presented itself? Then there was the question of the atom bomb, of guided missiles. With peace came the notion of the proportionate good and evil in the war, and wouldn't these proportions be accentuated in another conflict?

These are general notions and each GI had his personal problems, the old question of temptation and consenting to evil in his personal life. Various men reacted in various ways. I dare say that some exercised self-discipline. But what was the overall picture?

And what has been the tenor of the replies to our questions. "Yes, perhaps the pacifists have something." *Perhaps.* "The question will have to be investigated."

And yet no discussion comes up. "Look at the list of the soldier saints." "A man who dies in the defense of justice gains a martyr's crown." "The last Pope canonized ordered a crusade." But the soldier-saints, the martyrs, and that Pope didn't live in an age of unleashed atoms. Is it right to ask the mass of humanity to stand the test of martyrdom, of a life of heroic sanctity?

Most of us are not eccentrics. We don't want to be divorced from the common experiences of our fellows. That perhaps is the great temptation. We are sheep, not the shepherds. We are the laity, not the ordained preachers and theologians. We sheep are hesitant about following a lone voice here and there. We would like our shepherds to call to us and say in pretty much one voice, "Here is the path, this is the way," and not stand perplexed and unsure while the sky darkens and another storm gathers itself around us. Are we bleating in vain?

✤ House of Hospitality

JOHN COGLEY

TODAY THE CHICAGO PAPERS all carried headlines about the heat wave that for a week has been hanging over the city like a guilty conscience. "Heat wave breaks all records; no relief in sight" was the discouraging head in the evening papers, and tomorrow morning, according to the radio know-it-alls, there will be a repetition of the same grim prediction.

Everyone is talking about the weather. The still, hot air is clogged with platitudes about the heat, and the whimpered, wordless complaints of people too listless for more than a tired "Whew!"

There has been about the last week something of a movie twice seen. An incredible familiarity. The same dialogue, the same heavy movements, the same weary responses, the same inevitable sweating it out.

Older people go through their lines and their complaints with a knowing, querulous patience. They've all been through it before; it is as familiar as an ancient liturgy. Only babies and very young children voice their rebellion with any vigor, ignorant yet of the impotence they'll learn.

For the grown-up, the summer heat wave is familiar enough to recall a mood, to recapture an impression from the past, or to catch again some fleeting insight. Hearing the complaints, reading the headlines, exchanging the platitudes, it is something like hearing a snatch of some once-popular song. It brings back other times, other years.

I remember the summer of 1942, the first summer we were in the war, when the army's training camps, ubiquitous, were tightly crowded with fresh soldiers like cigarettes in a pack. Across the country that summer the air rang with the bellowing orders of drill masters and basic training instructors. All through the hot months, millions of men every sundown marched in elaborate formations for newly omnipotent colonels.

A handful were dying alone on Guadalcanal, but while the necessarily slow business of basic training held up the millions at home, the brass luxuriated in precision displays and the stylized devoirs that were their military due.

Oh, there were some parades in those days at the basic training camps, even bigger and better than those the seasoned veterans put on at the end of the war.

At a place like Jefferson Barracks, Missouri, tens of thousands of green GI's marched every late afternoon, eyes-right toward the colonel, haughty and proud in the reviewing stand, while the sun beat down and the ambulances stood waiting on the sidelines to carry away those who collapsed.

And when enough men had died of sunstroke that it was whispered around and four-letter curses called down on the parades, there was a notice on the bulletin board, brief and military, pointing out that the hot sun beat down on the Pacific islands, too, and on the deserts of Africa and the fields of India. This one men, it said, is a global war. After all, the sooner the better . . .

Marching out to their parade grounds and passing in review, the millions were a mass of men, soldiers row on row like poppies on Flanders Field or the white crosses of Arlington: each man swallowed up in the whole, moving, marching, saluting, almost breathing as one impersonal mass.

And if a fly or a mosquito challenged the ideal of military uniformity, then that was a moment of agony, a petty pain of war, to be accepted as such. "Don't move for anything less than a mad dog," the non-com instructors said. "And then only if he's actually biting you."

The blasted inconvenience of having nerves when the colonel was standing proudly with his four-year-old grandson in the reviewing place of honor!

The idea was to put off manhood for an hour and to melt into the mass like a drop of water into a sea, then move in unified precision as a proud army before a proud colonel.

"Like one man; move like you was one man," the non-coms kept saying. And sometimes it came off beautifully, like the Rockettes on a good day, and there would be reports that the colonel had been pleased. But, oh, the damage those sand flies did, the affronts they offered to West Point dignity.

After the parade was over and the colonel and his grandson went back to their quarters, while the stretchers were carried into the station hospital, the GI's marched back in squadrons to their tents.

Away from the parade ground and out of the colonel's sight, the order for "Route Step" was given, and this meant that you could be yourself again, could walk any way you wanted to, and you could talk if you had a mind to. You usually did have a mind to, to call down curses on the army, the war, the parade grounds, tradition, the colonel, and the mosquitoes. And because there were thousands of you, there was always somebody to talk to and to share your curses with.

At the sound of the sergeant's order "Route Step," personality seeped back into the men returning to their quarters, almost like God ordering life into the primeval slime.

The proud army became a group of men, each one an individual person. By a toss of the head, a gesture of the hand, a tone of voice, by these things it was now possible to pick out a friend, to know one man from another.

Now there were all kinds: the soft drawls and the slow carriage of Texans, each drawl unmistakable, each carriage unique; the hearty cheerfulness and the horseplay of the guys from Brooklyn, each with his own brand of horseplay, each with his own style of cheerfulness. And maybe someone would draw out a *Reader's Digest* from his back pocket and read as he walked, while two more might converse seriously in low tones.

It was possible now to distinguish the guys who were really unhappy in the army, homesick perhaps, from those who could take it with a grin. Happy men, sad men, troubled men, carefree men, serious men, pinheads, roughnecks, scholars, gentlemen and bums; the sanguine, the melancholic, the phlegmatic, the choleric and a thousand variations of each: at the sergeant's bellow each man was himself; and it's a shame the colonel never saw them that way. It's always a shame when men are not seen as individual men but as part of a mass, whether they be soldiers or Displaced Persons, slain German Jews or Bowery drunks.

Bringing people back to life, the way the sergeants did, is never as easy as it was in the army. In the world outside the army, it can't be done with the mere shouting of a command.

Outside the army, it's a slow business; and the price of life returned is patience and charity, understanding and sympathy. The price is often hospitality. Four summers before that hot one at the basic training camp, I knew another army that was dehumanized and stood silent and still, motionless in the sun. This was the tragic depression army, the mass that used to be called glibly "the great army of the unemployed."

They stood in the sun, stretching in a long listless line down the alley in back of the Chicago House of Hospitality; standing in line, tormented not by the clean sand flies of an immaculate army post but by the hateful, degrading vermin of unwashed bodies, they waited for a bowl of soup.

There were hundreds of them, but they were a silent, still crowd, with the quiet distraction of men who are missing something precious, call it the spark of ambition, interest in life, or whatever you want to call it. Anyway, whatever it was, it was gone; and it was something essential.

On the weary walks back and forth to the House of Hospitality for meager meals, on the fruitless searchings for "another chance," a job, a place to sleep, a way to kill a day; during the lonely futility of their day wanderings and the threatening insecurity of their night passings, they left behind them a trail of spent life, dripping from them like blood from an open wound.

A listless group of men, these men in the line taken as a whole, discouraged, indifferent, even to each other, shamed, and beaten by life.

How they got that way, what happened, why: there are a thousand different stories. It would be nice maybe if the eager people who want general answers to these questions could be satisfied;

but you just can't answer a silly question like: How do men get that way? or: What would you say is the cause of their present condition?

If you could answer, a flat "booze" (which is much more often an effect than it is a cause) or "laziness" or "bad home life" or "an unhappy marriage" or something resounding and satisfying, then the people who demand an easy explanation might be happy. But you can't account for a thousand human tragedies with a single phrase.

The point is that they were men. What was the cause, what happened, how do you explain, isn't it their own fault, don't you think if they had to do this or that or the other thing, etc.—all these things are beautifully beside the point.

When life is dripping away from men, it is not the time for speculation or self-satisfying theory-applications. This is the time to stop the flow, to heal the wounds, to bathe the sores.

A man is a man, a human person with intelligence and free will, living in a world of men, capable of heights and depths, of human tragedy and all the machinations of the world, the flesh, and the devil. Easy phrases and pet theories are no answer to human wreckage. God will mock us if we treat his great creature Man like a brute specimen in a laboratory.

And so, for whatever reason they found themselves there, the men in the breadline were a silent group; among them personality was as generally stifled as among any group of soldiers on a parade ground. The line was a sorry impersonal mass, and it moved as a single impersonal body; this one not proud but humbled and shamed.

There was room in the House of Hospitality for forty men. As an old man went off to a job or on to some other place, a man in the line took his bed in the House.

Then it was that life came back, slowly, painfully, almost shyly. Men we knew in the breadline for months as dour, wordless, dull people gradually took on a completely new (new to us, that is) character after they were established in the House of Hospitality for a while.

The security of the House, poor as it was, regular meals, a sure place to sleep, work to be done, the knowledge of being useful to others (such a little thing as slicing bread for the line or serving coffee was enough) and the casual but very real fellowship of the everchanging household of the place—these things were enough. It was often as if you could see a change taking place before your eyes, like something visible happening—color returning to a face after a faint.

Even the crudest kind of hospitality can work miracles. It is no wonder the wisdom of the Bible tells us to practice it in season and out of season and adds "without grumbling."

The slow miracle of restoring life to the joyless, of bringing back hope and a sense of belonging to the friendless, is more wonderful—much more wonderful—than the miracle the sergeant's short command brought about on the walks from the parade ground back to the tents.

But it can't be done with a word. What a man needs most is to feel like a man, to be treated like a man, to live in decency with other men.

What man can do for man! Man can raise other men from the dead, can rekindle hope, bring back the zest for living, inspire plans for the future, restore self-respect and pride in manhood— even mirror dimly the infinite charity of God.

This is the ideal of hospitality: being brother to brother, children of the same Father. Not scientific social work— hospitality. Not haughty superior dealing with "problem cases" —hospitality. Not condenscending judge dealing with errant accused—hospitality. No, hospitality is derived from the Latin word for guest. It expresses a relationship between equal men: host and guest. It is bound by the rules of courtesy and human companionship, and ruled by the law of charity.

There are always men and women who need hospitality, for one reason or another. There are, in an imperfect world of imperfect men and women, always those who need a calling back to life, a restoration of personality. There are always those lonely people, in all times, in all places, who need the knowledge of being respected as men and women, of living with other men and women with dignity, of sharing their own burdens with others and bearing some of the burdens for others.

Hospitality reminds people that they are brothers, children of God, dependent on others and capable of being depended on by others.

It is not a specialized work, requiring scientific training. It is something for everyone to practice according to the measure he is able to do so.

The House of Hospitality is a striking, almost dramatized expression of hospitality. But hospitality can be practiced by everyone, in the home, in the parish, in the club, sodality, school. It has a thousand forms and can be practiced in a thousand different ways.

The charm of hospitality, because it is peculiarly human, appeals to all men. And "the soul is naturally Christian": it is not surprising that often God should use the hospitality men give each other as an instrument of His grace.

DECEMBER 1947

 ## The Unwashed

TOM SULLIVAN

A MIDDLE-AGED MAN just walked into the office in search of a clean pair of socks. Informed us that he had a pair of socks on his feet, however they were in need of a washing. He pointed to his blue shirt and said, "You people gave me this several days ago." As he attempted to smooth out his suit coat he remarked, "This came from a Bowery mission." We didn't have a pair of socks to help the man out with, and glancing down at our own socks we noticed that they too were in a sad condition. We couldn't help but wonder as to the whereabouts of those new socks that we had at the early part of the summer.

We remembered our own mother's horror whenever she noticed holes in our socks, which openings frequently revealed dirty feet. She would generally mention how appalling and shameful it would be if we had an accident and strangers would be able to view our great unwashed feet. Our middle-aged visitor seemed to have the same terror of the dark night of the feet, and he promised to return the next day in search of socks. Before he left the office he insisted on telling his story.

"Yeh, I got drunk on paynight and found myself down on the Bowery where I was beaten up and rolled [robbed]. They hauled me over to the city hospital where they tossed me into the psycho ward, didn't even bother to put stitches in my wounds. I was released in a couple of days since it was decided that I wasn't psycho. Personally I thought the patients were saner than the people who work there."

HOW LONG?

A priest called here the other day. He wanted to know if we were acquainted with a Mr. ———. We replied in the negative. "Well," he said, "this man says he is in need of carfare to get over to Jersey for a job. And he states that you people have been giving him money for his bed over at the Union Hotel on the Bowery." We told our caller that we frequently give bed money to people whom we can't put up for the night due to overcrowded conditions. The voice on the other end of the wire inquired, "You mean that you don't know the names of these people you help and you don't keep a record of them?" We confirmed that. "Well, aren't some of these men unworthy and using you?" And we replied that they probably were if there is such a person as an unworthy case. However we don't feel competent to decide who is unworthy and who is not. Another one of those things we prefer to leave up to God. We were concerned with the present need and taking care of that. After further conversation our priest friend asked if he could not come over and discuss this matter further and get acquainted with the people here in the house.

 ## Pax

ROBERT LUDLOW

LOVE PROCEEDS from truth and Gandhi proceeded in love to the very end for he proceeded in truth—the truth as he saw it—he did not compromise; he was not a liberal or a relativist. His was devotion to an Absolute. And he could proceed in love because he could proceed without violence—it was the limit of his responsibility that he proceed without violence, that he *willed* no violence. It was his adherence to truth that, in the nature of things, brought about a violence that he never ceased to regret. But as life pushes forward, as decisions must be made, as truth must be upheld, and as it is impossible to uphold truth without running into opposition, so, in the nature of things, it was impossible that the nonviolent revolution of Gandhi should not have produced violence. But that violence was met with nonviolence on Gandhi's part—to the end he forgave, reconciled, loved. He was consistently pacifist. He was the subject of wranglings and hatreds. His acts set the stage for turmoil—and yet he was consistently pacifist throughout, he proceeded in love. Love which is never an easy thing, which can be harsh, which does not compromise truth, which penetrates revolution with pity, which forbids violence, which is indeed the very substance and meaning of divinity.

There is also the joy of life and the joy of death. Of life that is psychological freedom, of death that realizes the end of freedom in the Beatific Vision. There is the joy of Gandhi's death, the fittingness of his end—the baptism of blood. The blood of Gandhi, the redness of his blood, the joy of the soaked earth, the mother earth which receives him, receives his blood and his ashes till the resurrection. Rests, rests awhile in peace in the cool earth, to enter her life, to fertilize her vegetation, to have calm—respite from animated flesh, from the tyranny of glands, the ennui of physiology. It is tomorrow that the body arises; today, let it rest awhile, let it taste the earth, let insects crawl in its decay and worms wiggle their funny little paths in the debris. Today let there be no tiredness but only rest in the close hug of the earth; let it explore the secrets of matter while its life explores the creator of matter. Let it wallow a bit in mud, live with the carnal—exult and stretch lazily in the body brown earth, reach, reach out and spread. Spread to feed animal and vegetable in recompense for having fed on them when walking upright and setting foot ahead of foot as is the way with man. Drink, drink back the blood of baptism, the martyred soakings, the blood-mud. The glory of the blood, and the warm trickle of its spread, the slow spread of the blood penetrating the earth like the slow spread of revolution as it penetrates man. It is tomorrow that the body arises; today it is the wind, the gentle play of the wind with the ashes of Gandhi, today it is the coolness of evening, the red-blood sunset and the wind, the wind to scatter the dust of Gandhi. It is the wind today; tomorrow it will be the resurrection. The resurrection tomorrow—but today, today let the body collapse and enter the earth, let the tired body of Gandhi rest lightly on the earth, give him to the wind today, to the elements, to the flesh and to the material that he may enter into the very bowels of nature that she may cling yet to his resurrected flesh, for tomorrow is the resurrection.

According to what norm did Gandhi operate? He operated on the level of the absurd; in relation to the prevailing ethos of communities his norm lies in the regions of psychoses, as the Christian norm must ever be in relation to the things of this world. He moved in the supernatural and could not but appear strange to those whose concepts do not embrace this sphere. Even as Our Lord he traveled the earth in nostalgia for heaven and yet with no indifference to the multitude; he was detached from the things of time and yet through it all he loved man and nature, and his asceticism was tempered with pity and human warmth. His relation to the absolute was in no direct line, for it rebounded in his love for man; it encompassed a redeemed earth. I could not have much to say of the theory of mysticism to which he adhered, but there was in it enough truth and it bore fruit in the love of God and neighbor. As such it placed him in the soul of the Church. In a very real sense he was Christian and Catholic. I do not think that he can be classed with those mystics who, as Kierkegaard writes, become impatient of the revelations of God. For in that direction lies intellectual and spiritual pride and repugnance for the stench of the flesh, the sensual. Till finally there is conceived an impossibility of incarnation. So that one can no longer believe that God became man, that He stood on feet and saw through eyes and received nourishment. That He wept in sorrow over Jerusalem, sorrow that she was to go, for He loved her as one can love the strange beauty of cities, and the familiar streets and the noises of the streets. That He handled asceticism with indifference, as realizing its necessity and yet never pursuing it when higher claim was upon him. Claims of pity and hospitality, the call to souls that might lead through many channels and to strange places, so that oftentimes he ate and drank, but as a means to an end, as using things lightly, as keeping ever before Him the Divinity which He was. And the final criterion, the criterion on which He based judgment, was the love of God expressed visibly in the love of man. It seems to me that that was also the fruits of Gandhi, that he embraced a mysticism that went beyond preoccupation with self, even the self as related to God, and loved all men as an indispensable condition of perfection. It was for that he received the baptism of blood which brought him at once into the light of glory, the everlasting contemplation of God, having no further need of purgation.

We who walk the earth in sorrow! Who wear out the lonely watches of the night with our cries, who would all but despair if there were not in us the everlasting hope of resurrection, the absurd persistence of divinity, the unsatisfied longings for transcendance. And the strange beauty of night, the everlasting night of time, the cry of nature for liberation, the cry of those lost in the embrace of night, the sadness of night and the beauty of it. The beauty of Gandhi's death. Poor little one of God! Who is there left to wander the earth in your behalf, who to suffer for you, to join atonement in Christ? Have they buried their talents in the world, or are they hidden in convents and monasteries, or preoccupied with individual sanctity? Where are the Christians? Who among us to compare with this man of God, who to burst the black bowels of death, to pursue God down the night roads till the eternal dawn, to press revolution without violence, to give love for hate, to have joy in sorrow, hope in despair, victory in failure? Poor little ones of God! To whom shall we turn save only to Him who abides always in the heart of man, who in the days of time is lifted up as bread, who some time ago was lifted to the gaze of men at Golgotha. The eternal dripping of His blood fills the earth with divinity, makes holy the brown warm earth, redeems nature and man, takes to Himself the wasted body of His saint—for as He lives and as Gandhi lives, there will again be those who hear the whisper of His voice, the insistent call of the Absolute, the promptings of conscience. And once again there will be a pilgrim walking, walking the lonely stretches of the night.

Picking Cotton

AMMON HENNACY

HAVING A FEW FREE DAYS after the winter lettuce season at the large vegetable ranch where I had worked, I left my shack situated between a cabbage field and a lettuce field on land of the Russian pacifist Molokons and went to Phoenix to visit an atheist friend and spend the night in order to get the cotton truck before daylight. (This friend had bought a *Catholic Worker* from me in front of the library in Milwaukee one Saturday in 1941. He later read an article of mine in the *Catholic C.O.* His admiration of the courageous pacifist spirit of these papers led him to deviate from his atheistic norms.)

The next morning two bonfires were already burning along the curb where Mexicans, Indians and Anglos, many of the latter being "winos," were waiting to select the truck in which they would go to work. Just now there were only cotton trucks, there being a lull in citrus picking. Cotton pickers carry their own eight-foot to ten-foot sacks fastened with a strap around the shoulders and dragging behind them like a giant worm. There were eight trucks and several pickups. Most of them were shaped like the traditional covered wagon with canvas. There were benches on either side and in the middle. I walked around searching for someone I might know, but my friends of the lettuce fields were wary of cotton picking, considering this the hardest job to be had and one to be taken only as a last resort.

"Last call! Take you there and bring you back. Three dollars a hundred. All aboard gentlemen!" shouted a good-natured Negro in a bright mackinaw. The truck to which he pointed was box-shaped, of good veneer, with a short ladder leading inside from the rear. I entered and found a seat between a colored woman and a colored man. After a few more calls the doors were shut, and we could see each other only as one would light a cigarette.

Later on the truck stopped and we were joined by a large group of laughing Negroes of all ages. There were three whites besides myself, and one Indian.

Our destination was nine miles beyond Buckeye, which is about thirty miles west of Phoenix. After several sharp turns, when all in the truck were thrown this way and that, we came to the field. The Indian and I did not have sacks, so we rented them from the boss for a quarter.

This was tall cotton, and harder to pick than the small variety. The field was a quarter of a mile long and a mile wide. A young white man worked in one row, then the Indian, and then myself. I had never picked cotton before. The Indian, a Navajo, said this was to be clean picking, he understood.

Where the cotton was fluffy it was easy to grab, but where the boll was only partly open it was difficult to extract and hurt your fingers. As we worked along the row from the far end of the field toward the weighing scales and truck, my Navajo friend said that he was learning a lesson which he sadly needed. Now he had just enough money from day to day. Before this he had spent money freely and never had to count his pennies. He paid a dollar a night for a cot in a cheap hotel in Phoenix. He had an older brother who had been quite wealthy before the depression and was a big shot among his people because of his holdings in cattle. He drank, bought fine cars. Now with the "plowing under" and rationing system of the government he was a poor Indian indeed.

In speaking of the Navajo he said that they had always been poor in these last years, but that the suffering was now no greater than last year. If left to themselves in sheep and cattle raising and in growing corn they would be able to get along. But the government restrictions as to grazing and its refusal to provide schools for the Navajo according to treaty had given them little to do in their spare time except to succumb to the temptations of liquor and the allurements of the cities. The recent provision of half a million dollars for food from Congress was coupled with three times that amount to "rehabilitate" the Navajo.

This was another word for jobs for the white bureaucrats to feed on the misery of the Indian with boondoggling experiments.

Navajos do not eat fish, bear, pork; in fact any animal that does not eat grass is not "clean" to them. They will not kill a coyote for the bounty as do the whites.

We had worked three hours and took our cotton in to be weighed. I had thirty pounds and he had forty-two. The white man near us had eighty-five. In talking over this discrepancy we found that we had been picking only the clean white cotton, while the more experienced pickers picked the bolls along with the cotton and more than doubled the weight.

As we waited our turn for weighing our cotton, groups were shooting dice in the roadway. A Negro woman served coffee, chili, pie, weiners, etc., at reasonable prices. Some of the truck drivers sold food to their passengers.

Returning to the field we picked in more of an orthodox fashion, and in the total five and a half hours the Navajo picked eighty-two pounds and I picked sixty-two. Before we left I gave him *The Catholic Worker* to read with my letter about the Hopi refusing to go to war.

The next morning I met my Navajo friend beside the bonfire at Second and Madison. The truck of Negroes did not go out on Sunday. One truck took only those who had sacks. I got in a small pickup which headed westward about thirty miles to Litchfield Park. Several young girls kept us merry with songs. When we arrived at the field my Navajo friend came in on another truck. We happened to get sacks at different times, so did not work together.

An old man said that the rule here was "rough picking" which meant everything that had white in it, but no stems or leaves. When I emptied my sack, I had fifty-four pounds. The man next to me seemed to work rather expertly, and I asked him what time they quit on weekdays here. He replied that he only came on Sundays. "Make $1.25 an hour at my job in town, and time and a half overtime."

I commented that unless a person had a large family that was a good wage.

"I don't work here for the money," he continued. "I just come out here so I can keep sober. Was drunk from Christmas until yesterday—ten days. I can keep sober if I'm working, but I can't stand to be quiet or to loaf. And as I have eight kids, I need to keep working."

There was not much cotton left to pick in this field, and the word went around that we would quit about two P.M. At that time my second sack weighed thirty-one pounds, which, after paying for my sack, netted me $2.23. My Navajo friend had not done so well, picking only sixty-eight pounds. He said he had liked my reference to the Hopi in *The Catholic Worker*.

As we were going into town in the truck the man who picked cotton to keep sober was discussing the merits of different brands of liquor with another picker. This man was telling of going to a town upon receiving a paycheck as a "gandy dancer" on the railroad, going to the police and asking them how much the fine was for being "drunk and disorderly." They said it was $17.50 so he paid it at once, for he intended to get drunk and disorderly. I did not hear the rest of the story for the truck soon passed lateral 20, nearby where I lived, and I proceeded homeward with $3.93 for two part-days spent in the cotton fields.

Later in the day, sitting in my doorway, resting, I was asked by a man who drove up in a car to work for him for a week irrigating at $7.20 per day. Gladly I was willing to let this two part-days of cotton picking suffice. Good pickers can make from $8 to $12 a day, but I was not in that class.

Revolution and Compassion

ROBERT LUDLOW

IT IS IN ISRAEL that God revealed himself under the aspect of a national deity and it belongs to the Old Dispensation that there was a mission in the national state. And yet even there it was a state under law, subject to the moral law. There was distinction then between Jew and Gentile; there was not then fully realized the universal brotherhood of men. And so there was war. And yet even then there was realization of the sinfulness of war, there was the pacifism of the prophets, the cry of those who perceived what was beyond the law, who had a foretaste of the spirit of Christ, who longed for the brotherhood of all men that was to be proclaimed in the New Dispensation.

With the consummation of Christ's sacrifice on Calvary there was an end to the Old Dispensation, an end to morally justified war, an end to national states as desirable entities. For there is then no distinction between Jew and Gentile: all men take on the heritage of Israel, all men are admitted by the Divine Jew to the mysteries of Israel, all men are brothers in Christ. Therefore it is that, as the ideals of Christianity are realized, as they become exteriorized in society, so will national states wither away as being impediments to the realization of human brotherhood. And so will war be outlawed as rendering asunder the mystical body of Christ. And nations and peoples who today lie bleeding along the wayside, bleeding in the murder of war—will not be passed by and left in agony by the orthodox who dispute about "just and unjust" war and seek to lay down rules for murder. It will be seen that orthodoxy involves pacifism as the visible expression in society of that love for all men which is a precept of Christ.

It has been a slow process, this matter of realizing the social implications of Christianity—and it has not as yet been realized in any great degree. Mostly it has come about by indirection. Ecclesiastics suddenly realizing, or being forced by circumstances to realize, that the adoption of a new order, the success of a revolution, has not threatened religion but in reality has purified and brought out unsuspected implications of the faith. So slavery (formal slavery) ended and there is no theologian to defend it today—it is seen to be incompatible with Christianity that a man should own a man. So it may be with war; it may be seen that it is incompatible with Christianity that man should kill man. So it may be with the national state; it may be seen that it is incompatible with Christianity that man should be separated from man by artificial and antagonistic barriers. And so will be swept aside a whole host of casuistry, a logic that tries vainly to fit the spirit of Christ into syllogisms, a legalistic Catholicism that is concerned with how close a man can get to hell without tumbling in. And this is what is meant by Christian anarchism which opposes freedom to slavery, nonviolence to war, decentralization to the national state. It is a revolution which invites the cooperation of all radicals, which stretches out the hand to all men of good will whose consciences have been tortured in the totalitarian regimes of the day.

To our Communist brethren, to Communists throughout the world, many of whom burn yet with a zeal for righteousness, a love for the oppressed, a desire to see justice achieved, we would ask once again that they pause to reconsider the events of the past, the history of violence, the mockery the state has made of any attempt at unity with all men. And to consider if their good and laudable aims in the economic field are not being obtained because the *method* of obtaining them has swallowed up the end and become the end. That the state does not wither away, it becomes stronger; that violence does not disappear, it becomes the ordinary instrument of governance. And that a new slavery replaces the old slavery of private capitalism. That there really was no dynamism in the stupid materialism and atheism of the bourgeois and that to retain it as part of the Communist ideology is the height of reaction. For the truth did not end with Karl Marx, for he did not rid his thought entirely of the false progressivism and scientism and materialism of the nineteenth-century bourgeois. Indeed, in one sense he glorified them, he made them the criterion of justice. People like those connected with the Social Democratic Federation who are fast becoming professional anti-Communists (to say nothing of the Catholic press) are going also along this same road of illusions: the illusion that another war will at last settle the totalitarian business, that Nazism is done with and now we must have done with Marxism. And again war is to be waged by national states, and again it will not determine the right and wrong of anything. It will fashion other totalitarianisms; it will make a world of conscript slaves; it will pulverize the world. For if we will *not* use the Christian means of nonviolence, if we will not accept the example of Gandhi, then we have no right to expect the end will be any different than the means we use warrant; it will rise no higher, and there will be no redemption from this choice.

Someone said to a friend of mine that it seemed to him more compatible with the faith to be a Communist than to be an industrial capitalist. I think he is right. I could conceive of a Communism devoid of materialism and atheism and being in harmony with Catholicism; I cannot conceive of industrial capitalism being such. I know there are those in the Church who say that to be a Communist you *must* be an atheist. But they are wrong. Wrong as far as acceptance of the purely economic theories of Communism go. For if one rejects the philosophical basis of Marxism and the means advocated to obtain the goal of Communism, there is nothing to object to from a moral standpoint. And by rejecting those things the way would be opened for a great union of radicalism with religion in a last desperate attempt to achieve that justice on earth which would be the visible expression of the love of Christ. It is along that road the Church will triumph, never will she do so by coercion and personal intolerance. It may be the road to which she will eventually be forced.

But it is not the road in which Catholic Action tends, at least as we know it in this country. And the peculiar value of *The Catholic Worker* seems to me to lie in these largely unexplored possibilities. It gives opportunity for what, in the long run, may prove very valuable service to the Church. So it would seem to be a mistake to channel this into what most Catholics would regard as the "safer" course. It is well that it proceed pretty much as it has, reaching always more and more people and influencing minds rather than concentrating on organization and pressure group technique. There must be room also in the Church for these different approaches and for different temperaments and for as much freedom as possible. A good priest once said to me that the more canon law there is, the less religion, and in a sense it is true. For organization and rules only too often gain efficiency at the expense of the spirit—they tend of their very nature to stratify, to provide a framework for the mechanical performance of duties. So that here also there is room within the Church for a Christian anarchism. Which, because it is Christian, is never synonymous with disregard for morality or for revealed truth. But which is unalterably opposed to any coercion of conscience. And that is the freedom of which St. Paul speaks well.

But we are weighed down with many things: the flesh, the world, and the world of the subconscious. And there must be compassion. Christ and Freud taught us there must be compassion. And a revolution without pity can end only in a reign of terror, in a new slavery. There must be no coercion of conscience. But if we bear the marks of original sin we bear also that of the redemption and we too often lose sight of the fact that the new life made possible in Christ holds the possibilities of greater achievement than any man has hitherto known. And yet we continue to talk as though man's nature was hopelessly corrupted by original sin. As though there was no use in doing anything, as though Christ never came. There is a dangerous tendency in all of us to hanker for the Old Dispensation, for natural ethics. To forget that there are unexplored depths that could be possible with that new life coming from Christ. That He would lead us beyond slavery and beyond war and beyond national states to a realization, even in this world, of the Brotherhood of man under the Fatherhood of God.

But it will be a revolution with pity or it will be no revolution at all. It will leave judgment to God; there will be no guillotine, no torture chambers. There will be no Inquisition, for it will be seen that the way of love is superior to all else and that as one grasps more and more of truth so does he love more. If these things cannot be then let us sit down and weep, for we are indeed lost and it is as well that we depart from the face of the earth.

NOVEMBER 1948

 ## David

A Story of Love

WILLIAM GAUCHAT

DAVID CAME TO US last winter—to die. The doctor and his parents told us that almost casually. A week of life, perhaps a day, but not a month. Sometime that January, a spasm, a convulsion, a slight cry in his sleep, death would come like that.

He was six months old. The nurse who wrapped the last blanket about him told us, "He can't see—he is blind; can't hear—he is deaf; can't feel—atrophied; water pressure on the brain—hydrocephalous; lesion of the spine—*spina befida*." (There was a lump larger than a baseball, full of fluid, soft as a balloon, ready to break.) Dorothy got violently sick when we got home. I cried bitterly, the first time since I can remember. . . . We thought of our three beautiful girls—and David . . . waiting for death.

The first evening he was with us I made the sign of the cross over him—his dull eyes followed the motion of my hand.

"Dorothy, he can see!" Of course he could. The children verified that the very next morning, the way children will. . . . He chuckled at the antics of a torn teddy-bear. He loved it.

He grew into our hearts—instead of sobs and nausea, he was the Christ Child in the manger. He became beautiful.

After two weeks or so he wouldn't take his bottle. He sank into a coma, broken with little wails. His temperature, 105°. It lasted seven days. . . . We called his parents: "It is probably the end." We called the doctor who attended the birth. "Isn't he a mess?" And he said it so indifferently.

David pulled through that spell, and the next one, and so many more—but each time farther apart.

He could see, he could laugh, and he could love!

He was our boy.

June came and his parents took him. The house was empty. He had been the center of it for so long. . . . We never realized it until he was gone.

Remember, we'd say afterwards, how David used to laugh when Daddy came in from a trip to market and said, "How's my boy?" And so many other things like that.

And we used to remember when we'd question, "Why?" Why, but always unspoken—a broken, maimed boy child, in pain, doomed to die, why, God, why? The unspoken question in our eyes as we paced the rooms those nights his shrill voice protested. . . .

The sense of loss we experienced when he was gone gave us a clue to the answer. Six months later we saw him again and his parents. David had learned to talk a little—and his mother and father had learned to love him. That was the beautiful thing. . . .

There is no love without the cross, and no cross without a victim. And whether we be on the cross or beneath it weeping, there is Christ, and sorrow shall be turned to joy.

A Walk in Naples

JOHN COGLEY

"SEE NAPLES AND DIE." I heard the phrase first when I was still in high school. Then when I finally got to Naples, I almost saw an opera instead.

We spent all Sunday afternoon traveling down Italian roads in a sightseeing bus. The old man at the desk in the hotel had said that Little Vesuvius was a must for all visitors and that Sunday afternoon was just the time to make the trip. We took his word for it.

The night was coming on as we drove back to the city—via the scenic route along the bay, of course. It was sheer Fitzpatrick stuff, with Capri and Sorrento in the distance and the red sun hanging low over the blue, blue waters. Now that I think of it, I remember the time a few years ago when a Russian diplomat visited Chicago and was taken on a sightseeing tour by a group of city fathers. "Why didn't someone tell me that your city was so beautiful?" he was quoted as saying. The story was that he had been driven up and down the Outer Drive and through the parks all day.

The bus we were in was scheduled to pick up more tourists returning on the ferry from Capri so the driver was anxious to dump us at the travel office in Naples. Obviously, the guides' speeches were not timed for a fifty-mile-an-hour clip. All the way back the guides were breathless and unhappy but went through with their end of the bargain doggedly.

"On your right ladies and gentlemen, is the castle where Victor Emmanuel came after he left Rome," they would be saying, and then before they had the last syllable pronounced it would be time to point out the seaside villa where the aged Princess of Someplace still lives in retirement. Ever the diplo-

mats, the guides said little about the war damage which all day
had held the tourists' interest more than the untouched old
castles by the sea. But as we ooh-ed and aah-ed at some tremendous destruction, one of them bent down to us, both
Americans, and whispered comfortingly: "Don't worry, friends,
the Germans did their share of it, too."

After dinner back in the hotel, the evening was still young.
We asked the man at the desk what he thought we ought to do
now. "Well," he said, "why don't you go to the opera? Tonight
it's *Manon* with Beniamino Gigli. If you take a taxi you can still
make it."

So we took a taxi to the opera house and were there in plenty
of time. Immediately we felt a little foolish. We were both wearing bright plaid woolen shirts (at Sears Roebuck in Chicago the
man told me mine was just the thing for travel), no ties. The
crowd standing around in the foyer was very fashionable, indeed.
Most of them in evening clothes, and even the others wore dark
ties and starched white shirts. When the ticket man said he was
sorry but the house was sold out, we wondered about our shirts.
But later that night back at the hotel the old man said Gigli was
still very popular in Naples and that he should have warned us
we might not be able to get seats.

Anyway, that's how it came about that we saw Naples instead
of *Manon.* We decided to walk around, and for the next four
hours we kept at it. I don't think I'll ever forget that walk. And,
remember it took place in 1949, more than three years after the
war ended. Someone walking around the city tonight will see the
same sights. It was just an ordinary Sunday evening in post-war
Naples.

Most of the Neapolitans who don't have seaside villas seem to
live in crowded, smelly tenement houses of the kind that are to
be found on the Lower East Side of Manhattan. Maybe that is
why they escape to the streets at all hours of the day and night.
As soon as we left the opera house we melted into a crowd of
them pushing its way aimlessly up and down the streets. I say
melted. Not exactly. Everywhere we were recognized as Americans. Maybe it was the plaid shirts; more likely, something more

basic. Whatever it was, I don't think we missed a black mar-
keteer, a pander, or a shady proposition abroad in Naples that
night.

They came at us from all sides, sometimes literally running
down the street through the thick crowd, arms stretched out like
a football player's to catch up to us. They offered to sell us
everything from Rosary beads blessed by the Pope to their fifteen-
year-old sisters. Then when they had finally accepted the fact
that we weren't in the market for anything, they pestered us to
sell something to them: American cigarettes, watches, fountain
pens. Some of them were slick young characters straight out of
the gangster movies. But others were only raggedy kids with a
little English who had been sent out by their parents, they admitted, to bring back business for the adolescent daughters in
the family.

Neither of us, at this stage of the game, is easily shocked. We
had both run into prostitution before—in the tenderloins of
American cities, in wartime London, even in postwar Germany.
But to be approached ten times in a single block, and in every
block! This was not the canny business, the professional harlotry
of Piccadilly, of the Pigalle or North Clark Street, but the prostitution of poverty. The skinny kids marketing their sisters should
have been home in bed, getting enough sleep to go back to
school in the morning. But these kids don't go to school. Their
sisters themselves are at the age when, normally, they would be
having innocent crushes on movie stars and be busy electing class
presidents. But they, too, are still displaced persons. And their
parents? God forgive them. Who that is not as poor as they will
throw the first stone?

We were not the only Americans in Naples that night. A big
American aircraft carrier stood out in the bay. Its crew had shore
leave in the city. At the opera house we had seen an American
car drive up, two official stars marking it off as "command." But
the young sailors were not at the opera. They were wandering up
and down the streets of Naples, pursued as avidly as we were.
Most of them, it was obvious, had come a long way since gradua-
tion from high school last June or the June before.

As the night wore on, there were more and more drunken American sailors to be seen staggering out of bars, and more and more being led away from the center of town by the sleek young men and the ragged kids with a little English. Here was the corruption that war and poverty have brought to Italy reaching out to the youth of full-bellied U.S. But it is fair to say, too, that the drunken sailors were in the minority. At midnight, most of the American gobs were still wandering aimlessly and indecisively, as servicemen are forever doing in the loneliness of leave in a strange city. Some of them, arms loaded down with cheap souvenirs, were already on their way back to the ship. For these, every step of the way involved of necessity a "Begone, Satan." There was no let-up in the flesh-peddling as the night wore on.

The innocence of some of the little kids mixed up in this business hit us when one of them, after offering to bring us to his sister, refused to leave when we sent him away. Instead he stared worshipfully for a silent minute and then tagged along beside us, an obedient puppy. Finally we found out why. "You *camboys!* he said. "Bang bang! You bang-bang Indians. I never see camboys, only in cinema. Now I see you. You show me gun?" Those shirts again!

On the way back to the hotel, along the quieter streets, we saw dozens of the homeless children of Naples.

One little boy about eight or nine was propped up, asleep, against the side of a building. He wore a picket sign over his shoulder which told his story in emotional Italian. According to the sign (a homemade invention of brown wrapping paper and bright water-colored letters) he was a war-orphan who had no home and depended for food on the *lire* given him by "the good Christians" who passed him on the street. The very sign itself betrayed a professional hand somewhere. But the fact remained that here he was, after midnight, curled up on the street.

In a doorway, we found two more children, a boy six or seven and his little sister, four. The girl was sound asleep, but the boy heard us coming. He got up right away, holding the four-year-old in his skinny arms before us, like a priest lifting up a paten. Then he spoke in rapid Italian. We didn't understand a word he said.

But he might have been saying: "Look, this little thing is your responsibility, too." We understood, of course, that he was making an appeal for *lire*. The sleeping child never stirred through all this. God knows how many times before morning the boy picked her up and held her, accusingly, before the eyes of passers-by.

In still another doorway there were three little ones mothered by an incredibly filthy girl about twelve years old. The girl had the instincts of an overly dramatic actress. She stood before us and pantomimed wildly and shamelessly to spell out their needs. All the drama in her situation was exploited with a recklessness that belonged only on the operatic stage. She even went so far as to stretch out her arms like one crucified and cast her eyes, saint-like, toward heaven. For several minutes she kept at it furiously while the little ones gazed in wonder, first at her and then at us. Again, despite the stridently false notes, the facts were on her side. Here were the ragged little kids for all the world to see, and she alone with them.

There were others, too, usually huddled together in a doorway, clutching each other for warmth and comfort. Sometimes we would pass a lone child spread out flat on the sidewalk, dead to the world. Most of them did not wake up. In time we found ourselves whispering and tiptoeing carefully when we passed, as if we were going through some weird nursery after hours.

When we talked about the walk in Naples later, we heard many things. We heard that the Neapolitans "have always been that way." And it is true that we saw nothing like it in Rome or Florence. We heard that in Naples the very infants in the cradle are already crafty little beggars who know how to wring a couple of *lire* from an innocent stranger. We heard all kinds of explanations. But we heard nothing that could explain away the sights that sent us back to that hotel room, finally, with no words that made sense but only a deep, burning shame.

Picket Lines and the Cardinal

JOHN McKEON

IT IS, OF COURSE, yesterday's news now. Eight weeks ago the workers in Calvary Cemetery, belonging to Local 293, which in turn was affiliated with the International Food, Tobacco and Agricultural Workers' Union, voted to go on strike for what they considered just demands against their employers, the trustees of St. Patrick's Cathedral. The demands were for a forty hour week for the same pay as the forty-eight hour week and time and a half for overtime. The trustees did not see these demands as justified, feeling so they said, that they would put an undeserved burden on the public who owned graves in Calvary Cemetery.

That was the problem in essence. From there on in to the settlement of the dispute it became a classic lesson in how not to deal with a strike.

Eighty-five percent of the membership of the local and one hundred percent of the membership of the Calvary strikers were Catholic. Which is to say, all kinds, tapering down from the truly devout to occasional churchgoers. The peculiar slant this gave the strike became more apparent as the dispute went on.

The first day of the strike most metropolitan papers gave it minimum coverage and then left it strictly alone. To most of the non-Catholic population of New York, anything that is even remotely connected with St. Patrick's Cathedral is directly connected with His Eminence, Francis Cardinal Spellman, who is to them a figure of almost legendary proportions. No matter how rabidly anti-Catholic they may be, they still treat him with that odd mixture of vague distrust and respect that Americans usually reserve for visiting English royalty.

Because of his exalted position as a Prince of the Church, his being the most publicized figure in the American hierarchy and the best known the world over of all American cardinals, their patriotic, if not their spiritual instinct led them to anticipate his wishes by treating the strike as if it did not exist. The fact was, that in truth the Cardinal had nothing to do with the strike, until, weeks later when it had grown into an intolerable situation totally incapable of solution by the trustees, the trustees thrust it into his lap. Only then did the Cardinal enter the picture.

On the basis of some very strange information proffered him by an adviser, the Cardinal became convinced that the strike was Communist inspired and then that the strikers were using Communist tactics. Also that in some way the strikers had become guilty by association because the international union with which they were affiliated had been known to be organized originally by Communists—an issue that had not come up two years earlier when the trustees negotiated a contract with the local. When the strikers, bending over backward to please him, swore a solemn public oath that they were not Communist inspired, were not Communists, and abhorred Communist philosophy, the Cardinal was quoted by the papers as saying, "I am gratified, but they are getting repentant kind of late."

Each day in the last two weeks of the strike the papers credited the Cardinal with the strangest statements: "I am proud and happy to be a strikebreaker." "This is the most important thing that I have done in my ten years in New York," etc.

A sense of shock went through the Catholic population. News services grasped the statements avidly and flung them to the four corners of the earth through their wire services. Moscow took due note. The *Daily Worker* leaped gleefully into the fray, jeering, "Let Catholic working men and women note carefully the words of their Cardinal and realize that here, as in the case of Cardinal Mindzenty, the issue is not religion but the economic and political misuses it lends itself to."

We of *The Catholic Worker* came to know the strike and the strikers well. Early in the strike they started coming to us individually and in groups, having been cold-shouldered by all the other Catholic groups in New York, with the notable exception of the Association of Catholic Trade Unionists, who stuck by the strikers through thick and thin, giving unsparingly of their time, funds, and legal aid—convinced that the strikers' demands were just.

The Catholic Worker supplied pickets, direct relief, and encouragement whenever possible. We went among them, into their homes, attended their meetings, were on their strike relief committee, listened to their grievances, and formed our opinion: the strike was justified. We say it still.

It could have been headed off in the very beginning. The trustees could have shown the books to the workers if justice was on their side, proven in black and white that they were incapable of paying what the strikers asked. The strikers were not unreasonable or dishonest people. They were hard-working, simple people driven by what they considered intolerable conditions to strike. The dispute would have been settled there and then instead of becoming a fratricidal war.

It is all yesterday's news now: those strikers who had to drop their life insurance because they couldn't meet payments, the ones with savings dissipated, the rent owed, the vacation money laboriously put by and now swallowed up in the paying of bills owed to the butcher and the grocer. The striker whose only child was a boy of sixteen dying of a chronic kidney complaint, too ill to be moved to the hospital, and who needed money desperately for food, medicine, doctor bills, rent, who still stuck with his union and refused to scab. The striker with seven hungry children who said to us, "In the name of God, how can they keep saying that burying the dead is a work of mercy and we should be satisfied to take less and I've got seven kids to feed? Feeding my kids is work of mercy enough for me and it takes more than what they're giving me to do it on." And the shamefaced seminarians in buses, surrounded by heavy police guards, who drove through the picket line to help break the strike, past the signs in the hands of the strikers that read, "Is Calvary the Graveyard of Catholic Social Justice?"

Apart from all this a precedent of dubious worth has been set in the struggle of the laboring class for better conditions. Because of the Cardinal's refusal to deal with them so long as they were affiliated with the Food, Tobacco and Agriculture International, the strikers, on advice of legal counsel, voted to bolt their mother union, the CIO, and join the Building Service Employees International, affiliated with the AFL, headed by David Sullivan. Responsible labor leaders feel, and justly, that by forcing the strikers to do this the Cardinal has dealt a hard blow to the CIO in particular and labor in general. Hereafter whenever an employer comes to the conclusion that his workers' demands are unjust, he can use the Cardinal's action as a precedent to refuse to deal with their demands unless they give up their allegiance to what he can term a Communistic union. Today it is a local in the CIO but tomorrow it might be any labor organization at all.

It's old stuff now, except for those of us who went through it. And it will be a long time before we lose that nagging sense of shame and bewilderment that filled us when we first realized that there were eminent Catholic laymen surrounding Cardinal Spellman, advising him out of their own weakness, greed, and lack of diplomatic ability to follow a course that must inevitably lead him to loss of dignity and humiliation. And all because they, the lay trustees of St. Patrick's Cathedral, could not treat with Catholic working men as human beings and brothers.

MAY 1949

 Church in France

HENRI PERRIN, S. J.

I KNOW that a lot of your readers have been readers of my German diary and I would like to thank them by giving them some echoes of my actual life. For a year and a half I have been a workman in the district of Paris. I had sought work for a long time before finding it. Finally I was employed by a manufacturer of insulators and molded objects, a factory of plastic goods, plates, bowls, radio cabinets, etc.

First of all I worked as a molder on two steam presses; then they asked me to work as a turner. Interesting work, not too tiring, peaceful, too peaceful, because isolated. I was with a small crew of turners in a large factory of women.

In contrast to other factories, relations were slow to form; one talks little doing piece work, and salaries being small, the workmen concentrate on the job.

Only a few people knew that I was a priest. For various reasons I decided to try the experience of silence first of all for myself, to be more definitely one of them, to get in their rhythm, their thought, into their way of seeing things.

Later on, I believed that the moment had come to reveal that I was a priest; from each side they dissuaded me, saying how little we can imagine the distrust and the resentment at the heart of the people against priests and how little they are supposed to believe in our disinterestedness.

The reaction of my companions was at first some surprise, some curiosity, but there were no lively reactions or problems. Some believed that I must have been defrocked; others thought that I was forced to earn my bread; on the one side there was discreet reserve and distrust, on the other hand sympathy because of the companionship which had sprung up between us. It was only very slowly that my position was understood and confidence was given me, which was normal enough because this presupposes an occasion to explain myself and the occasion doesn't come up every day. Two kinds reacted more clearly on learning of my priesthood. The Christian sort, practicing Christians, C.F.T.C. etc., have received with joy and treated as a grace the presence of a priest in their midst. On the other hand, the Communists, except for a few militants among them who have all of a sudden become very sympathetic, have treated me for a long time with reserve and distrust—a reaction which I find very normal. They are awaiting my actions before forming any judgment. But with some of them, as with the others, a real friendship has been formed.

Then I left the factory in June and went to Paris in September. I could not find work until a month later. Then I worked for three weeks as a laborer in a sheet iron factory where I was fired by the owner as a bad worker, with a week's pay in advance. At this time I had a long and violent argument with the boss, who was on the point of striking me. I refused to take my discharge, which meant that I had to have a new interview with the inspector of work. Finally I gave in. I certainly was able to sense how the working man feels himself at the mercy of the employer and runs the risk of being from one day to the next deprived of his work.

Fortunately I found other work without much delay in an enterprise which in this district has four workshops and factories for manufacturing automobiles. I worked as a mechanic in a sheet iron gang which made fans for Ford trucks—work that was very new to me and which it took some adjusting to get used to. Because they cut off the current, we worked only four days a week, from Monday to Thursday, from nine in the morning until eight at night. Consequently on these days I could not say Mass in the evening because there is a meeting of the workers practically every night.

At this factory they don't know yet that I am a priest, except for the management and the union, but they suspect it, and I'm not going to wait much longer before I tell them. The union has given me an excellent welcome, which gives me confidence. When I was threatened with layoff because of lack of work (three workmen of our crew got their week's notice Monday), the union asked me to do everything possible to stay.

Once again I am amazed at the qualities that I find in my working companions, their faithfulness to their work. I don't say this is the way everywhere; I only say that here where I am I have again found real men, who to their professional pride, must often add the suffering and the greatness of a conscience in revolt.

Once again I have found the war between capital and labor,

the acute feeling on the workman's side of his exploitation, and the misunderstanding on the employer's side of the workmen's problems. Of course, my experience of the working life is too recent to allow a complete understanding of the problem in its entirety.

Still, I must say that, after a month on this job, my factory life has been a slow and increasing revolt against the capitalist world, from the inhuman attitude of the bosses who inspect the workers as one inspects a room full of machines, to the questions of salaries and production, the work of women and the union struggle, by all this atmosphere of the factory where the workman feels himself wrung out and exploited. Apart from my own personal experience, there is that of my own foreman who has behind him forty years of working life. For me he is the finest type of qualified workman, the conscientious sort of man I like and admire as much as a scholar or statesman.

When it comes to a small thing like the workmen not having the right to break for nourishment between seven o'clock and noon, when it comes to the control of his time or the organization of production, the hired man is not a free man. He is alienated; he is not a *man* who works with an engineer and a foreman's power, but a *capacity* for production which one has hired and which must be exploited to the maximum; he is not a man responsible for his production, but a mechanic whose output alone is interesting. The tactic of increasing the output without increasing the salary is one of the strongest proofs. To which one adds the inflexibility, to say no more, of the employers in regard to trade unionism and the sabotage of the management committees when they entertain the worker delegates with problems of sanitation or of feeding nursing mothers, while obstinately refusing to frankly open up the question of their administration.

Far from being a community of men who work together, it isn't even being administered by a human sense of production, but by the most apparent scramble for profits and money. In short, everything contributes to create more than ever in the working man a justified spirit of revolt, and only the hardness of the times and the experience of distress can take away tem-

porarily the hope and the material possibility of revolt. Capitalism distills more than ever in the conscientious workman the
feeling of alienation and rebellion.

The second point which has been brought home to me a long
time, as an experience hard won, is that of religious unbelief.
This first plunge into the working world, or the world of youth,
has brought me perception more and more acute of the profound
gap between this world and the faith of which I am the carrier.
The consciousness that the Christian message, as the people of
the Church express it and put it to work, is so completely foreign
to this world that it appears all the more as an object of curiosity
or of fabrication, but surely not as a response to human anxiety
which motives our generation as the others.

The reasons for this rejection of Christianity are often enough
expressed so that it should be easy to present some of them
here. Men don't discuss the Gospel, for which, nevertheless,
they maintain a longing, but they see in the Church only a temporal power, a political power, which has a past history of riches
and domination and which appears always anxious to assure its
influence. How many times have they not told me: "The Church
is clever. She feels that she has lost her influence. She is using
you to try to convert the left." The action of the Church appears
to be purely tactical; its practical life, its ceremonies, present
themselves to our contemporaries as enervated of all spiritual
vigor.

All that and many other reasons beside make our Christianity
appear to the unbelieving world as foreign as Buddhism. For
five months with the Ajistes, workmen and others, I have never,
so to speak, heard a question posed on the subject of religion.

I knew the external reasons that they give for this indifference,
but it is on the internal reasons that it is most easy for us to
act; the priest and the real Christians at present in the modern
world are still too few in number and too unsaintly; there are too
few saints among them for the demonstration of their faith and
their hope, their poverty, and their love to be a sufficient witness.

In summary, I have the profound and confirmed conviction
that it is normal and necessary for a priest to be in this factory as

a simple working man. He must experience it to understand how much that is necessary as absolute evidence and for a good many reasons that I unfortunately do not have the time to explain here. Finally, I have the impression that I have entered, after others, a new world ignored by the Church, a new mission country, a world that I must slowly discover; it will take months, years. Why does the Christian laity tell us so little about how foreign this world is to us?

Nevertheless, it is clear even on the brink of its unbelief that the real world is waiting for this witness to the truth from the Christian. It is easy to call this world materialist; it is often because one hasn't known the faith and the hope which profoundly bear it up. One could cite marvelous daily demonstrations of the faith and the love which spring from the heart of the working world, in the tireless faith of the Communist, in the will to love and liberty of the anarchist, in the brotherhood of the taverns and the songs with which they express themselves. I will only cite, in closing, this strophe of a poem whose author, Marcel, a twenty-five-year-old docker, gave me as a goodbye gesture the day I left the factory:

> One day peace will reign on the earth,
> When all the people clasp hands.
> There will be no more war.

> Then on this earth, where once
>   so much blood flowed,
> There will be the joy of living,
> Of love and of spring.

> From each nest
> Will wing the blessed songs.

> O people, my brothers,
> Unite, give me your hand!
> Do not make war any more.

I am afraid that the assembling of these impressions will seem pessimistic to you; I don't know enough English and I don't have enough time to acquaint myself by reading *The Catholic Worker* with how much our problems correspond to those facing the Christians of America. But I know that, here as over there, we cannot, we Christians, remain strangers to the sufferings of our people, whatever they are. I know that the love of God, in which we believe, has some practical demands that one cannot escape under pain of betraying the Gospel; I know that, with you as with us, one must pray ardently and humbly, so that slowly, across the history of our humanity, "the reign of God will arrive."

It is in this fraternal communion of prayer that I am happy to know you and to salute you and all your friends of *The Catholic Worker.*

JUNE 1949

 ## The Death of Peter Maurin

JOHN McKEON

WE WERE in a little, one-operator crossroads telephone exchange in the uplands of New Hampshire when we learned, in the course of a routine phone call to Maryfarm, that Peter had died the night before. Our mind registered the fact mechanically while we watched the girl beside us weaving the worries, the gossip, the hopes, the private lives of a whole county into an intricate pattern, as though the switchboard before her were an enchanted loom. No sorceress of old ever dreamt of such power at her fingertips, but it was exquisite boredom and a drag if the expression on the operator's face was valid. And yet she was living and young and apparently healthy.

When the call was over we thanked her and went out and started the long drive back, down out of the mountains. The mountains of New Hampshire are lovely in any weather and the weather of that day suited our mood, the mist shrouding the giant pines so heavily that the slopes seemed forested with ghosts, standing forever sentinel at the sides of the lonely, narrow, dirt roads.

On the way back I thought much about Peter. I had only known him briefly, in the past few months, when the walls of his mind had long since crumbled in ruin on his dream of a new society where "it would be possible for men to live and die as men, not as tortured animals." But even then, in his old age, uncaring, crippled in mind and body, he still had the power to attract, to seize the imagination. At Mass in the chapel at Maryfarm he would sit quietly in his seat by the window, seemingly oblivious, an old man, thickset, whose shoulders were still bowed with the heavy yoke of peasant muscle, but at the Sanctus he would rouse and force himself, unaided, to his knees. It was excruciating to watch, but an object lesson in spiritual discipline not easily forgotten. An old man, who all his life and now with his age on him and in great pain did not fail to render homage to his God.

An old man who all his life had sought to bring God and the vision of a Christian life into places that are usually left to themselves in our society: into flophouses and work camps and market places, among the foolish, the failures, the fanatics, those broken on the iron wheel of our time, the poor, the destitute, the homeless, the unwanted, the forgotten, the "weaker vessels." Those were Peter's apostolate and to the world that had formed them he addressed his mission.

Looking at him in the last few months, an old French peasant, sitting beneath the crabapple tree at Maryfarm, wrapped in a worn blanket and wearing a yellowed, ancient and donated panama, he might have been any old man sunning himself. There was nothing especially saintly about him, one sees hundreds such on park benches in big cities; the survivors—the ones who have outwitted their great enemy, winter, who sit warming themselves in the weak sunlight of a city spring. The ones who will, or will not, in the late afternoon go home to the meals cooked them by the wives of their sons, who will talk about their sons to you if you give them a chance, perhaps show you pictures of their grandchildren. The ones who will, or will not, be there next spring, and if they are not, the grave will be closed on them and they will be quickly forgotten.

But the old man underneath the tree at Maryfarm was different. He had no blood sons, no pictures of grandchildren to show, and the grave closed on him but he will not be quickly forgotten. He preached a mission clothed in language so simple that it appeared the speech of a fool or a child. Years ago, when I first read an essay of Peter's, I laughed and tossed it aside and the second time in impatience and the third time in anger. Did the man think he was talking to idiots? Did he actually believe anyone with the sense God gave a chimpanzee would spend his time reading such drivel, much less acting upon it? You would have to use better bait than that to fish for the minds of our time, minds that had slipped through the nets of prose cast by masters of the art, not once but many times, without effort. And yet, and yet . . .

He *was* speaking to fools, to minds weighted down by the dross of our time, the big ideas shouted from radio and forum, from newspaper and magazine, book and newsreel until the brain was dulled, surfeited, corrupted, unable to tell gold from glitter. The total of Peter's writing showed the same poverty that stamped his life; there is scarcely enough to fill a slender volume. Peter left as a legacy no weighty, hernia-creating tomes to be carried about by the future students of social action, no ponderous, inflexible terminology, merely a handful of ideas; but ideas of value, capable of buying many hours of reflective thought.

He was not an innovator, a prophet. The ideas and the ideals he preached were very old, the never-realized ideas, the ones that got lost in the shuffle centuries past and have been wandering in the wasteland ever since. The ideas of the Christian Revolution.

He was an agitator primarily, a very good one and fortunate. Fortunate because his star rose before him very early in life and all his life he followed it steadfastly and believed in it and never lost faith. Count on the fingers of one hand if you can those agitators of our time who followed into their old age the ideals of their youth without taint of either cynicism or opportunism. And the ideas of Peter's youth led him into some very strange places, with many opportunities for either.

He was poor by choice all of his life, eating by choice the poorest food, sleeping by choice in flophouses, on park benches, bus stations, content to wear any hand-me-down. And with all that keeping his humor and tolerance, his charity and understanding, the original force of his vision. Count on the fingertips of one hand the men who could do it and doing it could, incredibly, bind others to them, by force of personality, to do it also.

In the eyes of the world a man like Peter appears like a sorry joke. He wouldn't have fitted into a handsome office; his ideas didn't glitter; they didn't appear to have any drive; worst of all, they weren't practical. They left out too many buts and ifs and whereases and perhapses. The heads of corporations would have laughed at him if he had attempted to sell them his program; even ordinary people, those with a minimum stake in the system, often laughed. But Peter carried his ideas into the streets, explaining, exhorting, teaching, and there were those who listened. He had no car, no house, no speedboat, no stocks, no television set. He had nothing. And yet he had, in the end, what the heads of corporations do not have, people not of their families, not even acquainted with them, or who have ever seen their faces, who love them, for themselves and for their ideas and their lives.

There are tens of thousands living today who when they were hungry were fed because of Peter's efforts, and when they were naked were clothed because of Peter, and when they were homeless were harbored because of Peter.

He was an old man, dying alien and childless and a failure in the world's eyes, in a land not of his birth, and yet the spiritual seed of the poor French peasant, flung random on a hostile and uncaring world bore fruit, and many were the sons of his spirit who wept at his coffin and who walked behind it to his grave.

There is no stone to mark his grave, but if there were, it could bear a memorable epitaph:

PETER MAURIN
BECAUSE OF WHOM THERE IS
A LAY APOSTOLATE

JANUARY 1950

 # The Room with No Exit

JOHN McKEON

(SOMETIME during the night of New Year's Eve, at the St. Joseph's House of Hospitality here at *The Catholic Worker* in New York, Dick Conors, who had been staying with us for a week, fell from the roof of the building and was discovered the following morning by neighbors, lying sprawled in the courtyard that faces Mulberry Street, dead.)

The morning of the day that Dick Conors arrived at the CW he awoke in a Chatham Square flophouse, broke. When his eyes opened he found himself in a cubicle of boards, six feet long, three and one-half feet wide and six feet high, roofed with chicken wire and capable of being truly described not as a room, but as a coffin for cadavers who might be characterized as still alive by reason of the activity of the worms of hope that they contained.

He had difficulty focusing his eyes when he awoke. The retinas had a trick lately of partially refusing images, like a photograph taken with a camera jolted at the moment of exposure. He had been on cheap wine and short rations for weeks. But he could still remember his name. And where he was: newyorksomewhere-onthebowerydickconors. He didn't have a syndrome yet though he felt pretty sick and shaky, and the activity, the getting on his feet brought on the usual retching, the dry heaves that doubled him and brought him to his knees, hanging on desperately to the pallet, purple in the face. When he got back onto the narrow shelf with the paper-thin mattress and quietened a bit he must have smiled, looking up at the chicken-wire roofing, twin purposed, designed to prevent both theft and suffocation, because he could barely breathe and all he owned in the world was a torn shirt, pants, jackets, shoes and one sock. It was Christmas Day, in the Year of Our Lord nineteen hundred and forty-nine.

He might have dozed quite a while, there was nothing special to get up to, but at ten o'clock at the latest, he was roused by the kicks on the cubicle doors that the strong-arm assistant to the clerk renders impartially in his passage around the corridors. There could have been no appeal from the final decision. Five minutes after his first passage the assistant returns to fling open the doors to haul the still unconscious, the too weak or ill onto their feet and hustle them out of the building. The dead, if there are any, and there often are, he leaves lying until the arrival of the ambulance, the bored interne and policeman, the usual brief notes: DOA, dead on arrival, cause acute alcoholism, funds none.

When Dick got to his feet finally and out the door of the cubicle he could hear the muffled groans, snores and retchings of the last, late, living tenants. He must have made his way slowly down the corridor; he was in bad shape and all the corridors of flophouses are dark; the narrow passageways between the cubicle rows are lit by scattered twenty-five-watt bulbs that flicker dully, embedded in the ceiling like tarnished jewels in the forehead of an age-blackened idol. His lungs were laboring. One hundred years ago the windows of those lofts on the Bowery that became flophouses in the fullness of time were hermetically sealed, and the oxygen filters upward fitfully from the street-level entrance far below.

When he got out onto Chatham Square, he turned up his jacket collar against the cold and started to walk. The walking was instinctive first against the cold and then because he was still living and was in need. The needy, the truly destitute, are driven to movement, the ancient buried instinct whispering fiercely that life is movement, if you can still move you have a chance, seek, seek, seek. It is only later when the flame has become a flicker and starvation is far advanced that they become passive, quiet, apathetic, hoarding their energy.

All the streets that lead off westward from Chatham Square toward the Hudson, jinking to the right and left like a hunted hare through the maze of Chinatown, will, if you are lucky in your wanderings, lead you past *The Catholic Worker*. One of them he found and it was the line that attracted him. A line on the Bowery means food, conceivably clothes, and perhaps, just perhaps, by incredible luck, a bed, a chance to pull out of it. Things go with it in most places on the Bowery, religion chiefly, or signed pledges, passionate promises of reform as fragile as the paper they are written on.

It wouldn't have mattered to Dick Conors. When a man is beat to the knees there are few things he will not do to survive. We are a wise generation in our way, and concentration camp history has given us that little accretion of knowledge for meditation. A man on the Bowery, starving, will spin a Buddhist prayer wheel and chant the accompanying prayers with just as much gusto as he would sing a *Salve Regina* in different circumstances if he knows that by so doing he will eat. And Dick Conors wanted to eat. He knew it as an intellectual proposition, an abstract bit of knowledge: you have to eat to live. He didn't feel like it but he knew he should. But he had been off solids too long and after his turn came in the long line he forced down the pork, potatoes, vegetables and gravy only to have the familiar bitter acid bile boil up in his throat, and he rushed out of the dining room to lose it in the gutter. He came into the adjoining store that serves as the CW office and sat down, was noticed later in the afternoon, volunteered his brief story; he was thirty-five, a vet, combat service in New Guinea, separated from his wife, recurrent malarial attacks, had been in New York on the Bowery for six months. There was a bed free and it was given him.

He lay on it all that day and the next. He tried to eat but solids wouldn't stay down and then the withdrawal symptoms started. You begin to get terribly uneasy; everyone is noticing you, secretly despising you; they know that you're ill, bad sick, mentally upset. They don't care for you. They hate you, as a matter of fact. You should have noticed it before. You *would* have noticed it before if only your nerves were calmer. If you had a drink. A decent drink. Any kind of drink. Anything with alcohol will do: shaving lotion, rubbing alcohol, vanilla extract, whisky, wine, anything. But of course there isn't anything. That's because they want to drive you crazy. They're sick of you and they want to put you in an insane asylum. Bury you alive. But you'll fool them. You'll get out. You'll play it cagey. You'll get out. But you can't get out. You can't button your clothes. They've done something to your hands. They won't work. They're all thumbs. You can't feel them. And they won't let you out. They keep telling you to stay in bed, holding you down. They keep telling you to eat something, trying to make you, but they don't fool you. You know better than that. It's simple. They're trying to poison you. If you could only get out. If you could only get a drink. Just one drink. But you can't and you're helpless. And then you begin to cry.

If you're lucky when it happens you're in a hospital and the notes on your chart are simple and read: Pr. DT's, Vit. Def., Sup M. Meaning pre-delirium tremens, exhaustion, vitamin deficiency and supportive, remedial measures to be employed, probably massive vitamin injections and paraldehyde irrigations. But Dick Conors wasn't in a hospital and we know from first-hand experience of the bitter wrath visited on us by police and ambulance attendants when we try to get pre-DT and exhaustion cases hospitalized at the CW. "Take every crum bum on the Bowery who has a bellyache when there's a shortage of hospital beds? What the hell's the matter with you people? Are you soft in the head?" And so we didn't try, and besides, Dick didn't want it. It was our mistake. We should have fought, staged a sitdown strike in the hospital, refused to move, gone to jail, anything to get him attended properly. He was one of ours. We were responsible before God for his safekeeping.

With proper supportive measures he could have been saved: whole blood transfusions, massive vitamin injections, paraldehyde irrigations, none of which we are equipped to give or allowed to give. Barring the whole blood transfusions—blood that the medical supply houses like Sharpe and Dohme's and the city hospital blood banks cynically drain out of the veins of the men on the Bowery who are in crying need of every drop they have—paying five dollars a pint to the destitute and charging the solvent patient thirty. Glucose could have been used, barring that, steak, juice, milk and eggs, cheese, anything to enrich the impoverished bloodstream, support the laboring heart, the heaving lungs, the raveled nerve ends. But we didn't have it. We couldn't afford it. It isn't an excuse. It is an explanation. Dick Conors was our responsibility and he came to us for aid, as a last resort and we failed him for want of equipment, for money, the medium of exchange that could have been used to literally buy Dick Conor's life, pound by pound. He was a human life, a soul, a person in bad trouble.

But then again, we are fogged with trouble at the *Worker*. We eat with it, live with it, work with it and sometimes, no matter how much we fight the defensive rejection mechanism, guard against it, discipline ourselves, we become casual about it. The people who come to us are driven, compelled along the bitter path and we are the last way station on the road to nowhere, the last step down or the first step up. We get the failures of institutions dedicated to the salvage of failures. Alcoholics Anonymous sends us people they cannot handle and Traveler's Aid gives us their surplus to house. Those whom the City Relief cannot, will not, or refuse to handle are sent to us. The new ones in town come to us, the scared, the ashamed, those too shy or helpless to learn the ropes, the angles for survival that professional unfortunates know, come to us. We take all we can handle and more than we can handle. But it isn't enough to suffer with them. In the end, sometimes, you become casual. Man is an adaptable animal, it has been said, and you can not only learn to live with anything but you can make it acceptable, usual, commonplace and unnoticed.

So we treated him casually. We had been through cases like his many, many times before. On the fourth day, after we had gotten some soup into him, Don Klein, a CW member, took him to Gouverneur Hospital. Dick was a good tryer, shaky, but making the effort, joking about his trembling hands, not in a servile manner, but humorously, wryly self-deprecating. The trip and the net result was very much like one we took last winter with a friend of ours, English George, to Bellevue. George was also a pre-DT case, shaking bad, fighting hard for control. All the way up in the bus he sat with clenched hands, smiling nervously, fighting to hang on. We got off at Thirtieth Street, the dreaded entrance to the Psycho Division, and when we entered and explained our wants an interne interviewed us. The questions and responses are a set formula. The interne, a slim, small, darkhaired Irishman, let his eyes flicker briefly over George's face and asked him the three formula questions: What year is it? Who is President? What month is it? The questions are deliberately kept at a primitively simple level. Even the best of us might fail if we were asked quickly who is Vice-President? Who is the Speaker of the House of Representatives? Is the moon waxing or waning at the present moment?

George answered them quickly and nervously in his clipped British accent, proud that he could still think, still recall, that he wasn't lost yet. We watched him with pity and understanding knowing that what he most desired was hospitalization, but that he feared and dreaded the Psycho Division with its aura of electric-shock treatment and pre-frontal lobotomies. The interne smiled up at him in sardonic amusement and then addressed us. "He has no syndrome. Just a bit shaky. Sleep, rest and food. If he stays on Sneaky Pete and doesn't eat he'll probably contract pneumonia or pleurisy. We can handle him then. Right now he's not our baby." He was smiling as he said the words, looking at us and paying no more attention to George than if he were an ashtray. George flushed and looked straight ahead. We looked at the interne. It would have solved nothing to hit him. Either life would teach him or it would not. As we turned to go he called us back and scribbled a prescription on the clinic for vitamins and phenobarbital. Don Klein had less luck. All he got for Dick was four eighth-grain morphia tablets. Vitamins cost too much. We should know. Much as we would like to give the one-a-day kind to each member of the line with his bowl of soup, we can't afford them. They are doled out only to staff and house members whose need is immediate and apparent.

The morphia calmed Dick down that night, but the following day his nerves were gone. He talked quickly and nervously, about war, the Army, death. Death fascinated him and he was afraid of it. He spoke briefly of his wife, their separation, chewing his underlip until it bled. We gave him aspirin, hoarding the morphia against the long night. We tried to get him to eat solids. That night Don Klein couldn't find him to give him the morphia. Don is young, eighteen and conscientious. He hunted thoroughly but it didn't enter his head to search the rear courtyard where Dick was lying dead. Don was searching in the places a living man might be found.

When he was found on New Year's Day many people were interested in Dick Conors, a big man even as he lay crumpled in death; over six feet tall, well made, with a full head of prematurely gray hair. A Franciscan father from our parish church, Precious Blood, administered last rites, kneeling in his sandals and brown-cord-tied habit beside the body. And the Homicide Squad came. And the reporters. And the photographers. And three squad cars. The computed cost to the city in time and labor expended was eighty-five dollars. More than enough to have hospitalized Dick Conors and treated him properly while there was still time. He was a man in bad trouble who had gotten into a *cul de sac* that he couldn't fight out of. He was still young, life still had hope. The fate that overtook him is a common one today and there are none of us who can guarantee not ending the same way, God's grace refused. We live in an age that cannot guarantee security from one year to the next and walk a tightrope over the twin chasms of chaos and disaster.

For many of us the household of our time is a room with no exit—smooth-walled, circular, without recognizable angles—that we wander in forlornly, from wall to wall through the space of our existence, seeking the door that will lead us outward to the light, to the living and the life that we will, in the words of St.

Vincent de Paul, be conscious of. It is a door that we all seek, no matter where we are born, from our first breath to our last, with the crying intensity of strayed sheep, the flock gone, the range deserted, the fold far off and night approaching. And some of us are fortunate and find it. But the door that Dick Conors rose up from his bed of delirium at night to find led not to the light, but to the cold, dark, windswept roof of a decaying tenement, the flush edge without the guard rail, the long fall through the darkness to the stone courtyard—and death. We beg your prayers for him.

 ## The Shy Apostle

JOHN McKEON

THE MIDWINTER FOG clasped Union Square in the clammy, importunate embrace of an unwanted lover, swirling in heavy folds around the rain-blackened stumps of shrubbery in the park, swathing the equestrian statue of Washington in delicate scarves of mist, disembodying the voice that shouted hoarse defiance of life, ill usage, hunger and failure from the center of a silent clot of listeners directly beneath the statue. The illuminated clock in the tower of the Metropolitan Life Insurance Company could be dimly seen through the yellowish swirls, the giant hands standing at ten-thirty.

The night was too raw, too cold, for the benches to see duty, and they lay patiently in long deserted rows under the street lamps awaiting summer and the long days and nights of usage: the old men in the mornings in their clean shirts and pressed suits, retired from life, pensioned from usefulness, sitting, listening to the heavy passage of time; the office girls at noon hour, the hasty sandwich gulped, sitting with faces strained upward and legs conscientiously exposed to the indifferent sun, the lovers in the evening, the overflow of the political debaters, and then through the long night those tenants to whom the benches truly belong—the homeless, the far down, the city's poor.

There were perhaps thirty people in the park, the bulk of them concentrated around the speaker, one of the many Communist sympathizers who inhabit the place, and who are either too ideologically undeveloped or uncertain as political elements to be of any use to the Party save as volunteer speakers in their off hours. We paused, idly, on the outer fringe of the group, listening to him as we lit a cigarette. He was a man of forty-five or fifty, short, robust, powerfully built, and carrying the inevitable zippered briefcase of those who are aspiring to be minor Party functionaries, chairmen of front meetings, organizers of protest rallies, recording secretaries of union meetings or sparkplugs of rump caucuses.

His approach was orthodox, his manner heavy, and what he lacked in delicacy of casuistry he atoned for in the brutal sincerity of his statements, the heavy sarcasm of his appeal to the crowd, leaning heavily on the tactic known as "exposing" the reputed political knavery, the *agent provocateur* tactics, the fascist reactionary mentality inherent in his opponent's viewpoint.

His opponent, a shabbily dressed little man with a strong Yiddish accent and an obviously anti-Stalinist political background, baited him slyly, turning to the crowd with an exaggerated uplifting of shoulders at every new blast at his political antecedents, "I esk you, I appeal to you, did he enser me? Did he enser me? A tautologist, det's what he is. Polemics with himself he wants."

The crowd grinned in appreciation of the little man's antics. There are many lonely people in New York, and none lonelier than those who will stand late at night in fog and cold in a deserted park listening to debatable propositions they have heard ten thousands times before, and which have become as meaningless to them as the carvings on a rooming house newel post, worn smooth by time and the passage of many hands. It was not the truth they sought—who but a fool looks for truth in political debate, and they were not fools—but entertainment, forgetfulness of the ill-paid job, insomnia, poor health, the nagging wife, the lack of friends, the knowledge of failure, the unruly children with the silent, contemptuous eyes, or like ourselves, those who were made restless in the night, listening to the steep, condemning silence of all the sheets of manuscript they have never written on.

We turned aside to flip away our cigarette when our attention was caught by a group of men at the opposite end of the little amphitheater, huddled in various postures about a fire one of them had started in a wire wastepaper container, some of them perched on the railing, others standing, one of them seated on a crate, and all of them holding out their hands to the soft flower of light that bloomed with a fierce orange beauty in the fog, out of the improbable soil of old newspapers, bits of cardboard and fruit-crate lathes. They at least had accepted the reality of their predicament and had set about, with the few primitive means at hand, to combat it. We moved to them spiritually as well as physically. They watched our approach silently, and conversation languished as we broke into the circle and held out our hands to the fire. We stood silently for a while, and then took out a pack of cigarettes and lit one slowly, and slowly began to return the pack to our pocket. A little Negro opposite in a torn army blouse with the blue French-helmet of a famous colored regiment, lifted a finger and smiled: "You got one more, man?" We passed the pack, and he lit one, the eyes of the circle on him, and when he handed it back we shrugged: "Pass it around." When it came back at last, we put it in our pocket, and after a while felt gingerly inside it with the tip of an exploratory forefinger. There were three left.

The little Negro inhaled deeply and then, holding the cigarette parallel to his fingertips, exhaled a flat forceful stream of smoke, blowing the ashes from the glowing tip. "Man, I'm beat. This makes five nights I'm carryin' the banner. I'm about give out." The voice held no plea for sympathy and none was given.

It was merely a sociable comment. Among the destitute the value of the sympathetic word is nil. It is the action that counts. A figure opposite, half-hidden by the flames, said, "About time you went home to your wife, boy." The little Negro smiled mirthlessly. "You signifyin' to the wrong man. My wife died in '23." He inhaled again, and said as an afterthought, almost to himself, "An' the women I had since I wouldn't go home to if they wuz sleepin' on a mattress of ten-dollar bills." The circle shook with contained, appreciative laughter, acknowledging their group failure with all the women they had ever known, loved, left, deserted, buried or forgotten: those strange, capricious creatures who demanded sobriety, a regular pay check, monogamous behavior, security, a roof over their heads. As well ask a man to bring them on a honeymoon trip to the dark side of the moon, their laughter said.

An old man with dirty, matted hair and whose pulled-up, ancient overcoat collar formed a ruff, framing his flowing beard, rose from the fruit crate he was sitting on, and after smashing the staves under his heel, fed them slowly into the fire. "Trouble with you, Shorty, you don't live right. You oughta believe in God more." The group around the fire snickered. Obviously the old man's standing with them was that of an eccentric, a "Holy Joe" who, against the evidence of his senses, believed that God cared for his well-being. One of the figures alongside of him said, "He's beginning to sound like Angel." The little Negro took a last drag from the cigarette and, after pinching the coal, carefully put the butt in his blouse pocket, smiling at the old man, and when he spoke his remark was heavy with the pungent, embittered wisdom of the defeated: "God's a short blanket when you sleepin' in the gutter, Pop; you oughta know that." The old man clicked his tongue against the roof of his mouth in disapproval, feeding the last of the staves into the fire, and then said briskly, "About time for Angel to get here, huh?" We looked silently at the little Negro, who met our raised eyebrows with a smile. "Angel's ah meal ticket aroun' here, man. Comes every night this time. Brings Chinese food."

We looked at him with interest. A man, lately destitute, will sometimes make a point, if he gets a restaurant job, of bringing food to a buddy after work, perhaps to two, but rarely more. And never to a mixed group. The destitute also have their prejudices. The respectable "angels" on the Bowery are, were, few, and gave money, not food. There were only two within living memory— "Mr. Zero", the eccentric millionaire, now dead, who used to appear and disappear along the Bowery periodically, leaving a trail of dollar bills, and the unsung folk hero of our time, the young Italian bartender, who one Christmas a couple of years back, gave away his savings, some three thousand dollars, to the men on the Bowery, and who was promptly clapped in the Psychiatric Division of Bellevue on the strength of the obvious proposition that anyone who would give his hard-earned money to the men on the Bowery was undoubtedly mad. His wife, God bless her, in obvious sympathy with his gesture, got a court order for his release.

No one said anything further and the group fell silent. The political discussion had broken up and the park was utterly quiet, except for the crackling of the fire. Night pressed in, and the small noose of humanity drew tighter around the flames, united in common misfortune, having advanced, in all their living, no farther than Neanderthal man in their quest for security. Outside the circle the whining traffic lurched past the darkened office buildings of Fourth Avenue like a herd of hunted, metal animals wending their way through a stone thicket, the reflected stoplights leaving behind a blood trail on the gleaming asphalt.

There was the sound of footsteps coming fast over the pavement through the fog and the men half turned and shifted as a stocky, middle-aged man, bareheaded and with his arms laden with parcels, came up to the fire. He was breathing hard, as though he had come a long distance without sparing himself on the way. "I'm late," he said. "My friends were busy." We looked at him startled and almost laughed aloud. It was Raymond, a casual acquaintance at the CW whom we had met on odd occasions in the kitchen, speaking to Slim. Raymond had stayed at the CW years before we had arrived, been one of the house men and then had left abruptly. We recalled quickly the few facts we knew of him, that he was born in a small mill town in New England, was apparently well-educated, spoke in a soft, cultured voice and something else, something odd—Raymond, who apparently had a working knowledge of Cantonese and knew literally everyone in Chinatown, had many Chinese friends. One other scrap of information, the last, mentioned idly by one of the men in the house: he had a strange habit of going around the Bowery, on freezing winter nights, and picking up those men who had fallen on the pavement or in hallways, drunk, propping them against railings or getting them to walk.

Suddenly it was as though we were seeing him for the first time in his true perspective, as through binoculars, suddenly in focus. He was handing out food from the parcels to the men around the fire, egg rolls and what looked like omelets, "Chinese food." He must have begged it from his friends in the restaurants in Chinatown or the chop suey palaces along Fourteenth Street. The men around the fire knew him well, called him "Angel." It was apparently a regular performance with him. We had known Raymond over a year's time and he had never hinted at any such clandestine activity or work of mercy, but had always seemed to fulfill the comment a friend of ours had made of him: "The most dissipated man I know, in the classical sense; a wild and fruitless dispersal of energy."

We remembered how we had seen him often, late at night, when unable to sleep, we had gone into the kitchen for coffee. He would be sitting in a chair by the stove dozing, and would leap to his feet with an apologetic smile, making way for us. And suddenly, now, we saw him as we had always known him but never identified him as formally, a gentleman, "someone who is gentle with all alike." When he noticed us at the fire we held out our hand, palm upward, for the food and he almost dropped the package in startled embarrassment. "I didn't know you got up this far. I didn't see you," he said. We shrugged, smiling, and took an omelet. It was good, hot, greasy, brown-crusted and tasting of shrimp, bamboo shoots and water chestnuts. He seemed a little distracted by our presence and distributed the rest of the food quickly. We thought to offer him one of the remaining cigarettes but remembered that he did not smoke. To have spoken further to him, identifying him before the group, would have been a needless embarrassment so we stood silently with the rest, eating the omelet. He stood quietly, watching the men eat, nodding and smiling to those whose eyes met his. We watched their manner toward him. In the hierarchy of the Bowery, their place was very near the bottom rung; scavengers, the obviously psychotic personalities, those who would wear multitudinous layers of clothing if they could get them, the empty bottle, rag and wood pickers, the absolutely destitute and alone, those whose margin of existence was knife-edge wide. Eccentric themselves, their attitude toward him was as of one more eccentric than they in the sense of outraging all known standards of conduct. And truly so, perhaps. We had heard of the servants of servants, but never had we dreamt of meeting one who begged for beggars.

We looked at him closely, seeing him for the first time in his new role, but he was still the same Raymond, a man who must have had a naturally powerful physique in youth, with the mouse-colored hair of a blond person turned grey, and a wide, tired, faintly humorous face with no least trace of eccentricity in it. We pondered for the hundredth time the strangeness of individual human destiny: a man born with obvious gifts, who at one time enjoyed study, desired advancement over his fellows, money, success, who could have had them in fair measure, undoubtedly did, and who in mid-career was broken, deflected, turned aside from the road he had chosen, put to walk a path he had never dreamt of in youth.

He turned to us and smiled deprecatingly, fearful that we would be shocked by the strangeness of the meeting. "I come here every night," he said and hesitated. "My friends often have food that they throw away. No sense throwing good food away." There isn't of course. Futile also to comment on how few of us, recognizing the obvious fact, do so little to get it into needed hands. He nodded, looking around at the men, holding out his hands to the fire. "I have to get back downtown," he said. "Where to?" He shrugged. "The Bowery. I usually go there around this time." "What's doing?" we said. He smiled nervously at us, obviously disliking the trend the conversation was taking, but too courteous to break it off. "Oh, one thing and another. Just walk around." He stood for a moment longer and then, nodding at the men, held up his hand in salute and walked quickly away. "Angel's in a hurry tonight," the old man with the turned collar said brightly. "Things to do, places to go." The small Negro licked his fingers and fished the cigarette stub from his pocket. "I doubt that boy knows he's living," he said. The remark for some reason evoked the story in our minds, one that had puzzled us before, of St. Francis embracing the leper and kissing his sores. What was the leper's attitude as St. Francis dismounted, ran across the road to him and embracing him, called him brother? Was it, "Poor fool, were I as clean and healthy as you I would have better use for my time than this self-pitying behavior?" No matter. The deed was done, recorded, sped through time to serve forever as an example of the lack of fear and the wealth of love that those who trust in God possess.

We turned again to the fire and the men around it. It was possible, looking on them and claiming brotherhood, to envy the animals who live their given natures explicitly and with the implicit faith that transcends thought, untortured by the failure of reason to solve modern predicaments. For man the highest prize —to love God knowingly; for man also the greatest punishment— the gift of free will that enables him to make mistakes and worse, to be aware of them. An animal can be betrayed by instinct, but dies, if it must, integral; who cannot reason cannot make mistakes. And yet reason and its twin, faith, are the greatest gifts, peculiar to man and no other animal, part of his essential quality. How account then for his ability, peculiar to no other animal, to prostitute his virtues? "Who is greatly loved is greatly chastised." And the greatest chastisement can be freedom from restraint, freedom to let natural inclination have its will, to give pride and wilfullness full rein—all of them things that we deeply and instinctively wish—that passionate desire to avoid, circumvent, destroy authority that has its roots in our earliest struggles with apparent parental despotism, the hidden seed, cast random on the soil of our environment, chance and opportunities, that flowers into diverse fruit: great saint, great sinner, revolutionist or reactionary, affirmer or scoffer.

We looked after Raymond, hurrying past the equestrian statue of the Father of His Country, to be swallowed in the luminescent fog shrouding the neon signs of Fourteenth Street and thought what an unorthodox social worker God is: A mile below the Square, where Manhattan narrows to its tip, along those dim, dirty, ill-lighted side streets of the Bowery, haunted by the overhead rumble of the El and the whistles of tugboats from nearby piers, in a dozen darkened doorways, sodden with drink, forgotten or unwanted by every social agency, hospital or relief bureau in town, will be lying the bums, the unwanted, the far down. And among them Raymond will go, because the night is cold, the ground freezing and it is death to lie on it exposed and without covering, unconscious from drink. And he will haul them to their feet when he comes to them, try to get them to walk, talk to them, fight to fan the flickering flame of survival within them. And they will not thank him for dragging them back from the dearly purchased fumes of unconsciousness. They will kick at him and curse him, punch him if he is unwary enough or persists. But he will persist, because that is Raymond's apostolate. Out of a great city of eight million souls, we will all of us be too busy, or cold, or preoccupied this night with our own problems to go among the sodden failures, trying to get them to stand up, to walk, to struggle, not to die tonight, that they may live and go out and get drunk and fall down and freeze tomorrow night.

A fool's venture, any reasonable man would say, and out of pride and distaste would withdraw from contact with the diseased, vermin-ridden, ill-smelling bodies. And no one volunteers. But obviously God counts the work valuable, because every now and then He takes a man or woman of strength, and breaks them of the pride and reasonableness that they prize so much and sends them forth to do it and the work is done.

We shivered involuntarily; the fog was cold and the night advancing. We left the fire and began to walk to the subway entrance, thinking of Raymond hurrying through the streets, having refused even carfare. We had no least doubt that Raymond's was the better portion, his reward in store a greater one than we could ever hope for, and yet in weakness, looking around us at the fog, the high uncaring buildings, the whining traffic on the gleaming avenue, the casually hurrying wayfarers, we confess that the prayer rose unbidden in our throat, and though we strangled it quietly and no murmur of it escaped our lips the echo of it remained: Lord, Lord, allow us this: to accept Thy will voluntarily rather than be broken to it.

FEBRUARY 1950

 A Desirable Goal

ROBERT LUDLOW

GRACE, SAYS ST. THOMAS, elevates man to a higher condition than the natural condition of the highest angel. Grace, says St. Augustine, is to be esteemed beyond all the glories of heaven and earth. Grace it is that allows man to transcend nature, to live in the supernatural. And supernatural life is the *norm* for Christians. And since the life of the Christian is not a purely individualistic affair but societal, grace then has to do also with the social order as envisaged by the Christian. So that it presupposes that a social order in conformity with the teachings of Christ will be a social order which flows from grace. It is therefore most unfortunate that this magnificent truth is, in practice, disregarded by Christians and that a desirable social order is treated purely from a naturalistic and rational standpoint.

This explains, in part, why Christians look to the state and favor various forms of socialism rather than to the stateless society which would be possible as men become attuned to Christ. It is because we despair of grace that we look to the state to restrain man. And as emphasis is placed on the effects of original sin rather than on grace, which transcends these effects, so will it appear more and more that the state is indispensable and we will go more and more into slavery to the state.

Christian anarchism takes into account the divine possibilities in man. Socialism despairs of man working out his own problems without the state. Here I am using the term socialism loosely to include all those movements which are vaguely considered liberal but which all have this in common—that they wish to achieve their ends by political and parliamentary methods. And that, consequently, they end in surrendering more and more to the state, which becomes a polite dictatorship (the social service state) or a not-so-polite dictatorship (Bolshevism).

The important thing is that the Christian, if he is to take seriously the prayer, "Thy kingdom come on earth as it is in heaven," must have as a social goal an order that is inspired by the supernatural, and which consequently finds expression, not in statism, but in the free society of Christian anarchism. This is not to advocate angelism. It is but to advocate the utilization of the possibilities of grace which participates man in divine life and allows him to transcend the limitations that would make such a society impossible. And because this is so it follows that, if we are to keep this goal in mind, we will work towards a society that is decentralized and stateless.

The existence of the state is testimony to sin and as man, through Christ, overcomes sin—as the normal life of man becomes life in grace and as society is patterned on the normal— so will society be anarchist. For there will be no need of the restraining power of the state, and if there is no need of it there is no sense maintaining it. I say this should be the goal—unless we are to contend that Christianity will never be realized, that Christ gave us a useless prayer to say because it would never be possible of fulfillment. To hold that these things are impossible of fulfillment is to accept a mechanistic interpretation of history. It is to die to Christ rather than to live in Him.

Kropotkin has shown (in *Mutual Aid*) how instincts of mutual aid are as much a part of man as are egoistic impulses. Unfortunately, Kropotkin's unfamiliarity with Catholic dogma led him to suppose that his findings ran counter to the teachings of the Church, whereas they run counter to the Calvinistic conception of original sin. Man's nature, as such, was not harmed by original sin and there does indeed exist in him inclinations to virtue. And, with the help of grace, this inclination can be augmented to the point where a Christian anarchist society is quite possible. It might come soon or late—depending on man. But, as a goal, it is eminently Christian. And the objections to it are based, for the most part, on utilitarian considerations and on a faulty conception of the nature of man and on a pessimism that refuses to concede that, with grace, man—and man in society—can indeed behave as a divine being. Not by identification with divinity but by participation in the life of God.

This is the long-range view, and in our day to day existence we may have to make concessions in order to meet an immediate issue or solve a pressing problem. But we must not surrender our minds to the immediate—we must keep the vision, otherwise we will cease to fight the state and will succumb to the easy solution of the planned society by the state. It is because man is not a purely economic being that we have obligations to our fellows within an unjust system. I mean we must patch up the wrecks of Capitalism—not to prolong the system, but because we have obligations to man as man. To another person just because he is another person. Hence the relevance of the works of mercy. If this were not so the revolution would proceed without pity and a revolution that proceeds without pity is fascist to the core.

In the Christian revolution there must be no heads rolling, no consciences coerced, no third degree. If there are any of these things present then it is not a revolution in Christ and we might as well forget about it. Nevertheless, this should be no excuse for denying the goal, for adopting moderation, for avoiding extremes. But one of the extremes to which we should go is in maintaining a scrupulous regard for the individual person, to proceed always in nonviolence so as to safeguard even the bodily integrity of the individual. The Christian ideal is not the Aristotelian ideal of a golden mean. Christianity is not a mean between Capitalism and Communism. It is the extreme opposed to Capitalism and to what of Capitalism the Communists have retained. To Capitalist and Marxist atheism it proposes God. To Capitalist and Marxist materialism it proposes transcendental values. To Capitalist and Marxist technology it proposes personalism. To Capitalist and Marxist statism it proposes the stateless society. The society which, because it is permeated with grace, and to the extent with which it is permeated with grace, has less and less need of coercive government. And where the goods of the earth are distributed—not according to man's deeds but according to his needs.

We may have to go after such a society step by step—it may come overnight. But even the step by step procedure must keep the end of Christian anarchism in view—it must not be a step by step procedure to statism.

MAY 1951

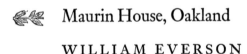 Maurin House, Oakland

WILLIAM EVERSON

In the ventless room,
Over the beds at the hour of rising,
Hangs now the stench and fetor of the crude flesh;
And at the grimed sink
We fill the basin of our mutual use,
Where our forty faces, rinsed daily,
Leaves each its common trace.

Is it then in this?
In this alone, then, that we find our oneness?

We never in cleanness, never in purity
Have ever truly met?

Oh my brothers! each brings our sin-deformed face to the greasy
    pan!
Is it not a terrible thing to come upon ourselves
Here in each other? In the inalienable commonality
Of our grosser selves? And found there
That sign and testimonial of our secret hearts!
Could it not have been other?
A true revealment of the soul's intent,
A freer gift, welcomed, and most dear?

Far off, in clefted rocks and dells, the springwater
Throbs out the faultless pulse of earth,
A lucent flow.

And God's sheer daylight pours through our shafted sky,
To proffer again the still occasion of His grace
Where we might meet each other.

JULY–OCTOBER 1951

 ## Chrystie Street I

(Excerpts from the regular column)

TOM SULLIVAN

WE WERE VISITED a few days ago by a young man in an army uniform. He said he had been reading the paper for some time and had several questions he would like to ask. However now that he finally arrived at our place he admitted that he couldn't remember them.

Nevertheless he did inquire as to what I thought of his wearing a uniform in view of the number of articles on pacifism found in our paper. I thought he looked quite sharp in his uniform and told him so. I also told him that I was not a pacifist and was not likely to give the retort that he expected. He expressed his pleasure at finding such diversified points of view in our midst.

Then he wanted to know what Peter Maurin would have said regarding the uniform. As I seldom knew Peter to give a direct answer to a question I thought it was a late date to start in now for him and I sort of thought that Peter would have told the young man to read the life of the Curé d'Ars who deserted army and uniform during his life.

Recently we heard from a woman up in Woodstock, New York, who knew Peter Maurin before he began *The Catholic Worker*. She tells us that Peter was teaching French up there at the time. One incident in connection with Peter that she revealed to us made us glow all over. It seems that he inserted an ad in a local newspaper stating that he was starting a fund of money to which all readers were welcomed to contribute. Also those in need were just as welcome to borrow from this fund. There were to be no interest rates and no one was to be coerced to repay his loan at any specified date. The story ended as everyone but Peter would expect. The initial deposit by Peter disappeared rapidly through loans that were never repaid nor were there any other contributors besides Peter.

No one seemed to know where this woman came from. But she was standing in the office looking for the one in charge of the money. She demanded in a strident tone, "Who is in charge here? I want to pay this seventy-five cents for my supper. You see a priest uptown gave me two dollars and I insist on paying for my meal. I know what you people are up against."

Since two dollars was all she had in the world we firmly suggested that she eat with us and hold on to her money. She flatly refused to eat unless we accepted, which we finally did. During the meal this middle-aged woman's story fairly gushed out.

"Christ knows my heart is broke. The city placed my baby boy in a home. I am what is known as an incompetent mother. Just because I have no husband and make my living singing in local taverns.

"Tonight being Saturday I was thinking of going over to Newark and see if I couldn't make enough to pay for my room rent. Then again maybe I would be better off if I went to confession and to communion in the morning. It may help me to get my baby back."

The poor woman left us that night and we learned during the following week that she had been committed to a mental institution in the process of trying to effect the release of her child. However a priest friend is following the case.

Each month I spend some brief minutes trying to visualize the make-up and the printed material of the next issue of our paper. The same question always rears its beautiful head: How would the paper look without this column for the month?

The identical answer is right there beside the question. I find it easier to write the column than to answer people's queries as to why I didn't write this month.

This is all due to the fiction that I am reluctant to write, at least until the very last minute. Besides which, I dislike writing due to my lack of talent. It kills you to know you haven't got it.

This month I came very close to not writing this column because of the New York Giants' and Brooklyn Dodgers' baseball series play-off. I became emotionally involved as to a choice of a winner. You have to know who your team is. And I didn't. I wanted the Giants to win since they were bereft of the pennant for thirteen years, but I also pulled for Brooklyn simply because of their universal appeal. Besides Brooklyn was the first major-league team to hire a colored player, thus breaking the racial discrimination practiced by all of the big-league teams.

What has all this to do with the Chrystie Street column? Well, that is what I was saying. You see, the lay apostles or reasonable facsimiles thereof as a rule are generally not interested in sports and usually peer at you very disapprovingly when you mention this indelicate subject.

So you can see that I am in no mood to be writing about the really important issues that we usually deal with. Such as the plight of the little people caught up in the terrible everyday predicament of life's injustices. Right now I feel cheated by having to meet a deadline with this tripe when I could be listening to the first game of the World Series.

A missionary priest who recently returned from his work in China spent a couple of hours with us the other day. He was probably the most informed person regarding the affairs of China that we have had the good fortune to come in contact with.

He sat in our office and spoke to us for almost two hours, commenting on one thing and another in China. Finally we asked him what political group in that country seemed to have the general welfare of the people at heart. This priest quickly replied that he thought that neither the former regime of Chiang Kai-shek nor the present rulers were the desirable directors of the people's welfare. He stated that the Chiang Kai-shek politicians were thoroughly corrupt from start to finish, at least from everything he saw and heard. He said that the present rulers aside from their persecution of religion were pestering the poor people to death with continuous indoctrination of their ideas from early morning till late at night. Although he did state that the present regime is breaking up the huge estates. This missionary priest saw only one group in the country that seemed to have the correct program for the country. They are a socialist group, small in number and lacking in any strong outside recognition or backing.

Before you dear readers begin to remind us, we do want to tell you that we are aware that the feast of the Little Flower is on the third of October. A couple of other careless proofreaders and I were responsible for permitting the mistake to slip by in our October appeal. If I had been properly impressed with the Little Flower's humility as described in the Office for that day I probably wouldn't have mentioned the other culprits nor I guess would I have mentioned the Office.

 A Friend of the Family

DOROTHY DAY

SOMEWHERE IN THE PSALMS it says that we can look forward to three score years and ten, if we are strong, but any more years are toil and trouble. Undoubtedly they are, but I suppose most people want to hang on to this life, life they know, as long as possible. Not that anyone will ever be ready for death in the sense that they feel prepared to face God and the judgment. Old Maurice O'Connell, who lived with us from 1936 to 1947 at Maryfarm, Easton, Pennsylvania lived to be eighty-four. After *The Catholic Worker* moved to Newburgh, Maurice remained behind. When the priest from St. Bernard's Church came to anoint him a few weeks before his death he announced jauntily that he would drop in to see him next time he was in Easton. His appearance there was not so casual. Yesterday, February 26, a requiem Mass was sung at ten o'clock and the body of Mr. O'Connell was laid in a grave in St. Bernard's cemetery, behind St. Joseph's Church, up on the Palisade over the Lehigh River. It was a clear, spring-like day, though the ground was hard under foot.

I thought, as the coffin was being lowered into the grave, a cheap grey coffin of proper shape but God knows what materials, the handles decorative rather than functional, that Mr. O'Connell had made a coffin for me back in 1940 or so, but that he had not made himself one. I should have brought him mine and let Hans Tunneson make me another. The coffin he made for me is of proper size and varnished with the bright yellow varnish that he had used on the altar, the sacristy closet, and the benches which he had made for our chapel at Easton, Pennsylvania, when Father Palmer and Father Woods first came to vacation with us back in 1937.

Mr. O'Connell put in a lot of work on that chapel. The altar, vestment closet and benches are all now in use at Maryfarm, Newburgh, and will be for many a year to come.

In addition to my coffin, which my daughter now uses to store blankets and other bedding, and the chapel furnishings, Mr. O'Connell took an old tool shed and made himself a comfortable little house in which he lived for all the last years of his life, until this last year, when he went to the Smiths and Christophers and boarded there. He had an old-age pension and so preserved a strong feeling of independence. He enjoyed being with the children. He helped John Filiger remodel his chicken house and he constructed the Montague and Buley houses, all of them long rectangular affairs that could be divided into three or four rooms, small and narrow like the emergency barracks veterans are forced to live in now, utilitarian, with tar-paper-covered roofs and sides, neither beautiful nor imaginative.

We had to remind ourselves very often of how much Mr. O'Connell had done for us in the years that we lived at Easton because he possessed a violent temper. He was, in fact, something of a terror. He came from Ireland so many years ago that he remembered, he said, when Canal Street was not a street but a canal. He was one of twenty-one children, and his father was an athlete and a carpenter. Maurice pictured him as a jaunty lad with his children, excelling in feats of strength and looked upon with admiring indulgence by his wife, who, according to Maurice, nursed all her children herself, baked all her bread, spun and wove, did all her housekeeping and never failed in anything. It was, indeed, a picture of the valiant woman that Maurice used to draw for us when any of the women were not able to nurse their children (not to speak of other failures).

He was an old soldier and had worn many a uniform, in South Africa, in India, and in this country. He had no truck with pacifists. And as for community!

According to St. Benedict, there should be a benevolent old man at the gate to receive the visitors, welcome them as other-Christs, exemplify hospitality.

Maurice's little cabin was on the road at the very entrance of the farm, and he never missed a visitor. If they were shabby he shouted at them; if well dressed, he was more suave. He had many a tale to tell of his fellows in the community. He was not a subtle man. His thought was simple, not involved. "Thieves, drunkards and loafers, the lot of them," he would characterize those who make up what was intended to be a farming commune. And if anyone living on the farm had any skill, it was, "what jail did ye learn that in?" One man who became a Catholic after living with us for a year was greeted with taunts and jeers each time he passed the cabin door. "Turncoat! Ye'd change yer faith for a bowl of soup!"

He was ready with his fists too, and his age of course protected him. Once when he was infuriated by a woman guest who was trying to argue him into a more cooperative frame of mind, he beat his fist into a tree and broke all his knuckles. A violent and enraged man, if any one differed from him, was Mr. O'Connell.

By the ninth year of Mr. O'Connell's stay with us, he had all the tools of the farm locked up in his cabin and would guard them with a shotgun. That first winter when Peter and Father Roy and the men had a dormitory in the barn, Mr. O'Connell became ill and was persuaded to be nursed in the dormitory. He was kept warm and comfortable, meals were brought to him on a tray, and he soon recovered his vigor. He decided to stay for the cold months and ensconced himself by the side of the huge pot-bellied stove. One end of the barn was the sanctuary, and was separated with curtains from the center where the stove, benches, chairs and bookshelves were. Peter and Mr. O'Connell sat for hours in silence, the latter with his pipe and a book, Peter motionless, his chin sunk in a great sweater that all but engulfed him. Mr. O'Connell was a great reader of history, but it was hard to understand him when he was trying to make a dissertation, especially when his teeth were out, as they usually were.

It was a difficult few months, especially in the mornings. We sang the Mass every day, thanks to Father Roy, and Mr. O'Connell did not enjoy this at seven in the morning. He had been used to sleeping until ten or eleven. On occasion his very audible grumbling was supplemented by a banging on the floor of the dormitory with his shoe. Taken to task for this he would snarl, "I was just emptying the sand out of my shoe." It was a winter when we had to dig ourselves out to the outhouses.

When Lent came we were reading Newman's sermons during meals, and whether it was because Maurice did not like Newman as an Englishman, or a convert (he decidedly did not like converts), or whether it was because he thought the reading was directed at him, he used to stomp angrily away from the table and refuse to eat. Stanley had always gotten along well with him (he had never worked with him), but Stanley had a habit when he was reading pointed chapters from the *Imitation*, or Newman, of saying, "This is meant for Dorothy," or "This is meant for Hans." Mr. O'Connell decided the reading was meant for him, and would put up with it no longer. He moved back to his cabin, and his meals were brought to him on a tray. When spring came, he came up to the kitchen and fetched them himself.

The cooking was good that winter. Either Hans or Duncan managed the kitchen, and "we never had it so good." Especially since Father Roy used to go down to the A&P on a Saturday night and beg their leftovers. They were very generous, especially with cold-storage fish or turkeys that would not last, even in the icebox, until Monday. Part of our Sunday preparation was cleaning fish and fowl and seeing what we could do to preserve them. I shudder now when I think of the innards, so soft that all parts seemed to merge into one. However, we had good cooks. And most of the time we had simple foods that did not need to be disguised.

It was about that time, spring and summer, when many retreatants came, that Mr. O'Connell took to telling them all that we never gave him anything to eat, never anything to wear. The fact was that we respected his distaste for complicated dishes, and he had a regular order in at the grocer's for eggs, cheese, milk, bread and margarine and canned soups. Not to speak of the supplies on our kitchen shelves which Maurice (or anyone else) felt free to come and help himself to. Our cooks had good training in "if anyone asks for your coat, let him have your cloak too. To him that asks give and do not turn him away, and do not ask for a return of what is borrowed."

As Father Roy would say, "If you wish to grow in love, in supernatural love, then all natural love must be pruned, as the vine is pruned. It may not look as though love were there, but have faith."

We were being pruned, all right. Not only through Mr. O'Connell but on all sides. Putting it on the most natural plane, I used to think, "How sure people are of us that we believe in what we say, that all men are brothers, that we are a family, that we believe in love, not in use of force, that we would never put them out no matter how hard we are tried. If they act 'naturally' with no servility even to an extreme of showing bitterness and hatred, then one can only count that as a great victory. We believe in a *voluntary* cooperation. Our faith in these ideas must be tried as though by fire."

And then I would look upon Maurice with gratitude and with pity, that God should choose him to teach us such lessons. It was even as though he were a scapegoat, bearing the sins of ingratitude, hatred, venom, suspicion for all the rest of us, all of it gathered together in one hardy old man.

And, on the other hand, to go with these subtleties, what about this business of letting the other fellow get away with it? Isn't there something awfully smug about such piety—building up your own sanctification at the expense of the increased guilt of someone else? This turning of the other cheek, this inviting someone else to be a potential murderer, or thief, in order that we might grow in grace—how obnoxious! In that case I'd rather be the striker than the meek one struck. One would all but rather be a sinner than a saint at the expense of the sinner. In other words, we must be saved together.

And so I firmly believe, I have faith, that Maurice O'Connell, in addition to being a kind of friend who built the furniture of our chapel and some barracks for our families, who sat and fed the birds and talked ever kindly to the children on the sunny steps before his little house, was an instrument chosen by God to make us grow in wisdom and faith and love.

God rewarded him at the end. He received consciously the great sacrament of the Church, Extreme Unction, he was surrounded by little children to the end, and even at his grave he had the prayers of kind friends; he had all any Pope or King could receive at the hands of the Church, a Christian burial in consecrated ground. May he rest in peace.

MARCH 1952

 ## Chrystie Street II

TOM SULLIVAN

I SAT IN OUR LIBRARY this afternoon listening to Bishop Fulton Sheen broadcast his Sunday sermon. The Bishop was in his usual style, which hasn't changed in years. He always conveys the feeling to me that I am now getting my final instructions just before The Last Judgment. As the Bishop preached, Frank, our radiodial jockey, addressed several comments towards the receiving set. When the Bishop mentioned the woman at the well asking Christ for the Living Water, Frank snarled, "Everybody is always asking for something." As the Bishop made the point that the worst sinners against impurity stood a better chance for salvation than those who had sinned against pride, Frank broke in at the pause and said, "I wish you would come down here and tell that to this gang who are running *The Catholic Worker*."

While Frank was indulging in this peculiar dialogue with the voice from the radio, a shivering stranger walked into the room in search of a coat. Someone found an extra coat for the stranger and he sat down to read a copy of *The Catholic Worker*. Shortly after he began to read the paper I noticed him study the Chrystie Street column. His eyes dilated and his cheeks puffed out as though he were going to spit on it. This, I couldn't watch any longer.

At the other end of the room an elderly woman sat waiting for the next meal; we had just finished lunch. Age had not proved any deterrent in her maintenance of a facial makeup, even to the penciled eyebrows. She was engaged in a cross-examination of another visitor from the deep South. He wears a railroad engineer's cap and an army overcoat plus a pair of blue jeans. He supplies a considerable amount of the intellectual life around the house with his comic-strip books that he fishes out of local garbage cans and wastebaskets. The woman was asking him about this Southern hospitality that she had so often heard about. She wanted to know wherein it differed from the New York variety.

One morning last week an irritated handyman from the theater next door paid us an unpleasant visit. He sternly informed us that the owners of the theater had mailed a protest to the city authorities. It seems that their complaint is against the men who line up for our morning and afternoon coffee and soup. To keep themselves warm in the early hours of the morning while waiting for John Derry to start the serving of the coffee, the men are wont to build fires against the walls of the theater. The fires blacken and soften the bricks, so the handyman claims.

We agreed to speak to the men along the line regarding this matter. We did not consider this fire-building detrimental and hated the thought of having to tell the men that they would have to freeze and like it during these bitter mornings. Consequently, we decided to bring an equalizer into the conversation with this emissary from the theater. Human rights and values come first before property rights. So we proceeded to point out several complaints we had against the theater. In a kind but threatening voice we replied to the visitor that we could make things awfully difficult for the theater owners if we cared to go to the proper authorities. He went hard for that line and finally left our house stating that he was sure that we could all get along with one

another.

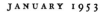

JANUARY 1953

 ## St. Francis and His Revolution

ROBERT LUDLOW

THOSE who placed their hopes in political means during the recent elections and were disappointed, as they would have been eventually disillusioned if their candidate had won, might do well to pause in this busy world of ours and think somewhat on St. Francis and the method of St. Francis. "St. Francis," states Father Meyers, "effected his revolution on an entirely different field. To effect the change, he did not kill a single human being, he sequestered not a single man's property, closed up not one man's business, inaugurated no new banking policy, initiated not a single repressive measure, wrote not a single law into the codes of the day, indicted no political instrument." But, it will be objected, that is all very well and good. It is an area of life that was open to the technique of St. Francis, but we are concerned with the political, with economic systems, with day to day living, and what else is there but that we should go about those things in the only way we know how? We must elect our man and then you will see our ideas realized. Yet this is precisely the point—St. Francis, who eschewed violence and politics, was more instrumental in effecting the downfall of an undesirable social system than were any politicians of his day, or any committees, or any organized groups of dissidents. Says Father Meyers: "Francis struck at the iniquity of it—especially with two provisions of the rule of the Third Order. One was the provision that Tertiaries must not bear arms, the other was that Tertiaries must bind themselves with no oath, except where duly constituted authority rightfully required it." And it must be remembered that literally thousands of lay people joined the Third Order, so much so that the feudal lords were beside themselves with wrath and appealed to Rome to stop this madness. This madness which deprived them of serfs because the Third Order members refused to bear arms or to take oaths of fealty to the lords.

And it must be remembered that St. Francis regarded the rule of the Third Order to be a rule that was applicable to the ordinary Christian. It was no specific rule for the clergy; it was meant for all of the laity. And how popular is this pacifism of St. Francis today, how popular with the Franciscans? How popular with the members of the Third Order? How many of them know the sixteenth rule of the Third Order, "They are not to take up lethal weapons, or bear them about, against anybody." Can we imagine the revolution it would cause should this rule be enforced among members of the Third Order so that they would all, as a matter of course, become conscientious objectors? But the same fate has befallen this idea of St. Francis as has happened with much else that he taught. Not only has this been true of St. Francis but of pretty much of all the pacifism in the Church. It has been made harmless by relegating it to the purely individual actions of clerics. St. John Chrysostom once wrote "We ought to be ashamed of ourselves, who act so differently when as wolves we rush upon our adversaries." (Breviary, June 11) And now, in the liturgy which bears the name of St. John Chrysostom (and which, of course, was not actually written by him) we are called on to pray, "For the honorable government of our country and its military forces . . .

to aid it in battle and vanquish every enemy and adversary." So are the saints dishonored when we canonize them to make them harmless! So may the day come when we harken to their message and eliminate the vestiges of militarism and nationalism that have found their way into our very liturgy.

Of St. Francis, Father Meyers states: "Coercion, therefore, of another person against the latter's convictions was as repugnant to him as sin. Violence had no appeal to him, not even against Saracen or bandit. Similarly whatever amounted to compulsion, such as reducing his neighbor to a plight where self preservation demanded his surrender to terms, was odious to him . . ." He was similarly opposed to repressive measures "because when you use violent repressive measures, you challenge secret resentment; what the victims cannot do publicly, they do in secret. Hence the tide of rebellious and satiric writings, mostly anonymous, characteristic of that day . . ." The attitude of St. Francis toward violence (he ignored the Crusades and went his own way unarmed to visit the Sultan), towards repression, is so much in advance of his time that many today look on him simply as a humanitarian born ahead of time. And, while there is a sense in which this is true, it must yet be remembered that, for St. Francis, it was merely a reiteration of what was contained in the message of Christ; it was no new teaching, and it was a teaching having supernatural sanction. It represented a development in natural law inasmuch as it applied to the social field the conclusions of revelation. It was superior to the logic of the philosophers who thought only in terms of a mechanical equality of justice; it went beyond that mischievous conception of ethics which, admitting the superiority of the Christian conception, yet felt called upon to accept an inferior brand suited to the condition of fallen man, hence, for all purposes, constructing a relativistic system in the name of Christianity. St. Francis did not so much oppose this as he ignored it and went about demonstrating the better way. He did not stop to argue theories about just and unjust wars, he simply stated that, should people (clerical or laity) wish to follow the path he laid down they simply did not bear arms; there was no argument about it, one accepted the position or one did not.

Wherein lay the strength of St. Francis? He traveled first the road of purgation. In Felix Timmerman's book, *The Perfect Joy of St. Francis*, we read of the days of sadness which burdened the soul of Francis as he wandered from place to place thinking of the flesh and feeling the pull of the flesh so that peace was a stranger to his mind; and we, who have not outlived this stage, feel kinship with him in his loneliness. But he emerged from the compulsive tyranny of the flesh, as those emerge who experience sex as liberation and joy. But for Francis, since he had chosen another path and was vowed to celibacy, his liberation came in a higher adjustment, in an awakening of consciousness, in the development of the super-conscious. "In the man whose thoughts dwell on the ranges of sense," we are taught in the Bhagavad-Gita, "arises attachments to them; from attachment is born love, from love springs wrath." And as St. Francis surmounted this, he realized that other saying of the Bhagavad-Gita: "He whose mind is undismayed in pain, who is freed from longings for pleasure, from whom passion, fear and wrath have fled, is called a man of abiding prudence, a saintly man." "My God and my all"—again and ever did Francis utter this phrase, for it was by participation in divinity that he became a free man, as light entered his whole being, as super-consciousness dominated, as he began to live outside of compulsive behavior, as much as it is given man to do so, then did he give forth in strength; as he lost himself in God, so did he resurrect a freedom undreamed of as long as it remains chained in potency by the ego.

St. Francis felt the redemption not only in himself, not only in all mankind, but in the earth itself and the birds and the beasts and the fishes of the waters. For St. Francis emerged from his purgation, not as a cold and austere ascetic, but loving and warm and tender. "Little brother rabbit," he cried, "come here to me. Why did you let yourself be trapped that way?" "Sister lark has a cowl like the religious have, and a humble bird she is. She is happy going along the road to find a few kernels for herself. Even if she must find them among dung she picks them out and eats them." "Notice that sheep there walking along so meek among those goats and their does: I tell you it was like that that our Lord

Jesus Christ went about meek and lowly among the Pharisees and chief priests. I beg you therefore, son, to have pity on this poor little sheep with me for love of Him." "Be praised, my Lord, through Sister Water, for greatly useful, lowly, precious, chaste, is she." For Francis all things partook in some sense of divinity. And so we bear an affinity to all things; in and through all things the light of God shines, the divine syllable echoes, the earth closes in and we become all, so that to harm another is to harm ourself, to kill another is to commit suicide. This is no meaningless pantheism; this is the recognition of divine origin that vibrates through all creation redeemed in Christ.

If the revolutions of the right and of the left are shallow, if they are too narrow to satisfy, if they exercise each their own tyranny over man, if political means have demonstrated their uselessness, is it not perhaps that we have left unexplored whole areas of thought and being? If we have debased God to the point where what we call God is a chimera unworthy of the worship of free men, and if, because we know not what to worship, we worship the state or the race or our own compulsions and if, in all these things, we have found no happiness, and if we then realize that Francis was divinely happy, may we not turn aside some day to learn of him and in doing so learn so much of ourselves that we could never turn back to the old ways or foster the old illusions or trust the old hopes but, in the eternal Francis, find the love and tenderness of God.

Five Years on the Land

JACK AND MARY THORNTON

WE READ DOROTHY'S ARTICLE in the December issue about the land movement and its hardships, and it inspired us to give a short report on our activities on the land.

It is now over five years since we have been married and have been gone from the CW, and, except for a brief stay in New York, and one year in Toronto, we have been on the land ever since. This is quite a while to spend at any activity, and one would suspect that we had learned quite a bit. We haven't learned very much. Having been born and reared in the city we did not know how to work, and this proved to be the cause of most of our troubles. Having had little capital, we never quite had enough tools and equipment. Spending quite a bit of time around the CW did not prepare us for the ways of the world of business, and we have been trusting where we should have been cautious, naive where we should have been wise. In short, we have been fools in the ways of the world, and, we hope, for Christ's sake. But in spite of all our trials and tribulations we are still on the land, though we haven't made much progress in farming it, and we still believe as Peter did, in Cult, Culture and Cultivation.

We have been on this farm since last May, and plan on staying here for some time to come. However, our record for sticking in one spot has not been enviable, for we seem to be only a little more stable than migratory workers. What this particular farm can use to great advantage is an experienced farmer and capital, neither of which we have. It needs an experienced farmer because the farm has been lying idle for fifteen years and there is not a decent blade of grass on it. It needs money because every building on the place is in need of repair, including the house. Only a few weeks ago we had to fell the ceiling in the living room as it was hanging precariously and we were afraid it would fall on someone. We have the new ceiling ready to put up and are waiting for someone to come along and help with it. Frank Coyle arrived the last time we had a ceiling problem.

The farm consists of eighty acres, a house, and several dilapidated outbuildings. There are no modern improvements in the house, such as running water, bath or toilet. We do have electricity though, and also propane gas. The water can be had by just stepping out the back door. Recently we purchased a tractor, on the installment plan, and expect to get something accomplished next spring. So far we have managed to plow up enough ground to put in an acre and a half of wheat. The whole process took well over a month. First we had to get the money for the seed and fertilizer, then we tried in vain to borrow a grain drill. People in this area do not like to lend their equipment. Finally we got a man to promise to come and plant it for us, but it rained before he could get around to it. It rained for about ten days and it was another two weeks before the ground was dry enough for planting. Finally, we hired a man to put it in and he came with a mammoth rig and did the job in about ten minutes. As one neighbor put it, it cost us more to put that wheat in than it would to go down to the feed mill and buy the same amount we might realize from the harvest. Next year it will be different though, at least with the wheat.

After we got the tractor we went to a sale to see if we could get a little equipment and some stock. We purchased a pair of small pigs, a side-delivery rake, a buzz saw and an old phonograph. The next day was Sunday, and after Mass and a leisurely breakfast, Mary shouted from the yard that the pigs were loose and headed for the highway. I bolted out the front door just in time to see them rounding the house onto the highway. I gave chase but they slowly widened the gap and never stopped running until they were clean out of sight. I chased them all over the countryside to no avail. We finally captured them after three or four hours, by hiding in the brush and diving on them as they came by. Things like that always happen on Sunday when you are in your good clothes. Several days later we decided to hook up the buzz saw and saw some wood. The wood was cutting fine, but the ashes were hitting me in the face, which seemed odd, and several times the log I was sawing cut loose and flew away. Finally one of the logs hit me on the wrist and I knew something was wrong. The trouble was that a John Deere tractor pulley runs backward and you have to put a hitch in the belt to get the saw to run right. These are some of the obstacles that you run into when you are trying to learn to farm by yourself.

We are partial to horses and would like to have gotten a team, but since we have no hay and no fencing they were out of the question. Besides, if you work off the farm, as we always have, it is difficult to get anything accomplished with horses. On the other hand, the fertilizer the horses provide is invaluable to the good life of the farm, and if there is one thing this farm needs above all others it's manure. I am employed as a janitor for the local grade and high school. It is a job that certainly is important to the community; there is a good deal of responsibility attached to it, and plenty of hard work. It is an ideal job in these respects. But like all jobs of this nature, it is low paying. In point of fact, only an old man who has raised his family or a single person could get by on the wages it pays, and most generally, those are the kind of people who are left with the responsibility of these jobs.

Are we discouraged? Well, somewhat. Who wouldn't be if we didn't seem to be able to do anything right? It is not encouraging to work the better part of a day on something without success, only to have someone come along and solve the problem in a matter of minutes. But we had little or no experience in any of these things and the mistakes are perfectly natural. However, this is the kind of a situation that eventually breeds discouragement and finally abandonment. It is all too true of the land movement, in this country and in England, that many people were interested in it and liked to talk about it, but few took positive steps to prepare themselves for it. We are some of those many people. We would like others to avoid the same pitfalls. However, we still think that if you want to get settled on the land, the thing to do is to get on it and wrestle with it. But if you are young and not married it would be wise to learn something about farming.

Several years ago there were a series of articles or letters in *Commonweal* on the land movement. I recall that one gentleman remarked that it was a shame and a waste of talent that many young couples went onto the land, underwent almost unbelievable hardships, and returned to the city, sadly disillusioned and almost misanthropic, when otherwise they might have made a valuable contribution to society. This is always the risk that is run by people with idealistic tendencies. They seize upon an idea, and without stopping to consider the whys and wherefores jump into a situation, only to find that it is a spot where even angels fear to tread without preparation. But we think that the greater shame lies with those many who felt the call to the land, and for one reason or another put it off and are now engaged in other activities. There were many who saw the vision of the green revolution and liked what they saw. Many who dreamed a dream once, but never quite got around to doing anything about it. If all those who felt the call to the land had done something about it, their contribution to society would be great indeed. Some wag said that few people carry radicalism and idealism past thirty-five, intimating that by that time they learn something. This seems to be the awful truth. Sure it is tough on the land. The hardships and humiliating defeats are sometimes almost impossible to bear. But life is a struggle, and who wants to be afraid of life? Do not all spiritual writers tell us about the invaluableness of suffering? Yet most of us bend our every effort trying to avoid suffering, poverty, discomfort.

It is always a temptation to avoid suffering, but once you get on the land it quite naturally becomes a part of your life; you can hardly avoid it. It is not easy to rise in the pitch-black darkness on a cold winter morning, praying that there is a little bit of fire left in the stoves, and hoping you remembered to bring the kindling wood in the night before, to drive off to work long before most people are up. But it is a chance to suffer, a chance to put yourself in harmony with people all over the world who have few comforts, little to eat, no leisure. But we really have so much more than over two-thirds of the peoples on earth. We are indeed rich in earthly goods. While burning brush the other day, because it was in our way, we thought of the people in France, in the Middle East, and the boys on Chrystie Street waiting for the morning line to start. How much warmth they could have gotten from all that brush, and how they would like to have had it. Besides, what other alternative has one who wants to raise a large family, who wants to encourage them to accept responsibility, who wants to make an honest living, who is interested in catering to the whole man, who believes in poverty?

But to get back to our particular situation, our farm is like all other CW farms in that it has to be nurtured from without. We do not have the business acumen required to get the better end in a trade or even to break even; to recognize a bargain when we see one; to save for a rainy day; to give service for profit, etc. It seems to take all these things and more to be a successful farmer. Instead, we believe in mutual aid; in helping our neighbor even if he is better off than we are. It is unlike other CW farms in that we see few people, we get little opportunity to attend meetings, engage in discussions, make retreats, or a host of other things peculiar to CW farms. We do not mind receiving alms, in fact were it not for the help we have gotten up till now we would be poor indeed. Our children are all outfitted in cast-off clothes, as we are too; the furniture and household effects we have were given to us. In fact we seem to be getting without being able to give in return. We would much rather be engaged in a program of mutual aid, wherein we get according to our needs and give according to our means. It's true, as Dorothy points out, that the worst position people think they can get in is to be beholden to someone. This seems to be the cardinal sin of this decade. People have got to get even.

We would like to say that the future looks promising for us. Our two pigs are becoming fat, our goat is with kid and will freshen in the spring, our twelve chickens have quit laying but they are keeping the pot filled, and a reader of the CW from Texas is coming up to look for a farm in this neighborhood. And, though we are broke and it is cold out now and the snow is flying, it will not be long till spring when everything in nature will take a new lease on life, including us.

We would like to invite anyone who is interested in settling on the land to come visit with us, or work a little while with us, to become acclimated to some small extent to some of the problems of rural life. It would be an attempt at mutual aid. We would give a little and receive a little. If anyone is interested in purchasing a farm, we would like to say that farms are fairly reasonable in this part of the country and we would be glad to be of some assistance in locating places. We would like very much to give land to some families who would like to live in the country but not necessarily farm, as Lou Murphy did at the Detroit CW farm. However, we will not have title to the land for at least five years, and not a clear title for five more years.

———————————————————————————— JULY–AUGUST 1953

 Meditation on the Death of the Rosenbergs

DOROTHY DAY

AT EIGHT O'CLOCK on Friday, June 19, the Rosenbergs began to go to death. That June evening the air was fragrant with the smell of honeysuckle. Out under the hedge at Peter Maurin Farm, the black cat played with a grass snake, and the newly cut grass was fragrant in the evening air. At eight o'clock I put Nickie in the tub at my daughter's home, just as Lucille Smith was bathing her children at Peter Maurin Farm. My heart was heavy as I soaped Nickie's dirty little legs, knowing that Ethel Rosenberg must have been thinking with all the yearning of her heart of her own soon-to-be-orphaned children.

How does one pray when praying for "convicted spies" about

to be electrocuted? One prays always of course for mercy. "My Jesus, mercy." "Lord Jesus Christ, Son of the living God, have mercy on them." But somehow, feeling close to their humanity, I prayed for fortitude for them both. "God let them be strong, take away all fear from them, let them be spared this suffering, at least, this suffering of fear and trembling."

I could not help but think of the story in Dostoievsky's *Idiot*, how Prince Myshkin described in detail the misery of the man about to be executed, whose sentence was commuted at the last moment. This had been the experience of Dostoievsky himself, and he had suffered those same fears, and had seen one of his comrades, convicted with him, led to the firing line, go mad with fear. Ethel and Julius Rosenberg, as their time approached and many appeals were made, must in hoping against hope, holding fast to hope up to the last, have compared their lot to that of Dostoievsky and those who had been convicted with him. What greater punishment can be inflicted on anyone than those two long years in a death house, watched without ceasing so that there is no chance of one taking one's life and so thwarting the vengeance of the state. They had already suffered the supreme penalty. What they were doing, in their own minds no doubt, was offering the supreme sacrifice, offering their lives for their brothers. Both Harold Urey and Albert Einstein, and many other eminent thinkers at home and abroad, avowed their belief in the innocence of these two. They wrote that they did not believe their guilt had been proved.

Leaving all that out of account, accepting the verdict of the court that they were guilty, accepting the verdict of the millions of Americans who believed them guilty, accepting the verdict of President Eisenhower and Cardinal Spellman who thought them guilty—even so, what should be the attitude of the Christian but one of love and great yearning for their salvation?

"Keep the two great commandments, love God and love your neighbor. Do this and thou shalt live." This is in the Gospel; these are the words of Jesus.

Whether or not they believed in Jesus, did the Rosenbergs love God? A rabbi who attended them to the last said that they had been his parishioners for two years. He followed them to the execution chamber reading from the Psalms, the Twenty-third, the Fifteenth, the Thirty-first. Those same psalms Cardinal Spellman reads every week as he reads his breviary, among those hundred and fifty psalms which make up not only the official prayer of the Church, but also the prayers which the Jews say. We used to see our Jewish grocer on the east side, vested for prayer, reciting the psalms every morning behind his counter when we went for our morning supplies. I have seen rabbis on all-night coaches, praying thus in the morning. Who can hear the word of God without loving the word? Who can work for what they conceive of as justice, as brotherhood, without loving God and brother? If they were spies for Russia, they were doing what we also do in other countries, playing a part in international politics and diplomacy, but they indeed were serving a philosophy, a religion, and how mixed up religion can become. What a confusion we have gotten into when Christian prelates sprinkle holy water on scrap metal, to be used for obliteration bombing, and name bombers for the Holy Innocents, for Our Lady of Mercy; who bless a man about to press a button which releases death on fifty thousand human beings, including little babies, children, the sick, the aged, the innocent as well as the guilty. "You know not of what spirit you are," Jesus said to his apostles when they wished to call down fire from heaven on the inhospitable Samaritans.

I finished bathing the children, who were so completely free from preoccupation with suffering. They laughed and frolicked in the tub when the switch was being pulled which electrocuted first Julius and then his wife. Their deaths were announced over the radio half an hour later, jazz music being interrupted to give the bulletin, and the program continuing immediately after.

The next day *The New York Times* gave details of the last hours, and the story was that both went to their deaths firmly, quietly, with no comment. At the last Ethel turned to one of the two police matrons who accompanied her and clasping her by the hand, pulled her toward her and kissed her warmly. Her last gesture was a gesture of love.

Max Bodenheim

DOROTHY DAY

EVERY DAY at twelve-thirty a bell calls us to the rosary in the library at Chrystie Street and those who wish to, gather together from the house to pray for peace. Sometimes mothers and children waiting for clothes are caught sitting there, and participate in prayer if they wish, or just sit. Slim goes on rocking in his chair, a cigar stuck in his mouth if he has one. Generally the attitudes are those of reverence and attention. Some kneel, some sit, some crouch over chairs in strange grotesque positions.

One day last February Max Bodenheim and his wife Ruth came in around eleven-thirty and said that they had been evicted from their furnished room, that he had a broken leg in a cast and they needed shelter. Could they go to one of the farms? There was more room at Maryfarm, and Charlie would drive up that day, so Max settled himself in the library, directly in back of the table where the statue of the Blessed Mother stood, to wait for Ruth to bring their few belongings from a friend's house. He was caught there when the rosary started. My glimpse of him in back of the statue, the flowers and the lighted candle was such that I was distracted indeed; I could not help but think, "Poor Max, suddenly caught like this, with dozens of ragged down and out people coming at the ringing of a bell into the room, planting themselves all around him and praying. He must think that he is being besieged, that they are praying at him, or for him." Afterwards I found Ruth sitting on her suitcase in the hall, a picture of abandon, reading some of Max's poems which she was sorting out from a broken suitcase by her side. I apologized. "We're not forcing prayers on anyone," I told her. "It's just that it's the only place we have to pray."

"Max is a Catholic," she said then. "Baptized, made his first communion, he was confirmed too, down in Mississippi where he was born. His mother was from Alsace-Lorraine." Later I found that she herself was baptized. According to her story one of her parents was Catholic, probably her mother since her name was Fagan. She herself was a Libertarian Socialist and attended the meetings of that group, and carried around with her pamphlets about the labor movement. I have one of them in my desk now.

They went with us to Maryfarm and stayed there for a month or six weeks, and then because she had become embroiled with a Russian guest who kissed her hand and flirted outrageously with her while he crudely insulted her husband, I drove the Bodenheims to Peter Maurin Farm on Staten Island. It was a bitter day and she had a touch of the flu and didn't want to leave. She had been enjoying her flirtations. She was thirty-five and her husband was sixty-five. She was a beautiful woman with strong Jewish features, with a splendid figure and a great warmth of manner. She could have played the part of Judith or Esther.

Max occasionally came to Mass, but Ruth said she believed only in love. And perhaps she should have added compassion, because certainly that is what she felt for her husband. She had met him on the street one rainy night and found him in such a forlorn condition that she had started taking care of him. They were married two years ago, not long after they met. Max had been divorced by his first wife Minna, had not seen his son for eight years.

I had known Max for many years, in New York, Chicago, and later in Staten Island. When Gene O'Neil recited "The Hound of Heaven" to me in the back room of an old saloon on Fourth Street, Max had been one of the habitués of the same place, writing poetry then on the backs of old envelopes. I remember one long poem he and Gene and I wrote, taking turns at writing the verses. Max didn't drink much then and he was a hard worker beginning to turn out novels and books of poetry, which never sold very well, and trying to get money by poetry reading, which used to make us all laugh. He had lost most of his front teeth then, and between his pipe and a lisp and a stammer it was hard to understand him. He was never a very prepossessing person, in spite of the picture the newspapers drew of him as a Don Juan.

I ran into Max later in Chicago, still reading poetry, and then some ten years later, when I was living on the beach in Staten Island and taking care of a number of children for the summer from the Hoffman School for Individual Development; his son Solbert was one of the number. He was ten years old, a serious little boy, good and diligent, playing and reading, eating and sleeping, and giving no trouble at all. Max used to come down once a week to see him and give him lectures on ethics and conduct. When Solbert grew up and his parents parted he didn't see Max any more, and when he married and had children of his own, they had nothing to do with their grandfather. Max told me this when he was staying with us.

He and Ruth remained with us at Peter Maurin Farm until after Easter, and on Easter Sunday Max went to Mass, and I was glad that it was a sung Mass. Ruth used to go into town once a week to try to sell some of Max's poetry so that they could get a room again. Once she sold one to *The New York Times* and they rejoiced for weeks. It didn't bring them much more than ten dollars. When she was away in town Max would not eat and every now and then, from a long silence, he used to ask me, "Do you think my beloved wife will be back this evening?" He didn't do much talking, but every day or so he would produce another poem.

He lay on one of the two beds we set up in a warm hall bedroom, and rested and smoked his pipe and wrote.

When spring came and the warm weather and his leg was better, Max and Ruth disappeared. Ruth came back later to get some things she left in a seaman's duffle bag and she and her companion, a young lad, rather somber and silent, walked down the road to the train about eleven. It was the last I ever saw of Ruth or Max. Last week they were murdered on Third Avenue, in the room of a young fellow who had given them shelter. Max was shot and Ruth beaten and stabbed.

The police caught this demented friend, Weinberg, three

days later, as he himself sought for a place to sleep in the basement of a rooming house on Twenty-first Street.

I read the account of this brutal slaying in all the papers February eighth and it was an ugly story indeed, with all the worst of Max and Ruth portrayed, the story of a drunken Bohemian, a clown, an exhibitionist, a lecher and of a woman who was loose in morals, depraved in appetite, loving Max for his prestige as writer and poet and finding her satisfaction in the passions of younger men. Only the *Daily News* gave him some credit for achievement and mentioned that he had won poetry awards, that he was the author of fourteen novels as well as several books of poetry. In spite of this achievement, his life had been spent in dire poverty.

Ruth herself had told me that he had been married a second time to an invalid on whom he had lavished what care he could from the sale of the popular rights to his books which came out in twenty-five-cent editions. For a few hundred dollars to pay for food and medicines, and doctors and later her burial, he had lost all his royalties.

The whole story was an ugly, sordid tale of poverty, drink and passion.

How often I have felt that a solid tide of evil is held off from us by the Blessed Sacrament in our midst, here at the farms and houses. By our daily communions we hold it back; it is dissolved like a mist by the sun of Justice.

We each of us could say, as we read this tragic story of death, "There, but for the grace of God, goes each one of us."

Max was buried in a family plot in New Jersey and a rabbi officiated at his funeral, the expenses of which were paid by the poet Alfred Kreymborg. He had many friends at his funeral and many followed him to his grave. There certainly was no possibility of a Catholic burial, since he had not practiced his faith since childhood.

Ruth believed only in love, she said, but she was in love especially with herself, her own beauty, which she used to inflame others to desire. The horrible part of it is, I have seen good and pious girls playing with mens' feelings, playing with their own, taking delectation in temptation, using those dark deep forces of sex "to influence for good." Their kindness is particular kindness, their friendship is particular friendship. As St. Augustine says, we need to love all as though we loved each one particularly. In spite of jealousy each one must see that we love all, all the others, most dearly. And it is so hard to love some, and so often whatever we do in love is repaid with bitterness, hatred and reprisals. This is good pruning for us, of our self-love. By the very pain we feel, we know the measure of our pride, our desire to use our influence, our love.

How little we were able to do for Max or Ruth. The bare bones of hospitality we gave them. If we had loved them more, if Ruth had found more love with us, perhaps she would not have wandered around trying to bestow it, trying to bestow the only warmth and light and color she knew in the ugly grey life around her. We were able to do so little; God must listen to our prayers for them, and maybe it was by the very violence of their death, the terror and pain of it added to Christ's suffering for them, their sins were wiped out that last awful moment and the gates of eternal life were opened up for them. I see this through a glass darkly.

And poor Weinberg, child of no home, placed in a Hebrew orphanage at an early age, kept in a mental hospital at ten years old, and never once visited by his mother, released at the age of seventeen to go into the army, serving there for seven months and then released again as unfit for public service, shut off from life and from people, without faith, without hope, without love, earning miserable meals by miserable work, dishwashing, that only job open for the unskilled, the unorganized, the crippled mentally and physically. He took the only kind of love he knew, bodily love, from wherever he could find it, in this case from a woman as mentally clouded as himself. In papers found among her things there was a record of her having been in a state hospital herself.

There was violence in Ruth. She wanted men to fight over her. It is instinct in many women to wish to be so desired that men will pay any price for their favors and where there is no money, blood will do.

The murderer cried out, "I have killed two Communists; I should get a medal." There was malice in the smile he turned on the police and the reporters.

But Max was only a poet, and his sympathies with Communism were because they spoke in terms of bread and shelter, and he had lived long with hunger. Drink was his refuge, because drink is often easier to get than bread. When he was young he wrote free verse, but those last years, when he was most disorganized, his verse became formal and stylized. Every day that he was with us he worked on a series of sonnets, dedicated to each one of us, polished, stately, courteous, often obscure, and he came to meals happily to read them aloud for our applause. I remember one especially that he wrote to Agnes, widow of a barge captain, who had been helping us for some years. And I loved this delicate appreciation of her sweetness and diligence, her care for our comfort.

Agnes had charge of the second-floor bedrooms and the linens and bathroom, and never a word of criticism comes from her lips for such wild disorder as accompanied such guests as Max and Ruth. No matter how comfortable a room—how tidy when they entered—it was soon a shambles of dirty clothes, rags, dust, cigarette butts, tobacco, newspapers, bits of food, onions, bread, apple cores, empty coffee cups, paper bags, scuffed shoes, dirty socks.

The newspapers commented on the sordid unheated room on Third Avenue and Twelfth Street where their bodies were found, and I thought, as I read, how over and over again in our houses of hospitality, I have seen just such rooms, reflecting the grim and cheerless chaos of the minds of its occupants. There is a comfortable disorder and the sordid disorder of people who do not love the material, though they seek all their pleasure in it. In trying to save their lives, they lose them.

In trying to live the life of the flesh, the Bodenheims were most hideously tricked. May their poor, dark, tormented souls rest now in peace.

❦ A Re-evaluation

ROBERT LUDLOW

DURING THE EIGHT YEARS I was at *The Catholic Worker* I accepted certain principles, advocated certain ideas, some of which I still accept, others which I would modify, and some which I do not accept because I never accepted them though many had the impression that I did simply because I said nothing in print one way or the other about them. The underlying principles of the CW I hope I shall always accept—the ideas of personalism, social justice, respect for all. The ideas of racial equality, of resisting the growing power of the state, of refusing to go along with the hate campaigns necessary to wage war these days and a refusal to participate in wars which of necessity must also use weapons whose very composition makes for their indiscriminate use. I do not think I have to preface any critical evaluation of ideas which I myself helped to spread by protesting my loyalty and indebtedness to the CW. I left not because of any personal or ideological disagreement, and these re-evaluations I express after a year and a half of absence.

I now think it was unwise that we employed the term anarchism or "Christian" anarchism. Because I think it useless to take a term which has a well-established meaning, to which certain groups have a prescriptive right, attach to that term specialized meanings which very few people understand, and then use the term as an expression of policy. It was inevitable that the term would create more misunderstandings than it ever cleared up. And I do not exclude myself when I state that I very much fear that a good part of the psychology behind the use of the term was a somewhat immature desire to appear more radical than the next fellow, to out-left the leftists, to shock without enlightening. If you ask hit and miss on the street where the nearest Catholic

Church is, you will almost always have pointed out to you a Church in union with the Roman See. The commonly accepted meaning of Catholic is just that. As such the Church in union with Rome has a prescriptive right to this term. However certain Anglicans (to give but one example) insist on using the term "Catholic" in a specialized non-traditional sense. They call themselves Protestant Catholics. Now if you grant their premises (which I do not) their position is logical. They mean they are Catholics who protest against what they regard as the unwarranted claims of the Roman Pontiff—as such they are Protestant Catholics. But I very much fear that most people would be quite confused by this, because this small group has combined two words which have a history behind them, divested them of this history, and so, far from making clear their stand, they have only served to obscure it.

So with the word anarchism. It has a history behind it and that history identifies it in the minds of most people with groups who, in theory at least, reject all authority. Not only all temporal authority but all divine authority. One has but to consult the accepted interpreters of anarchism to realize that their position on authority is one no Catholic could consistently hold. And when you mention anarchism to people, that is what they take it to be. And those who do reject all authority have, by this criterion, as much prescriptive right to the term anarchist as do adherents of the Roman See to the term Catholic. So it is only leading to confusion and obscurity to insist on its use. Similarly with the term Christian anarchism. Who has a better prescriptive right to this term than the Tolstoians? And yet we have only to read Tolstoy to realize how unacceptable his religious notions on authority would be for the Catholic. Is it not then somewhat childish to insist on grabbing these terms from our anarchist friends as though we had more right to use them, when all history shows *they* have more right to the terms?

As for the ideas of anarchism, I never felt that individualist anarchism was at all compatible with the Catholic ethos. Consequently I used the term syndicalist anarchism. Individualist anarchism is the sociological counterpart of Protestantism. Viewing the individual in an atomistic, isolated sense, it despairs of all cooperative ventures for the common good and finally can offer nothing but a one-man revolution. But that is far from the Catholic conception of man as dependent not only on God but on society—on government. Syndicalist anarchism escapes this somewhat by advocating cooperation, by working through unions, by not making the individual the all-important item in the revolution. And indeed a case could be made for syndicalist anarchism as a form of government *provided* it were the will of the people. For as I pointed out sometime ago, St. Thomas states that the people, if they so choose, may retain governing power in their own hands rather than delegate it to others. But the mistake of syndicalist anarchists lies in this—that they assume that it *is* the will of the people to retain authority in their own hands (or at least it is the will of the people *if* the people only knew the facts and were enlightened) and thus to advocate a here and now rebellion against legitimate governmental authority. Nor can we as Christians escape this reasoning by saying, "If you do not use the things of Caesar you do not have to obey Caesar." For in matter of fact we unavoidably use the things of Caesar and so we cannot escape that obedience called for by Christ to Caesar in all things that do not invade the realm of God. And it is simply not in the Catholic tradition to make the realm of God so large that there is no room left for Caesar. If that were so, Christ's words would be meaningless.

This by no means should be taken to imply an acceptance of the status quo, for the Church has recognized the right to criticize, to advocate change, to disobey when the government is clearly in the wrong. What we should not do is go under an *a priori* assumption that all government is evil and unjust *per se* and is to be automatically disobeyed. As long as the people choose to delegate authority, that delegated authority has the right to demand our obedience in all that is not sin. And, as a general rule, it is for the Church to determine when it is sin. On matters on which she has not ruled, we are of course free to differ. So that there are good Catholics who refuse to bear arms and good Catholics who do bear arms—as one example of this permissible divergence.

I can then no longer hold with those who present anarchism as a goal capable of realization or those who, while stating that it cannot be realized (short of a miracle) nevertheless continue to propound it, apparently as a result of a psychological imperative, or because they deem protest as protest its own justification. To insist that mankind as a whole become such (by personal reformation) that an anarchist society would be possible, is like insisting that all become celibates or that all become Trappists. The Church wisely holds that this is possible only for a selected few, that the great majority must work out their salvation otherwise. And so the Church does not demand that the average Catholic live like a Trappist, and her moral theology takes into account the frailties of the generality of mankind so that she does not place on us a burden too heavy to be borne. In the secular sense perfectionist anarchists are akin to the Jansenists in their rigorism, and just as the Jansenists consigned most of mankind to hell, because most of mankind could not approximate *their* standards, so one hears frequently from this type of anarchist that "the masses are asses."

It remains true however that the national state is a hindrance to man—not because it is a state but because of the concept of national sovereignty which makes of each state a strutting, egoistic maniac ready to pull the trigger at any offense to its vanity. Through labor unions, through non-governmental organizations, and (most importantly) through the Church we may help to oppose this concept, and work for some union in which the individual states will agree to surrender national sovereignty in favor of a world society.

 # Death of a Boy

EILEEN FANTINO DIAZ

RAIN FELL DULL AND LISTLESS on the roofs for the second day puddling on the black tar as a young boy high over the blurred street came to the edge and started down the fire escape. High in his hand was a flash of white and grey, bright against the darkly moving sky. It was a pigeon, one of the many that streaked over the tenements and soared away into the blue air on brighter days when sunlight shoots through the settling dust of afternoons.

He had caught a piece of flight in his arms and was bringing it down into his world, to his cavern of a street where the sky is unconquerable. And his heart was wild with rapture, the wings soft and wet; the eyes of the bird looked into his own as it shook to be free. With his hands full of stirrings, he dropped down like a puppet falls to the stage, dizzy and crazed, six flights down to the sleekly wet street, his head split open by his return.

One small boy came first to gaze at the body, the twisted looseness and the outpouring of anguish which was left of him. This spectator grabbed the pigeon out of the limp hand and beat it with all his strength against the moldy wall of the building until he had only strength for crying. Death again the sudden and cruel joke without sense or beauty or grace, shock breaking the steady humming beat of the rain.

The neighborhood came to express sympathy to the boy's parents and sit in a small room with the still body, strangers came and lived an image of the fire escape slippery with rain and the boy coming down holding a pigeon, and of the fall. Children talked about it, mothers shuddered. The complacency of life looking at death stilled the question, always that question.

The flight of birds is the bright streak of hope in a dark and fearful city. How many hushed wings had those eyes followed off the roofs and into the sky, like a vision of life not shadowed in the rooms of his life and the incessant coming of days. And there on that one dark day-in-his-hand all secrets, the meaning and striving and patience, his face wet with the world's tears falling from the abyss of the sky—this thing in his arms, the soft wings, the power of flight and life outside the prison of his confinement, this moment perhaps he touched God and died.

NOVEMBER 1955

 ## Our Fall Appeal

DOROTHY DAY

DEAR FRIENDS OF THE CATHOLIC WORKER:

In the light of our present difficulties it is necessary to restate our position and tell our readers again just what it is we are trying to do—what it means to us to perform the works of mercy, spiritual and corporal. The most important thing in the world to us is to grow in the love of God, to try to do His will. Our Lord Jesus told us that what we do to the least we do to Him. St. Paul told us we are "members one of another, and that when the health of one member suffers, the health of the whole body is lowered."

We believe not only in St. Thomas' doctrine of the common good, but feel it can be affected only if each one of us, alone, realizes his personal responsibility to his brother, that his love for God must be shown in his love for his brother, and that love must be expressed in the works of mercy, practiced personally, at a personal sacrifice. So we live together, here at *The Catholic Worker*, pool resources of money and ability, and so are able to take care of far more than just ourselves.

People have so far lost that sense of personal responsibility that our country is becoming a country of institutions, and a gigantic part of our income goes to support them. State responsibility has come to take the place of personal responsibility. Doctors at mental hospitals and veteran's hospitals have said that a tremendous number of patients could be cared for at home if their families would take the responsibility. On the other hand houses and apartments become smaller and smaller so that there is "no room at the inn." We are able to have fifty in our own home here at Chrystie Street because it is two old houses thrown into one, built at a time when people wanted space. When people come to us we cannot say, "Go, be thou filled," and refer them to an agency. So we have come to be feeding and clothing a vast number of people who come in to us day after day, the lame, the halt and the blind.

But we are not organized as an institution of any kind and the city does not know how to classify us. We are not a multiple dwelling, a rest home, a convalescent home, a shelter or an asylum or a convent. We are a group of people living together under one roof, with one head, which is Charlie McCormack, now that Tom Sullivan has gone to the Trappists. Often I am considered the head, being older and the publisher of the paper. I get the summonses, the complaints. We are not registered as a charitable agency, it has been pointed out. But we hope our dear Lord recognizes us as charitable people. We try to keep the laws and regulations about housing, health and fire prevention, and take as good care of our family as we can. But we find we are always coming up against some ordinance, some infraction. We will always be in trouble with the city and the state because, though we also consider ourselves good citizens and lovers of our country as well as children of God and try to bear our share of the responsibility of brother for brother, the city and the state have come to feel that this is their field (since it has been left to them). A western Bishop said to me once that he did not believe in state ownership of the indigent. God wants man's free service, his freely bestowed love. So we protest and cry out against every infringement of that great gift of God, freedom, our greatest gift, after the gift of life.

That love of brother, that care for his freedom is what causes us to go into such controversial subjects as man and the state, war and peace. The implications of the Gospel, teaching of the works of mercy, lead us into conflict with the powers of this world. Our love of God is a consuming fire. It is a fearful thing to fall into the hands of the living God. It is a living God and a living faith that we are trying to express. We are called to be holy, that is, whole men, in this life of ours. We are trying to follow this call. It has led many of our workers into the priesthood, into Trappist monasteries, into convents. But we as a group, not having *this vocation*, are not classed as a *religious* group, not even as a *Catholic* group, and so do not have the protection of that classification. We are individual Catholics, not Catholic Action.

Many have left us to marry and raise a little community of their own, and endure all the sufferings of trying to lead this life in the factory, on the farm, enduring the frustrations of seeing their talents unused, their best energies of all their work days put into meaningless work in the cities, and not having the help we have of our community life and the assistance of our friends in our houses and farms.

We never intended to have breadlines, to care for so many, but it is aways so hard to turn people away. Men out of hospitals, with no place but the public shelter housing other thousands, turned loose on the streets by day. We have had people come in to us from the streets who have died a few weeks after, from their long endured miseries. We still have people coming who sleep in doorways and spend their days with us and share our meals. It is so hard to limit oneself, and then too our Holy Father, Pius XII, told some Sisters once never to be afraid to run up bills for the poor. Of course it always comes back to the fact that we are not an accredited agency. We are not a charitable institution. And we are never going to turn into that because we are trying to make the point, by our lives, by our work, that personal responsibility comes first. We are born alone, we die alone, we must, each one of us, do what we can for God and our brother, not God and country, but God and our brother, as Christ stated it.

We are in difficulties now, not only with our bills, but with the state, with the city. We cannot print our usual fall appeal, without pointing this out. But we are begging you to help us keep going with these ideas of ours about mutual aid, voluntary poverty, and the works of mercy. If we were forced to cease, how great a burden which we are bearing now would fall upon the state or city—mental hospitals and convalescent homes, relief rolls and the breadlines of the Municipal Lodging House. And how many would be just wandering the streets, crouching in doorways. Oh God, look upon the face of Thy Christ in these poor, and help us to keep going.

So we are asking you, as our Lord Himself told us to ask, for your help once more. And may God and His Blessed Mother whose month this most specially is, bless you a hundredfold, heaped up and running over.

In His Love,
DOROTHY DAY

PART IV

Radicals in Action
1956–

A Small Disciple

ROBERT GRANT

WE ARE SO BUSY running these days that we scarcely notice anybody. Not even the very fat or the very thin or the very beautiful or the very ugly can get more than a glance out of us. James William Smith was one of those least likely to attract our notice, being middle-aged, middle-sized and with a face halfway between attractive and unattractive. He did have a certain mild light in his green-grey eyes, it was true, but with jewels and plastics and electricity scintillating all around us we are hardly apt to pay much attention to a certain mild light in a man's eyes.

But James William Smith did get noticed once, and this is how.

He worked as a janitor in a few stores of the neighborhood, and in his free time he read almost constantly, though he only owned two books, the Gospels and the *Imitation of Christ*. The shopkeepers, realizing they could get his services for practically nothing, paid him practically nothing. Whatever they gave him Smith accepted without complaint. The neighborhood believed that Smith was a fool, yet an honest fool who never stole merchandise and cleaned stores thoroughly well. Once in a while a grocer gave him a cake that had gone moldy, or a haberdasher gave him a pair of pants that couldn't be sold. Sometimes they were gifts and sometimes they took the place of wages. Smith said nothing but thank you.

One night, while Smith was sweeping up in the "More 4 Less Grocery" two men broke in. They grabbed him, tied him with clothesline, and hit him over the head with a bottle of Pepsi-

Cola, knocking him out and almost killing him. They rifled the cash register and fled.

The two thieves were caught and arraigned for trial and James William Smith became the principal witness against them. He was brought to the witness stand but he never testified. He refused to take the oath.

The court clerk stood there with the Bible in his hand, and the judge leaned down and asked what the delay was in swearing in the witness.

"The witness refuses to take the oath," the clerk said, shifting the Bible in his hands as if it had suddenly grown hot.

"What was that?" The judge's face compressed with incredulity and annoyance. He did not wait for an answer. "Please, let's have no delay; we've got a heavy docket to get through this morning. Will you kindly swear in the witness and let's get his testimony."

The clerk again held out the Bible to Smith, who shook his head politely, like someone being offered food whose stomach is full.

"The witness refuses, your honor," the clerk replied.

He said it loudly and now everyone in the court, including the two thieves, was staring curiously at the witness. This was a low court, and there weren't many people present, but probably more people were looking at Smith now than had looked at him in his whole life. The judge inclined toward the witness, squinting and excavating the hollow of his ear, as if to remove whatever it was that was distorting his hearing.

"Is this true, Mr.—" The judge consulted the record on his desk: "Is this true, Mr. Smith, that you refuse to take the oath?"

"Yes, sir," Smith said, in a dry weak voice.

"Yes, your honor," whispered the clerk who had put down the Bible.

"Yes, your honor," Smith said, a little louder now, but nervously.

"And may I inquire," said the judge, annoyed yet intrigued at the same time, "just why you refuse to take the oath on the Bible as required by United States law?" He pronounced "as required by United States law" much more forcefully than the rest.

"It's against my religion, sir." Smith said.

"Your honor," whispered the clerk.

The judge waved his hand. "That's all right, that's all right . . . and Mr. Smith, what sect do you belong to, may I ask?"

Smith seemed confused by the word "sect."

"What is your religion, Mr. Smith?"

"Christian, sir."

The judge lifted his eyebrows at the rest of the court, including the thieves. Then he began to talk to Smith with an exaggerated patience, as if with a child. "We are all Christians, Mr. Smith. I am a Christian. I go to church, I believe in God. This is a Christian country, Mr. Smith. I mean what is the name of your group, your organization?"

Smith again seemed confused. "Christian, sir, like I told you."

The judge glanced at the clerk as if figuring how many moments he could allot to this comedy.

"Look, Mr. Smith, I'm trying to be patient with you. We've had thousands of Christians there on the witness stand and you are the first to refuse to take the oath. How many others belong to your brand of Christianity?"

"I don't know, sir."

"Then," snapped the judge who had once been a prosecuting attorney, "I take it we are looking today on a one-man church."

There was laughter; even the thieves smiled. Smith said nothing.

The judge tried one more angle. "These two men are accused of assaulting you, Smith; it was just luck they didn't kill you. Don't you wish to see justice done, see them punished?"

At these words a strange smile began to play with the corners of Smith's mouth. But he said nothing.

"I must warn you, Smith. This is a very serious offense. It shows your utter contempt of this court and for the government and people of the United States of America. It is in my power to indict you. But I don't believe you are a criminal, Smith, but just a victim of misplaced zeal. I've studied the scriptures quite a bit myself. Is there any particular passage which in your mind authorizes your behavior?"

"Yes sir, Saint Matthew, sir. 'You have heard that it was said, you shall not swear falsely, but shall perform to the Lord what you have sworn. But I say to you, swear not at all, neither by Heaven, for it is the throne of God, nor by the earth, for it is His footstool, nor by Jerusalem, for it is the city of the Great King. And do not swear by your head, for you cannot make one hair white or black. Let what you say be yes or no. Anything more than this comes from evil.' "

As he spoke, the mild light in Smith's eyes seemed to glow brighter than neon or diamonds. Maybe the judge noticed this, for he did not say another word to him but angrily recessed the court and had Smith taken into custody for contempt. The foreign minister of Russia made a big speech that day, so Smith's case did not get into the newspapers. No psychiatrist was called and Smith was speedily tried and found guilty and ushered noiselessly into prison to be punished to the full extent of the law.

The neighborhood shopkeepers complain now. Janitors belong to the union and must be paid ridiculous wages. You can find children or women of course, but they do slovenly work and they steal. Once in a while you still hear talk about Smith; the other day, for example, the haberdasher said to the grocer, "Wish old Smitty was back. Crazy as a bedbug but . . . but a good man."

"U.S. Keeps Detention Camps Ready"

AMMON HENNACY

THIS IS THE HEADING in *The New York Times* of December 26, 1955, describing the camps ready for subversives when a "national emergency" arises. They are located at: *Allenwood, Pennsylvania,* near the regular Lewisburg Federal Penitentiary; *Avon Park, Florida,* forty miles north of Lake Okeechobee, formerly a federal prison camp; *El Reno, Oklahoma,* formerly inhabited by prisoners of war from Rommel's Afrika Korps; *Tule Lake, California,* near the Oregon border, formerly occupied by twenty thousand Japanese in the hysteria of World War II; *Wickenburg, Arizona,* northwest of Phoenix, formerly a glider school of the Air Force; and *Florence, Arizona,* formerly a prisoner of war camp for nine thousand Italians, situated between Phoenix and Tucson.

While there is space in these camps for only five thousand at present they could hold scores of thousands if the "emergency" became frightful enough to the politicians in Washington. These camps were authorized under the McCarran Internal Security Act of 1950, and in 1951 one and a half million dollars was appropriated to fix up these six camps. Elmer Bendiner in the *National Guardian* discusses these concentration camps also, stating that six liberal senators who had fought McCarran were somehow maneuvered into settling on these camps as the lesser of two evils. These senators were Kilgore of West Virginia, Lehman of New York, Kefauver of Tennessee, Graham of North Carolina, Douglas of Illinois, and Humphrey of Minnesota.

Mr. Huston, who wrote *The New York Times* article, visited the camps at Florence, Wickenburg and El Reno. Describing the latter as containing twenty-nine buildings, each about one hundred feet long with three iron stoves in the middle to provide heat. This is on the old Fort Reno military reservation of eight thousand acres across from the El Reno Federal Prison. This is a country of cold winds in winter and hot winds in summer. I hiked through there in December, 1945.

The Florence camp is about a mile away from the state prison in Arizona. I saw its grey buildings when I came back from picking cotton in Eloy. One hundred and fifty federal prisoners now live there. They have renovated the buildings which now number twenty-six, capable of holding three thousand subversives. Strange to say, this is the only air-conditioned prison of all the three-score federal prisons in the U.S., with a chapel, television room, library, and well-equipped hospital. Sewage disposal is ready to serve twenty thousand people. About eighty acres are cultivated and their own pork is produced. But do not let this fine atmosphere make you feel happy, for if you had a notion to escape there are the bloodhounds of the state prison handy, and in every direction is the lonesome desert where it is very easy to get lost. In the spring for forty miles around the desert flowers bloom. Mother Bloor hiked across the U.S. when she was sixty-five and describes this Florence area as the most beautiful in the U.S.

I have been in Wickenburg many times but did not notice the camp there. Mr. Huston says it would house about eight hundred and because of its more substantial buildings, venetian blinds, etc., it would be more suitable for women prisoners. The Wickenburg climate is delightful when Phoenix and Tucson roast in the summer, and it is not too cold in the winter. Dude ranches abound and here we see the "western atmosphere" advertised in the magazines.

It is anybody's guess as to who will inhabit these camps. The FBI does not tell us in advance what they are going to do, and the brother of Secretary Dulles who runs the American spy system is even more secretive. It is certain that all those left of center can be accused of any form of "guilt by association." Mr. Huston says: "After Pearl Harbor, for instance, a great many Japanese were rounded up and interned. . . . It was later acknowledged that not all of them were disloyal or a menace to national security. Undoubtedly objections would arise over the detention of certain individuals if another national emergency arose. The Government's employee security program has been criticized as unjust to hundreds who are not bona fide security risks. In the climate of a national emergency hundreds, perhaps thousands, could be sequestered in security camps who were not actual, or even potential spies or saboteurs."

DECEMBER 1956

 ## Pacifism and the Crisis of Revolution

EDMUND J. EGAN

IT IS ALWAYS WELL to examine one's beliefs at times in which the challenge to them seems most real. So in this time when innocent men and women are being murdered in Hungary with cold brutality and profound cynicism, let us consider pacifism in the perspective of the agonized moment.

Seldom in the past has a situation presented a picture of the problem of war at once so perplexing and clarifying. For those, of course, who maintain an absolute pacifism on scriptural grounds, no change in situation can have any bearing; the violent use of force, like the commission of blasphemy, is evil in itself.

I am dealing here, however, with that attitude of pacifism which derives primarily from the workings of human reason, albeit inspired by the Christian command to charity and to moral absolutism in general. For this position of "philosophical pacifism" has of late lost some of its tangential props. What is happening in Central Europe today is not one of those conflicts between the masters of states, in which the people are dragged in to wage the battles of power-hungry leaders. Nor is it one of history's money wars in which the blood of a people is sacrificed for the profit of a class. It is rather the revolution of an entire people against a tyranny which has dared every extreme of cruelty in order to re-assert itself.

The purpose of these observations is not to fulminate against the Soviets; they no doubt consider themselves justified by reasons strategic and political. Their cynicism, it is true, seems a more blatant evil than America's blundering hypocrisy, yet is what they have done at Budapest at root a greater crime than what this nation did at Hiroshima?

The reason for emphasizing the injustice committed against the Hungarian people is to strip down the standard argument for pacifism to its moral center, and this is best done by granting there to be a "just cause" in the use of force; and a revolution by workers and students seeking bread and freedom allows us to assume such justice. Likewise, men and women attacking armored divisions with clubs and pistols removes the standard objection to the immorality of means used in warfare.

It is in the face of a situation such as this that we must examine what I consider to be the inviolate center of the moral position of pacifism, or in this case to be more specific, of conscientious objection. Perhaps the greatest single moral objection to war is the necessary abnegation of individual conscience which it entails. For whatever the war policy of a nation, real or alleged, may be, the dominant policy must actually be military success, and therefore strategic considerations subsume moral ones. The individual who joins a military service may follow one of two courses in this regard. First, he may join with a head full of mental reservations as to orders he will not obey, action in which he will not participate. This position is however an academic one largely, since: 1) it requires that the individual place himself in a situation in which heroic virtue is likely to be necessary for him to obey his conscience; 2) modern war and training for it abound in actions which are morally objectionable, especially to the Christian, and 3) most important, the war effort, itself, to which *all* actions under the military aegis are directed, is rendered unjust when unjust means are proper to the war's conduct. It is therefore the usual procedure for the soldier to choose the other course, and give over his conscience to his military superiors, who tell him whom, where, and when and how he will fight.

In the recent Hungarian revolution, as in any such popular struggle, such considerations cannot be said specifically to apply. The spontaneous use of violence by groups of civilians in the cause of an immediately perceived good cannot be called *military action* as such; it is on the contrary, *individual action*, communally channelled. Let us however examine the character and results of this kind of "war." It is first to be noted that action such as that undertaken by the Hungarian rebels cannot succeed *in terms of force* so long as it retains the spontaneous, relatively individualistic character of which we have spoken. It might succeed by some combination of military consolidation and external aid, or it might succeed, as it seemed to for a moment in Hungary, by the moral pressure of a people so nobly offering their lives.

But as soon as we speak of moral pressure, we are dealing with a focus of meaning different from that of armed force, and the pacifist contention of the ultimate futility of violence becomes illuminated. In thinking of the Hungarians our consideration shifts towards those rebels who advanced on the Soviet tanks armed only with their flags; here we are closer to the marches of the Indian *satyagrahi* than to the movements of a modern army.

None of this is to detract from the nobility of the armed revolutionaries; to eschew violence in such a situation demands education to a value attitude which is not in the tradition of the West. The above remarks only attempt to point out that the challenge to pacifism made by a "noble war" like the Hungarian revolution is not so severe a challenge as it might at first seem.

Indeed this revolution points up a contention central to pacifist thought, especially in the Catholic theological context. That is the fact that in an armed conflict there is an insuperable advantage on the side of the less morally scrupulous combatant, an advantage which the other side must meet in kind if it hopes to win the war. This is the inner dialectic of force, and it obtains whatever the justice of the cause fought for. In this light we may note the swell of revenge and anti-Communist terrorism on the part of the Hungarians during their brief supremacy. It is of course true that the decisive factor in this conflict was the extent of Soviet military power; it is however relevant that in the early stages of the revolt, before that power had fully asserted itself, the above-mentioned "dialectic of force" became manifest, and the idealist who associated himself with the revolution was given pause by the reports and newsreels of the mass shootings and hangings of captured Communist officials.

It will be said that such actions will always occur when men's passions are stirred by war, but we must object that this indicts the war before it excuses the actions in question. And it is when we look from the Hungarian microcosm to the overall world political struggle that means to any end are limited by moral principles, and especially by the supreme moral principle of determinations of actions by individual conscience. Now, when the moral errors of past wars and past selfishness are bearing fruit in the suffering of innocents, the call to arms is in the air; new barbarities of nuclear war and total mobilization offer to replace the present evils.

And when we take pains to expose this vicious circle of despair, our only excuse in doing so is that the despair is not total. The old way has run out of possibilities: in the old way there is no hope, and the new way of pacifism is not the way of nations or of societies. The only hope remaining is that the individual may refuse to enter the vicious circle, that he may be true to himself, and to his fellow men, by accepting his necessary alienation from their sad and noble struggles.

How Do You Like Our Jail?

DEANE MOWRER

WITH THE STIFF BEARING of authority, starchily efficient, you sit behind your desk which is at the very center of things, there in the main hall of the seventh floor, right next to the bulletin board and the elevators, between the dining room and the recreation room, looking toward either end of the hallway where the long corridors lead off like the arms of a cross down the rows of cells squatly frowning behind their ponderous barred gates. The morning hubbub has subsided. Most of the girls and women— they are preponderantly young, it seems—have taken the elevators to work assignments in laundry, kitchen, clinic, or prison offices. You can relax now; at least a little. And so it is I find you sitting, with your slightly sardonic eye and gleaming badge, as I pass somewhat awkwardly by with mop and pail toward my own particular cleanup operation in corridor A. This is my second day, the second of a five-day sentence. Yesterday you had said: "I remember you gals from last summer. You're not American. You're just impossibles." A woman prisoner at work nearby had caught up the derisive "impossibles" and sent the unflattering label tumbling down the corridors. To refuse to take shelter in an air-raid drill—no self-respecting criminal would be guilty of such. But then there had been that priest to see Dorothy—and Father McCoy he was, too—and all those telephone calls full of concern for her. You say no more about "impossibles." But as you see me coming, you can't resist hurling the question in your strident official voice: "How do you like our jail, Deane?" Again volatile guffaws of a prisoner proclaim this an official witticism, and the ensuing parrot-like cacophony covers my confusion as I falter a would-be non-committal, "It's interesting."

Now with the free unhurried view of retrospection, I recall your question and try to phrase a more specific reply.

How do I like "our jail"? You were right to say *our*; for ultimately each of us participates, I think, in the guilt of our time, is jailer as well as jailed. But to answer your question—suppose I said I liked it. Would you conclude that I am homesick for that narrow cell with the two uncomfortable cots, the cold toilet seat by the window, the slow-draining lavatory, the hard concrete floor, the dirty tiled walls, the cramped space where we could only sidle circumspectly? Yet there was a window cleverly contrived to open, pane by narrow pane; the good fresh air came in; and on a sunny day a large splash of sunlight fell across the little metal table where we could take turns sitting—toilet seat for chair—and write letters with a borrowed stub of pencil. And we could pray; even say our rosary, though our beads had been confiscated. Counting the *aves* on our fingers served with us as it has with many others; but then a fellow prisoner lent Dorothy a rosary which we shared to both pass and redeem the time.

How do I like our jail? Suppose I said I thought that it was holy. Would you think that I am referring to the chapel which we were not permitted to visit? Or to the religious literature and spiritual guidance which were so markedly not in evidence? Nor do I mean the touching little shrines which some of the longer term prisoners had been permitted to construct in their cells. Nor the many acts of kindness which we experienced and witnessed. Yet I found holiness there—great holiness. I saw Christ templed in suffering, in those imprisoned ones whom He commended to us so particularly: "I was in prison, and you came to me. . . . Amen I say to you, as long as you did it to one of these my least brethren, you did it to me." I heard His voice over the wailing love-hungry dissonance of Negro blues, the flamelike abandon of Spanish song, the defiant shriek of obscenity. I heard Him cry again: "Father, forgive them, for they know not what they do." And I knew that He was speaking not only of them but also of me, of you, of all of us who are imprisoned in this world, who wear the shackles of selfishness, who have participated actively or passively in man's inhumanity to man, who have forgotten or remember so seldom that we can love God only through loving our neighbor.

Life Behind Bars

DOROTHY DAY

WHEN I THINK of the long sentences served by so many others in so many miscarriages of justice, when I think of the accumulation of prisons, outmoded and futile, that dot the land of the free, I am not particularly interested in writing about my few days in jail last month. I am just glad that I served them, and am ready to serve again if there is another compulsory air-raid drill next summer. It is a gesture perhaps, but a necessary one. Silence means consent, and we cannot consent to the militarization of our country without protest. Since we believe that the air-raid drills are part of a calculated plan to inspire fear of the enemy instead of the love which Jesus Christ told us we should feel toward him, we must protest these drills. It is an opportunity to show we mean what we write when we repeat over and over that man is here on this earth to love God and His brother. We love our country and have no wish to give up citizenship. Peter Maurin felt himself to be not a Frenchman or an American, but first of all a Catholic, but just the same he loved both the country of his birth and his adopted country, where he had worked for forty years.

It was good to have the opportunity to "visit the prisoner" which is one of the works of mercy, even for so brief a visit, by being a prisoner oneself. One of the Little Sisters of Charles de Foucauld has had herself committed to a prison in France in order that she might live with her less fortunate sisters, and in her confinement live a life of work and prayer.

We have no complaint to make of the prison or of the attendants there. Our physical needs were supplied: blankets, sheets, towels, clothing. What if the clothing was a bit coarse, unbleached muslin and not cut to fit? What if the dress was a

193

purple sack coming just below the knees! I would not say we were clothed with modesty, nor in Christian fashion, but we were clothed. Our food was coarse but adequate, a little too much rice and spaghetti of course. The cells were tiny and crowded but they were both warm and airy. One could open the window as wide as one liked, one or all of the five little panes. One pane of glass even was clear so that we could look out on Greenwich Avenue, on the swirling snow, the slushy streets, the people rushing to and fro, the brightly lit stores, the flower shop, food stores, all in the heart of Greenwich Village.

We were given thorough physical examinations, even to X-rays and Wasserman tests. There was a recreation room on the roof, a beauty parlor, a craftshop and in the few days we were there we were taught by a gentle teacher to make some brass enameled ashtrays. If there had been more time we would have worked in clay, leather, bound a book, dressed dolls.

The "ladies" as they called us, worked in the laundry, kitchen, sewing rooms, cleaning and so on. We were given mop and pail to clean the corridors. But there was never enough work for the five hundred or so prisoners, so there were many idle. I saw one girl display with pride a dress she has made for herself, so there is a chance to learn a few useful things.

But the sadness of it all is that aside from talking day in and day out about freedom, and "how much time you got" and "when do you get out?" there are some there who are truly happy. Quite a few of the women who have lived with us at St. Joseph's House of Hospitality have spent short terms for disorderly conduct and drinking, and I remember one Jean especially. She was staying with us on Staten Island and as we all sat around the table one night sewing and talking (she was playing solitaire) she suddenly said, "I never was so happy as when I was in the clink." Born and bred on the Bowery, of a drunken father and mother, all her family scattered, she looked upon the jail as a place of comfort and security, a place where she could not get into much trouble, where there was warmth and companionship and movies on Saturday night and television every night until nine, and nobody expecting much of her, just taking her as she was. It is sad too that there is nothing much to come out to, not enough hospices, just the prospect of going back to the same old taverns to find your friends, to the same old work with its tensions and dirt and insecurity, and far more expected of you than you are able to give.

"I don't like to work," one little Puerto Rican said to me. She spent most of her time lying on her cot, singing melancholy songs. "What kind of work were you doing?" "Laundry work and I'm here for being a pickpocket," and she covered her face with her hands in mock shame and laughed at me.

Why are the jails so full, and why are the searches so rigid? And why are they all so young, these girls that fill the four corridors on the six or seven floors of the House of Correction which are used as cell blocks. It is mostly drugs, and the girls themselves say the problem is hopeless. "We will get out, and then we will be here again."

I remembered an article I had read in the magazine section of *The New York Times* on drug addiction, and the way it is handled in England and the way it is handled here. "Of course it is not a crime," one of the officers said to me. "But it is treated as a crime, and it certainly leads to more crime." The *Times* has also called the Women's Detention Prison a "black hole," because it is overcrowded, because girls are held there long before trial as well as after conviction. But physically speaking, it is not a black hole. The sad fact remains that it is more comfortable physically than many a slum tenement with its overcrowding, its vermin, its cold and dark and lack of hot water.

Our physical needs are cared for, but certainly not the spiritual. If you go in on Monday, you do not see a priest until the following Saturday, and if you ask for rosary or prayer book or Bible, you do not get it. And you wonder if there is any visitation, any preaching, any telling the stories of the lives of the saints, any glimpse for these prisoners of any other kind of life than the one they know of the flesh. Or is it only a half-hour Mass, one half-hour out of the one hundred and sixty-eight hours of the week, thirty minutes out of the ten thousand eighty minutes of the week?

CW Staff Member Arrested by FBI

CHARLES BUTTERWORTH

"DON IS A DESERTER from the Army," said Agent McKeon and showed me Don's picture. He had found me alone in the office that day. "I don't want to get into this," I replied. "You will have to talk to Bob." Maybe Bob was somewhere around, so I left the office to look. Going back to the kitchen, I saw Don. It all happened so quickly. "There's a man in the office you don't want to see." "Who's that?" smiled Don. "A man from the government." There was a kind of a serious pause and then Don turned, got his jacket, and left.

About two weeks later agents McKeon and Stratton returned. They had learned that I had chosen to help Don instead of the FBI. It was suggested I go with them to talk to someone at the U.S. Court House, and I went voluntarily to clarify our general position. There was a wait and Agent McKeon asked with interest about my coming into the Church and all about the farm, the chapel, the crops and the animals.

The man I was to talk with didn't want to see me, and Agent Stratton arranged a complaint against me. He mentioned that my failure to cooperate would mean that much more money would have to be spent to find Don.

The complaint reads in part: "Butterworth, the defendant herein, knowing that an offense against the United States had been committed, did unlawfully, willfully and knowingly receive, relieve, comfort and assist the offender in order to hinder and prevent his apprehension, trial, and punishment in violation of 18 USC Sec. 3."

I was confused and felt fear that day and failed to tell them exactly what I had done. So the next day I handed in a written statement of how I'd warned Don and hadn't seen him since. It ended with the following statement of the reason for my action.

"I believe that modern atomic war is contrary to God's will and that God is calling many people to refuse military life. The best position a person can take is to openly refuse cooperation and accept the punishment due. It requires time and understand-to reach this position.

"Meanwhile it is not my duty to help the government force a person concerning a decision on military life. Instead I would try to help a person reach his own decision and would tell him if he was in danger of forceful return to the military."

Thanks to Ammon Hennacy and Bob Steed I'm out on $1500 bail. The trial should come in late May. I am not sorry, but grateful that I acted as I did. It gives me the chance to make a concrete choice for a nonviolent society as opposed to a military one. Therefore I shall plead guilty and accept the punishment due. I shall try not to back down on my choice to live now as we shall all live when God's peace comes.

JUNE 1959

 ## Grand Jury Indictment

CHARLES BUTTERWORTH

THE UNITED STATES case against me for refusing to give up Don to the FBI is still in process. The indictment had to be passed on by the Grand Jury and I went down to the Court House for that meeting.

There was a long wait so I told Agent McKeon how in the old days a fugitive could obtain sanctuary in a Catholic Church. He established his right of sanctuary by grasping a large ring or knocker on the church door. I said that a priest who refused sanctuary could be excommunicated. But maybe that's wrong. The Catholic Encyclopedia just says, "Violation of the protection of sanctuary was punishable by excommunication." Bob thinks this penalty probably applied to the person who tried to take the fugitive away, not the priest. But the position seems clear: No one can both "turn people in" and remain at *The Catholic Worker*.

Then I was called into the Grand Jury room. It was medium sized with a large table in the center and the jury of sixteen people on a raised platform nearby. I was seated at the table with Mr. Starkey, the prosecuting attorney, and several other officials. There is no judge; the district attorney instructs the jury on their duties. This arrangement helped to put me at ease; I was glad there was no raised witness chair.

The hearing lasted about a half-hour. The questioning was thorough and fair and a secretary wrote it down for the record. "Did you write this article?" Mr. Starkey showed me my article in the May *Catholic Worker*. Bob had sent a copy to the FBI. It was entered as evidence and then Mr. Starkey read it to the jury.

My statement was vigorous but not smooth. Several people got up and walked around, maybe to go to the washroom. Some paid good attention, but others showed by their wandering eyes they were waiting for the next case.

As near as I remember, this is what I said: "It is likely, it seems to me, that this law has been broken. If you find that to be the case, then it will be your duty to grant the indictment the government asks.

"But I want to draw your attention to something else. This law is part of the war system. It is part of the old way of trying to get peace—by arms, military service, and laws supporting them. Perhaps there is someone here who is beginning to lose faith in that way to peace. Now we at *The Catholic Worker* are pacifists; we reject the old way to peace. There is a new way which the world must learn that Gandhi used in freeing India. It is called pacifism or nonviolence. You can learn about it from

The Catholic Worker or from the Quakers or you can learn it as I did from studying the life and teachings of Gandhi."

Then I spoke about an apparent contradiction. *Catholic Worker* policy is to encourage people to refuse military service but to refuse on moral grounds and openly by returning and accepting a possible jail term. In time a man can gain both his dignity and freedom this way. But I had told Don, "There's a man you don't want to see," and let him leave. My words don't deny our policy. They show that I thought Don wasn't ready yet for this open way.

In closing I told the jury that I was convinced, first, that the destruction of all life by war and atom bombs is not the future. A great era of peace lies in the future, and all present fears of total destruction are false. Second, that God is a living Person fully in control of events and the true leader of history. "Our God is a God of Peace."

That ended the statement, and Mr. Starkey, Agent McKeon and I waited outside for the decision of the jury. It wasn't long, and a "true bill" was granted.

The next step, ten days later, was the pleadings. This time Ammon went with me because he had to sign my bail papers again. Judge Dimock was very careful that I understood the meaning of pleading guilty to a felony, that I couldn't vote any more. He read the indictment, listened to what I'd done, and checked the law. After consideration he allowed me to proceed without a lawyer and agreed that a report on me should be made by the Probation Department.

In these hearings good men are seeking only to do their duty under law. That is as it should be. I am not fighting Mr. Starkey or Judge Dimock, or the rule of law as such. I am fighting the war system which I see now as essentially immoral. But if law is used to support that system then such law becomes infected and loses all moral sanction. If such a war law touches me, I must react by non-cooperation to the limit of my strength.

The day at the Court House closed with a talk to my probation officer. He showed understanding and respect for our moral position. He had been assigned five conscientious objectors from

Union Theological Seminary before the last war. The sentence will be given on June 10. Gandhi says do not exercise the imagination in such matters, expect the best and be ready for the worst.

My reading recently has been seeking a better understanding of the way of prayer of the Little Brothers and Sisters of Jesus. Their way is friendship, prayer, and sacrifice among the poor. This is the true way to peace: prayer and sacrifice. Jail is part of our sacrifice, penance for the social sin of war. And we have the certain promise of Christ through Mary at Fatima in 1917 that our efforts are not in vain. The problems of war, persecution and Russia will be solved and "a certain period of peace will be granted to the world."

 ## A Dime from a Poor Man's Pocket

(Excerpts from the regular column)

AMMON HENNACY

"I WAS JUST GOING to ask you for a dime," said a well-heeled non-Catholic acquaintance of mine to a young man on the Bowery who had asked him for a dime for a cup of coffee. The young man looked dazed, stammered a bit, and, reaching in his pocket, took out a dime and a nickel and handed my friend a dime. This was too much for my friend whose conscience hurt him. He ran after him saying: "Here, I'll trade you the dime for a quarter," which he did.

The moral, as I told my friend, is not to be sentimental and weak-minded. My friend robbed the young man on the Bowery of whatever faith in human nature he might have had. To do one good deed that day would perhaps have built him up, but now he would think, "I have met another phony." As a general principle I do not believe in giving men on the Bowery any money "for a cup of coffee," for as far as I know if they are sober they are collecting enough to get drunk, if they are drunk they don't need any more liquor. I have given something in weak moments to men who approached me saying with a smile, "I need eight cents more to get my bottle." And I have weakened other times too.

I have met two cases, not on the Bowery, but in more respectable places, where a cripple and a blind man faked their condition, and owned houses and cars, preying on the weakness of others and perhaps the "bad conscience" of those who pass by. To give food, clothing and shelter to those who need it without asking any questions as to whether they are "worthy" or not is the work of the CW. (The poet W. H. Auden, when asked on the radio what the CW did, said, "They help the undeserving poor.")

DECEMBER 1959

 ## A Death in the Family

DOROTHY DAY

DURING THE FIRST WEEK of November, Beth Rogers called me from the farm and said that the body of a man had been found in the woods about a half-mile from the Peter Maurin Farm. It had been lying there for so long that it was just bones. The police had called the farm because we had reported George Clements as missing last March. Beth and Charles identified the clothes on the body, and it was taken to the morgue at the Farm Colony, in the center of the island, before the coroner had a chance to examine it to find whether the body was of a hunchbacked man, as George was. But it was George, as we knew from the clothes, even from the special shirt that Tommy Hughes had given him because he himself had outgrown it. If it had just been a matter of the clothes which came into our clothes room and which to a large extent outfit us all, we could not be sure. But Tommy knew his shirt. In the absence of any known relatives, the body was turned over to us, and George was buried with Father Campbell, our pastor, offering Mass. He was buried in St. Joseph's cemetery on a little hill in back of the Church.

George Clements had become interested in *The Catholic Worker* when he lived on Skid Row in San Francisco on welfare and attended a meeting at which I spoke at St. Boniface Church, his parish. He was so fascinated by the work that he wandered around among his friends, among whom were priests, and collected enough money to take the bus to New York. We were surprised, of course, to see him arrive, but not at all surprised when he found the CW not at all the Utopia he had expected. He stayed for some months, and was able to make enough friends and write to enough friends in California to get the bus fare back again to San Francisco. But nostalgia for Mott Street drew him back, and in another six months he was back again, bag and baggage, this time to remain. I cannot remember whether it was fifteen or twenty years he was with us, getting older, quieter, more bent than ever. Probably his most animated moment was when Kieran Duggan chose him to act Santa Claus in the Christmas play he put on two years ago, called "The Trial of Aaron Heresy." Many in the house acted in the gay little skit, which drew people together in hours of practice down in the basement of Chrystie Street. Kieran's verses were sung to the popular tunes of a current Broadway musical and everyone enjoyed the frivolity.

Last January, when we were evicted from Chrystie Street, Slim and Molly and California George, as they called him, were moved down to the farm. They all settled down nicely and neither Slim nor George seemed to be disturbed by the move.

Except that George kept writing to friends in San Francisco, asking for money to go back. So many years had passed that most of the letters were returned to him as *not found* or *deceased.* Once in a while he took a walk in the woods, but he was last seen, according to report, in front of the post office in Pleasant Plains.

When the police could find no trace of him through the Missing Persons Bureau, we began to think that, by some miracle, some friends of George had gotten the money together to send him back to California. He was always secretive. People who are forced to live in community often take pains to have a private life of their own outside of it.

It was a grave shock to us all to find that George had wandered off like a sick animal to die, covered over with leaves, hidden from the road, merging with the earth, overlooked by the mushroom hunters who scour the woods spring and fall, and finally found by a schoolboy playing in the woods on Sunday afternoon.

This Money Is Not Ours

DOROTHY DAY

The Catholic Worker
39 Spring Street
New York 12, N.Y.
July, 1960

Treasurer
City of New York
DEAR SIR:

We are returning to you a check for $3,579.39 which represents interest on the $68,700 which we were awarded by the city as payment for the property at 223 Chrystie Street which we owned and lived in for almost ten years, and used as a community for the poor. We did not voluntarily give up the property—it was taken from us by right of eminent domain for the extension of the subway which the city deemed necessary. We had to wait almost a year and a half for the money owed us, although the city permitted us to receive two-thirds of the assessed valuation of the property in advance so that we could relocate. Property owning having been made impossible for us by city regulations, we are now renting and continuing our work.

We are returning the interest on the money we have recently received because we do not believe in "money lending" at interest. As Catholics we are acquainted with the early teaching of the Church. All the early councils forbade it, declaring it reprehensible to make money by lending it out at interest. Canon law of the middle ages forbade it and in various decrees ordered that profit so obtained was to be restored. In the Christian emphasis on the duty of charity, we are commanded to lend gratuitously, to give freely, even in the case of confiscation, as in our own case—not to resist but to accept cheerfully.

We do not believe in the profit system, and so we cannot take profit or interest on our money. People who take a materialistic view of human service wish to make a profit but we are trying to do our duty by our service without wages to our brothers as Jesus commanded in the Gospel (Matt. 25). Loaning money at interest is deemed by one Franciscan as the principal scourge of civilization. Eric Gill, the English artist and writer, calls usury and war the two great problems of our time.

Since we have dealt with these problems in every issue of *The Catholic Worker* since 1933—man's freedom, war and peace, man and the state, man and his work—and since Scripture says that the love of money is the root of all evil, we are taking this opportunity to live in practice of this belief, and make a gesture of overcoming that love of money by returning to you the interest.

Insofar as our money paid for services for the common good, and aid to the poor, we should be very happy to allow you to use not only our money without interest, but also our work, the works of mercy which we all perform here at the headquarters of *The Catholic Worker* without other salary or recompense than our daily food and lodging, clothes, and incidental expenses.

Insofar as the use of our money paid for the time being for salaries for judges who have condemned us and others to jail, and for the politicians who appointed them, and for prisons, and the execution chamber at Sing Sing, and for the executioner's salary we can only protest the use of our money and turn with utter horror from taking interest on it.

Please also be assured that we are not judging individuals, but are trying to make a judgment on *the system* under which we live and with which we admit that we ourselves comprise daily in many small ways, but which we try and wish to withdraw from as much as possible.

Sincerely yours,
DOROTHY DAY, Editor

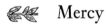 ## Clothes

MARY LATHROP suddenly jumped up from her chair in the office and screamed. She had left a man in the toilet for half an hour while she was supposed to be mending his trousers. A discussion had started and she all but forgot him. The oversight was remedied, but it goes without saying that the man was in a plight. He had only one pair of pants, as is usual with folk who come to us. We need pants, coats, sweaters, jackets, socks, etc., etc. We get many women's clothes, but need men's badly and we need also sheets, pillowcases and towels. Can you spare something? Please? Thank you. God bless you.

Mercy

DENIS KNIGHT

HEROD, HOESS, there is a word that has not been spoken yet
The last word man will utter
Under trumpet thunder:
Mercy.
Some words look pretty good from a distance, like freedom,
Nation, free world, responsibilities and right, America;
But slump round somehow in shadows when you drive up close.
Mercy is adamant. Mercy is awkward, ungrammatical, alone,
Not an easy word for a man to pronounce in company.

To pick this word you'd have to climb up rock beatitudes
I think, get knocked about on pity, peace, and love,
Which might prove tricky.
Mercy is dear toy of Christ baby.
Mercy green bud and flower of flesh that quilts with honeycomb
Dead tree of nerve and bone. In warm and silkworm skin
Treasures the tinkling blood and springing soul
Of this whole man-assembly, planet, and camping ground of men,
In ragged tents by Eden.
Ask the question: Will the word of mercy be spoken by men
Unto men, before it's disaster and angel of death too late?
I think so. I think there is no too late. I think
Easily will the iron center of the world be smashed
Upon the Child's toy; upon the young Man's heart
(And arms aloft) in kisses of His mouth, kissing the burnt skin
Clean, Who waters His garden with His right hand, healing
    Hiroshimas.

<hr>

FEBRUARY 1962

 ## Letter from Thomas Merton

DEAR JIM [FOREST],

It is really quite providential that the peace article I wrote for the *Commonweal* Christmas issue was held up by the censors and is now appearing this week, in conjunction with the General Strike for Peace. I do hope it helps even a little bit. Anyway, my heart goes with it, and I am with you all in spirit. I am glad that in that article I explicitly mentioned the point that all people, the ordinary people, the ones who don't want war, the ones who get it in the neck, the ones who really want to build a decent new world in which there will not be war and starvation, these should know the power of their witness against war, and the effect they can have by protest and refusal of cooperation in immoral war efforts.

Of course the tragedy is that the vast majority of people do not understand the meaning of this kind of witness. In their pitiful, blind craving for undisturbed security, they feel that agitation for peace is somehow threatening to them. They do not feel at all threatened by the bomb, for some reason, but they feel terribly threatened by some little girl student carrying a placard, or by some poor working man striking in protest. Somehow they feel that it is after all possible for people to change their minds and revise their whole attitude toward a setup that has its enormous disadvantages but—at least it is "what we are used to, and please God don't ask us to get used to something else." Unfortunately, the bomb is going to impose a terrible adjustment on those who may be left around to adjust. And it is with this that people want to defend themselves. We have to have deep patient compassion for the fears of men, for the fears and irrational mania of those who hate us or condemn us.

My Mass on February first, the Feast of St. Ignatius Martyr of Antioch, will be for all of the strikers everywhere in the world and for all who yearn for a true peace, all who are willing to shoulder the great burden of patiently working, praying and sacrificing themselves for peace. We will never see the results in our time, even if we manage to get through the next five years without being incinerated. Really we have to pray for a total and profound change in the mentality of the whole world. What we have known in the past as Christian penance is not a deep enough concept if it does not comprehend the special problems and dangers of the present age. Hairshirts will not do the trick, though there is no harm in mortifying the flesh. But vastly more important is the complete change of heart and the totally new outlook on the world of man. We have to see our duty to mankind as a whole. We must not fail in this duty which God is imposing on us with His own Hand.

The great problem is this inner change, and we must not be so obsessed with details of policy that we block the deeper development in other people and in ourselves. The strike is to be re-garded, I think, as an application of spiritual force and not the use of merely political pressure. We all have the great duty to realize the deep need for purity of soul, that is to say the deep need to possess in us the Holy Spirit, to be possessed by Him. This takes precedence over everything else. If He lives and works in us, then our activity will be true and our witness will generate love of the truth, even though we may be persecuted and beaten down in apparent incomprehension.

Thanks for the issues of last month's CW. Did I thank you for the Christmas letter? The singing outside the Ladies' Jail warmed my heart. I wish I had been there with you. Small things like that have very great Christian meaning, so much more than a lot of more formal and pompous gestures.

I got a beautiful letter from a nun in Haiti, talking about the people there. Maybe they are among the very poorest on the face of the earth. One feels that Christ is almost visible among them, in them, in their poverty, in their abandonment, their destitu-tion: why does not one look to see the face of Christ and to come to Him with help? But meanwhile His Heart has assumed all their sorrow, all the injustice done to them, and while He will comfort them, He will also do what He does, in mystery, to re-store the balance, the violated order.

God was seemingly never more absent from the world and yet His Christ, the Word, is walking about all around us all over the face of the earth, and in a terrible hour.

With all affection to Dorothy and to all of you. Thank her for her good letter which I will answer. I am praying for all those intentions, tell her please.

God's love and blessing to all Christ's poor and all who yearn with Him for peace.

What Is To Be Done?

KARL MEYER

I CAME HOME from work this evening firmly determined to excommunicate from St. Stephen's House of Hospitality (to cut off from all communication with) one of those men who was among the first to come to us, an alcoholic, who has been with us on and off, mostly on, for over three years. Not to cut him off because it is the Christian thing to do, or the Catholic thing, or the redemptive thing, or the kind thing, but because it is a thing that must be done. It must be done because he hasn't gotten any better over the years with us. He has in fact gotten much worse. He used to be amiable and pleasant, now he is bitter and often belligerent. He used to have some physical resilience; now he is groggy and confused. He was never sober enough to know the meaning of consideration for others, but he used to listen when you asked him to do a considerate thing. He used to have more control over the bladder when he slept on other people's beds without asking them, and sometimes he even took off his shoes.

It must be done because I haven't gotten any better over the years with him. In fact, I've gotten worse. I used to be gentle, sort of sentimental; now I've gotten hard-nosed. I used to be patient (my friends will laugh), but I haven't much patience any more. And then, I used to sleep in the back room where I couldn't hear him knocking on the front door at three A.M. which he always did, and the other people had to get up and let him in, or curse him and argue with him until he agreed to go away, which he used to do sometimes.

No, it must be done because he'll never go away and stay away until he knows that he doesn't have a chance here. Give him an inch, and he'll take a mile or two, and I don't have it to give any more. Give him a cup of water and he'll take the kitchen sink, and the rest of us have to wash our hands there, and our shirts and our dishes, because it's the only sink we've got.

So I came home from work this evening, and there was a letter from Jim Forest, asking me to write about Houses of Hospitality and why there should be more of them and what they should be like and how you start one. So I have to take time away from other things and people and write quickly what I know.

In his book, *What Is To Be Done?*, Leo Tolstoy tells of taking the census of a slum district in Moscow, and of the comprehensive institutions and plans he envisioned for eliminating destitution in the city. While he was planning, his old friend Sutaief came to his house for a visit:

> He sat immovable, dressed in his black-tanned sheepskin coat, which he, like other peasants, wore indoors as well as out. It seemed that he was not listening to us, but was thinking about something else. His small eyes gave no responding gleam, but seemed to be turned inward. Having spoken out to my satisfaction, I turned to him and asked him what he thought about it.
>
> "The whole thing is superficial," he replied.
>
> "Why?"
>
> "The plan is an empty one and no good will come of it," he repeated with conviction.
>
> "How is it that nothing will come of it? Why is it a useless business, if we help thousands, or even hundreds, of unhappy ones? Is it a bad thing, according to the gospel, to clothe the naked, or to feed the hungry?"
>
> "I know, I know; but what you are doing is not that: Is it possible to help thus? You are walking in the street; somebody asks you for a few kopeks; you give it to him. Is that charity? Do him some spiritual good: teach him— What you gave him merely says, 'Leave me alone.'"
>
> "No; but that is not what we were speaking of: we wish to become acquainted with the wants, and then help by money and deeds. We will try to find for the poor people some work to do."
>
> "That would be no way of helping them."
>
> "How then? Must they be left to die of starvation and cold?"

"Why left to die? How many are there of them?"

"How many?" said I, thinking that he took the matter so lightly from not knowing the great number of these men. "You are not aware, I dare say, that there are in Moscow about twenty thousand cold and hungry. And then think of those in St. Petersburg and other towns!"

He smiled. "Twenty thousand! And how many families are there in Russia alone? Would they amount to a million?"

"What of that?" said he, with animation, and his eyes sparkled. "Let us unite them with ourselves; I am not rich myself, but will at once take two of them. You take a young fellow into your kitchen; I invite him into my family. If there were ten times as many, we should take them all into our families. You one, I another. We shall work together; those I take to live with me will see how I work; I will teach them to reap, and we shall eat out of one bowl, at one table; and they will hear a good word from me, and from you also. This is charity; but all this plan of yours is no good."

These plain words made an impression on me. I could not help recognizing that this was true; but it seemed to me then, that, notwithstanding the justice of what he said, my proposed plan might, perhaps, also be useful.

But the longer I was occupied with this affair, and the closer my intercourse with the poor, the oftener I recollected these words, and the greater meaning I found in them.

I indeed go in an expensive fur coat, or drive in my own carriage, to a man who is in want of boots: he sees my house which costs two hundred rubles a month, or he notices that I give away, without thinking, five rubles, only because such is my fancy; he is then aware that, if I give away rubles in such a manner, it is because I have accumulated so many of them that I have a lot to spare, which I not only am never in the habit of giving to any one, but which I have, without compunction, taken away from others. What can he see in me but one of those persons who have become possessed of what should belong to him?

I have my own Sutaief in Lemont who has been with me longer even than the alcoholic whom I mentioned above. I would not have you believe that all who come to a House of Hospitality are a burden. Quite as many are a source of joy and strength. There are good men and kind men and gentle, poets and wise men, scholars and philosophers.

Lemont has long hair and a long beard and wears his black coat and gloves in the house and washes less than most, so that the respectable suppose that he is very strange and alien. But he is more kind and wise and scholarly than all the bourgeois I know. He loves that passage from Tolstoy, and he always counsels me not to try to do too much for too many, because just as we must all bear one another's burdens, so too any one of us can only bear the burdens of a few. But there are so few of us here and the needs of the poor press in upon us overwhelmingly, so that "never to be safe again is all our lives."

It isn't that the man I must excommunicate could not be helped, but that behind him stand ten thousand more, and I can not take them all, starting with him. If you open the door they will come in by hundreds; I have seen them with my own eyes. At one time we fed eighty men a night in a kitchen ten feet by ten feet. The first thing is to survive, the first year and the second and the third. If you don't survive yourself, you can't do anything for anyone. There have been Houses of Hospitality where the householders drove themselves to insanity. Lesson Number One: Do not burden yourself beyond the limit of grace, humanity and survival.

We need more Houses of Hospitality where the strong will share the burdens of the weak. The more houses the better, because the more there are, the lighter will be the burdens in each house, and the lighter the burdens, the more the weak will be strengthened to walk. I am not saying that you should take alcoholics and psychotics into your house, because few can bear it or know what to do, but I am speaking of the sick and old and unemployed and orphans (so many of the alcoholics and psychotics were raised in orphanages).

I mentioned that I come home from work in the evening. Why am I not home all day? I come home from work in the evening because I work all day to earn a living for my household. Dorothy and my good priest often tell me I should quit work and beg for our living, so that I could do more for the poor. But if I did more for the poor by begging money from people, the people would do less for the poor by paying me to do a bad job for them. You can have a real estate broker and an insurance broker, but you can't have a broker for your charity. If people gave me money they would not be able to take the poor into their own homes, nor would they be able to ask their boss for a reduction in salary so that the low-paid workers in their hospital or restaurant or business could be paid more, nor would they be able to go into a high-class restaurant and offer to pay double the check so that the fifty-cents-an-hour dishwasher could be paid a decent wage, nor would they be able to cut their pay in half so that the unemployed could be hired to share the piled-up work that puts such pressures on the employed and often breaks up homes and ruins lives. I have to fight with my employer to keep from doing overtime and getting home even later in the evening. I tell him, "There are thousands unemployed. Go out and hire them to do overtime."

Yes, if people were to give me money, we would have one big House of Hospitality in every major city, and one hundred would be inside and ten thousand would be outside, and the people would say "We have a House of Hospitality in our city. Let the poor get themselves over there before it closes at eight p.m."

Now I hope no one will say, "Well, I was going to send you a dime, but I see you don't want my money so I'll go out and get an ice cream cone instead." In that case I'll take the dime; but it isn't the better way.

So that is why we need Houses of Hospitality, and why I work and have a small House of Hospitality.

Now, when and how do you start a House of Hospitality and what is it like?

I started my first *Catholic Worker* house in Washington, D.C., when I was nineteen years old and not even a Catholic. I was working as a messenger for Dean Acheson's law firm, one of the biggest, and most of our work was defending giant corporations in anti-trust suits. Not every anarchist starts out by being perfectly consistent.

I rented a store on the roughest street in the roughest neighborhood in town, on O St. between Sixth and Seventh, though I didn't know about it at the time. It was just where I happened to get a store. There were more murders around there than in any other precinct. I was the only white man in the block, and when I came home from meetings late at night the police used to stop me and warn me to get out of the neighborhood. My father wasn't in Congress yet; my parents were home in Vermont and my mother never really knew.

The store had a middle-sized front room with a show window, a very small kitchen with a sink, and in the back, a larger room with no windows and a small alcove with a toilet. The floor was of concrete, and water used to come in and stand around in various spots in the back room. For this I paid fifty dollars a month, cash on the barrelhead, and I had not a grain of trouble renting it in spite of my age, its location and the strange purposes I proposed for it. I bought a stove, refrigerator and a gas heater in successive months. Instead of getting beds and chairs.

I got fifty dollars worth of lumber and constructed six benches to do double duty service for sleeping in the back room and meetings in the front room. The neighbors, and also some cops, came in to see what all the hammering was about, and they wanted to know what kind of racket I was setting up, but I didn't say much. Some of them wanted to buy the benches then and there. I should have sold them. I had everything set up and was ready to receive my guests. But I sat there and sat there and nobody came. I started in June and for several months nobody came. Summer passed. In early autumn I was walking along the street and I saw a man lying on the steps of a Protestant church. I wakened him with difficulty; he was loaded. I loaded him into a cab and brought him home. I was exultant.

In *The Catholic Worker* of January 1962, I wrote of my exultation after my first venture in alley picking. It could not have compared with my joy in my first action of hospitality. But within three days my joy was to turn to desperation. My new guest was stone drunk, and if I had known anything about it I would have observed that he was absolutely punchy from years of drunkenness. But I immediately determined upon his redemption from wine. I put him to bed, or rather to bench. For the next two days I tried to sober him up, but what was my despair to discover that in the morning he was as drunk as the night before. Somehow he managed to elude me and to oil himself up frequently. I didn't get much sleep because he didn't seem to keep regular hours. All he could eat was sugar with coffee. By the morning of the third day I was exhausted and desperate.

I called my friend Jim Guinan of Friendship House (who was to become my godfather at my baptism a few months later) and he told me to bring him over. As soon as the poor man was delivered into Jim's old hands, I went upstairs, lay down on a couch and cried for half an hour. After that I was all right. I had learned a lesson—Lesson Number Two: Don't demand prompt success from anyone else, or from yourself. After five months of operations and one three-day guest, I closed my first House of Hospitality. I would only mention that Jack Biddle drove me home once with Ammon Hennacy from a meeting where Ammon spoke, and they stopped and had a look at my place when they dropped me off. That was before Ammon knew me at all, but perhaps he remembers that house.

After all this I went to New York and, the following June, joined the people of *The Catholic Worker* in their Civil Defense protest, and served my first thirty days in jail.

A year later, Ed Morin and I started St. Stephen's House (I got the store and he got the people), which has met with some success in its almost four years. I have written all of this preface so that you might say, "If such a fool as this can do it, perhaps I can too."

As my Washington experience illustrates, setting up house is easy: it's the hospitality that brings problems.

St. Stephen's House is located with a view to the major relevant factors. I am poor and I am taking the poor into my house, so we are going to be even poorer. Therefore we are set on the edge of a small slum pocket, a back pocket just three blocks away from Chicago's glittering Gold Coast. We are in a poor neighborhood because slum landlords are tolerant of poverty, slum tenants are tolerant of poverty, and police and building department officials are tolerant of poverty, in poor neighborhoods; we get along well with our neighbors. It is no crime to be poor here. Some houses have had to move time and again because they kept moving into places where it was a crime to be poor.

Furnishings and food we get from the Gold Coast alleys. Fortunately, it evidently is not a crime to salvage the criminal wastes of these rich neighbors. They think us quaint, seeing us going about at late hours poking our heads in garbage pails or dragging bed springs through back streets.

We live in a store on account of the marginal nature of small business in the slums; storefront properties offer more space for less rent than regular housing units. We have five rooms with steam heat for seventy dollars a month. The steam comes once a day, if it comes at all, but the kitchen oven warms the whole house. There are four floors of tenement flats above, and at least once a month the plumbing breaks down above us and water pours from floor to floor on its way to the sea, but I haven't met a pipe I couldn't plug. In between the floods we are warm and dry and life is pleasant here.

In ten months of 1960 (I was in jail for two months) my expenses for the house and personal concerns totaled $2,102.56. Monthly expenses ranged from $131.28 up to $347.97. The basic monthly costs were approximately as follows:

Rent	$ 70
Gas	10
Electricity	10
Phone	8
Laundry	12
Food	40
	$150

Miscellaneous costs include the following:

Raincoats for an American Friends Service Committee peace vigil	$18.48
Payment of a fine and costs to spring Ed Bodin from the city jail	29.00
Leaflets for the protest in behalf of Eroseanna Robinson	15.00
Travel to and from peace conferences and meetings	49.74

There were ten beds in the house, always taken, and occasionally extra people would sleep on the floor for several days, or even several weeks.

Around six or eight men came from outside each night for supper.

We had clothing for those who needed it, and bread for some of the families in our building.

Three of the men in the house lived here through the entire year, and I was able to claim them as dependents for non-tax purposes.

The meals were cooked and the house was kept by Joe Patrofsky, who worked seven days a week, because he was a working man "too old to work" and the work was there and who else did it, and all he got for it was sixty minutes an hour, as Richard says when he mops the floor. I realize now that we exploited him by not giving him more help, and my only excuse is that I worked as hard myself, though I took a day off whenever I pleased.

Well, what of these people to whom we offer hospitality? They are of every shape and sort, and every state of poverty and destitution. Three may be old or sick and "unemployable"; two may have mental illness or psychosis; one may be an alcoholic, or a wandering man of God, an indigent student or an unpaid peace worker, or simply an unemployed worker. We have had here a journalist, of the Jewish faith he always made clear, who was unemployed because the FBI kept going around and telling his employers that he had twice refused to testify before the House Un-American Activities Committee about his activities in behalf of integration in the South. We have had here a poor rich young man who was doing alternative service as an orderly in a Catholic hospital and trying to meet the payments on a small sports car. We have had here a generous, kindly, handsome, strong, hardworking young gentleman, who happened to be a Negro, and who didn't just happen to be employed except for occasional work as a porter in a cheap drugstore, and who happened to wind up in a penitentiary for attempting armed postal robbery. We have had connected with us Mr. Cable, a madman whose behavior was shocking by his own account. We have had here an inferior decorator, of checks that is; he didn't make a good living by it. There are only two of us who don't eat meat, but we managed at one time to keep two butchers unemployed. One of them has died now, but the other is still unemployed.

There are workers and scholars and non-workers and non-scholars. If a house is small and the people are different and individual, the strength of one gives help for the weakness of another. The house is a center of thought and action. It is a microcosm of the world. Many visitors come and take away more than they bring. The workers and the non-workers and the non-scholars hear the discussions among the scholars about peace and love and politics and sociology, and they become informed and aware by diffusion. The non-workers and the scholars see the workers at work, but I can't see that it does them much good.

I believe that a dying man is more alive here, and a living man is more alive still. We have here a community of need, where the first man who comes in need is received, and a community of diversity, where all are welcome. We have a communion between the living and the dying in the natural order, and are often dying unto ourselves in order to live unto others in the supernatural order, but I believe that we become more alive ourselves.

I have walked across the world from Chicago to Moscow, and the scene bored me much of the time. But I am not bored here. We don't walk past the world and its problems. The world comes in with its problems and sits down for a cup of coffee and a word of consolation.

This Night I Carry the Banner

KARL MEYER

Holy Thursday
164 W. Oak St.
Chicago, Ill.

AT FIVE O'CLOCK we went to Mass at St. Dominic's Church, and as on Palm Sunday, the people were called to join the procession, for which we were grateful.

After Mass we held a Paschal supper at St. Stephen's House. Eleven residents and guests sat down to feast on lamb sent us by Father Damian, and a twelfth sat down to vegetables, having some concern for the poor lamb.

After the supper we had a reading of St. John's story of the Last Supper.

At nine-thirty, seven of us set out for St. Dominic's for an hour of vigil and prayer, a part of the actions of the Week for Peace in Chicago. Seven of us—four Romans, two Jews and one Anglican—set out for a vigil of prayer before the Eucharist for the intentions of the Pope for world peace. Is it strange that two Jews and an Anglican should go out with four Romans to such an event? Each man has his own Christ, though we seem in this movement to have a power to draw the estranged together. We had plotted together, and had it in mind to bear him away and make him a king over a pacifist kingdom, to bring the people into subjection to his universal law of joy. "Each of us," said Mauriac, "makes Christ a prisoner of his own limited way of thinking and feeling." But somehow he always resisted.

Down on skid row they are "carrying the banner"—a euphemism of the destitute meaning to walk the street through the night with nowhere to sleep, taking only a temporary refuge from cold or rain in all-night coffee houses, movie houses or taverns, hoping to be spared cops, night court and jails. This is the night when Christ "carried the banner." To commemorate his night of prayer and his arrest, I walk the chill streets without sleep, taking my refuge for a few hours before the Eucharist.

I walked down North Clark and over on Madison. The street was empty. Everyone was seen through dingy windows slumped at bars. I began to say to myself, here is a man seeking to emulate Christ in his presence to the destitute, and yet he has never stood at the bar with them to drink a glass of beer. How shall he know them? How shall he be present to them? So I began to ask myself, will I dare to go into one of these places and ask for a glass of beer? And if I dare, how shall I ask? Will I know what brand of beer to name? Will I be conspicuous to them in all the newness of this experience? Will the bartender question my age, who have no draft card to prove it?

So discussing with myself, an hour passed quickly and I found myself beyond Madison and Morgan. I turned back toward some likely bar I had passed.

I had gone a few feet, when, looking down just to my left, I saw a small white pigeon standing against the wall. I bent to touch it and it backed away, then flew off weakly, almost settling in the middle of the street, and then, reaching the far side, stopped against the opposite wall. I crossed the street and now took the bird in my hands and sheltered it under my coat and brought it home to rest safely.

What is the meaning of this omen on such a night, the night of these words: I am going away—but I will ask my Father to send you another—peace I leave with you; it is my own peace that I give you; I do not give peace as the world gives it.

Tomorrow, we will carry the banner of protest in the Easter March for Peace. Yes, let us go on doing that. But if we really would go in search of peace, we must carry the banner of poverty, of cold and sleepless nights, walking the pavement among the poor in spirit. Down there on Skid Row (not Park Row), down there on Madison Street (not Madison Avenue) we will find the love of peace, weak and unsheltered in the darkness of the shabby night.

The hour going down, passed in meditation, moved quickly and carefree; but the hour returning was very long and I was impatient, weighted down under the burden of a small pigeon carried under my coat. When I had brought the bird home and placed it in my room, I went back to the Church. A Methodist came too in the small hours.

Later on I went out onto the streets again and made the Gold Coast rounds, digging up a couple of cleft potatoes and some fruit in a small basket. When I had brought that home, I set out for the Church again. Along the way I heard boxes rustling in an alley and being interested in such things, I stopped to look, and behold, there was Brother Rat trying to make a go of it too.

<hr />

JULY–AUGUST 1962

 ## Life Among the Leeches

JAMES E. MILORD

THAT AUGUST JOURNAL of inflammatory opinion, the *Chicago Daily Tribune*, despite its frailties, has one steadfastly redeeming spot: the Help Wanted ads. Whether you are a scientist with brains or a drifter with brawn, a bi-lingual forty or fresh fifteen, employable or not, there, on those bright pages, you will find hope and courage. Your fires of inspiration might sputter, fade, and all but die with the polite "We'll-let-you-know" response, but tomorrow's fresh crop of hyperbole will rekindle the glow.

As a liberal arts student and worker-without-portfolio, with sweeping and shoveling skills to my credit, I usually bypassed the dazzling Executive, Professional, Clerical and Sales columns, pausing to lament not having earned a doctorate in galactic physics, or run up ten years in synthetics. The luminous four-figure salaries fell to the earthbound, one-figure realities in the unhappy hunting ground of the hard pressed, the *miscellaneous* column.

This nebulous catch-all section often came up with clever ads. Having passed the course as a proofreader between lines in that flotsam of decoys, I should have known better than to bite on the tempting bait. But this ad began with an artful dodge, though slightly on the shop-worn side now. It was steady enough to bring this college idler up hopefully. Besides, it was February, and a more bleak one I had not seen. It read:

> Wanted: Young man with pleasant voice to do telephone con-tact work. Call Superior—

Whoever said that flattery will get you nowhere has never consulted the Help Wanted columns.

The office door read "General Research Corporation" in the boldest of letters. And bold was the man, indeed, who conceived its shady inner workings. A nondescript, cubbyhole place, one among thousands like it up there on the Near North Side. It boasted two tiny rooms: one served as the manager's office, the other as the "boiler" room.

The manager waved his disgustingly large diamond around on a fat hand, effusive, enthusiastic about the "Bureau" and its work. What work? Down to brass tacks now. It was really very simple. They were pushing children's encyclopedias. A worthy cause, I reflected naively, and signed on as a "statistician." This category was the euphemism of those primitive days for book drummer. I was given a sheet from the Chicago telephone book, a dial phone, some file cards and three pitch sheets, typed in single space on the wall before me.

You began the pitch like this: "Hello, Mr. or Mrs. D.? How are you today? (Pause) That's good. Mr. or Mrs. D., this is the General Research Corporation calling. Yes, we're gathering educational statistics in your section of the city. We'd like to verify the number and ages of the children in your family." (Pause)

Sometimes the answers were amusing: "Children? I don't got no children. I ain't even married." Or, *"My* children? Well, there's Myrtle—she's forty-two, and Henry is thirty-eight."

Without further ado, the statistician bowed gracefully out of this as soon as he could say goodbye.

Every fifth or sixth house struck grist for the money mill. It was amazing the number of people who unwittingly gave out information on their children. While they were enumerating the details, we hastily scrawled the bare facts down on an index card. In a week's time, we exchanged our "statistics" with the man next to us on the boiler line and rang the number. We now shifted our titles to "contact counsellor," and began to pitch away. This polemical gambit was a masterpiece of double talk, superlative and nonsense. It was pasted at eye-level for convenient reading (and eventual smooth memorization), and contained three disputations: Introduction, positive, and negative rebuttal.

The whole point of our contact was to involve the element of surprise.

"Hello, Mrs. S.? (Yes . . .) This is Mr. M. of the General Research Corporation. (Yes . . .) Mrs. S., our statistics department called you last week to verify your children's ages?" (Oh, yes . . .) A quick look at your "data" now.

"How are Billy and Mary today?" (Oh . . . uh, fine.)

Keep talking now, on through the first paragraph, following well into "introduction." If no adverse comments from the other end came bouncing back, proceed through "positive." If any questioning started, shift over immediately to "negative rebuttal." Swing the tone up to an oily level now, easy does it, get singsongish, indulgent, authoritative, elaborate.

All this ritual and cant and hypocrisy to sell a very sad, shabby set of books! The phenomenal inventiveness of the lies! Throughout the "introduction" phase of this operation, and well into the "positive" accentuation, our main product, if you will, *books*, were never, but never to be mentioned. Finally, nearing the climax, we told our harassed housewife:

"Now, for a limited time only, to select families, we are placing the educational *service right in the very homes* by the 'educational counsellors' from our Bureau."

There was never any mention of prices. As a contractor-statistician my objective was securing appointments for the counsellor, for which I earned $12.00 if the sale went through. The salesman and the manager also took their generous cut of the pie. I often wondered what the sets were purchased for by this bogus outfit.

The manager had the unhealthy habit of monitoring our pitches occasionally, and when things were waning on the sales graph, he would storm in to chide us for our lack of sales technique. His boast was that he could sell books to a Chinese who couldn't read English!

I placed a solid lead for a counsellor, after a few dozen pitches, with a weary housewife whose husband was a streetcar conductor. Crying children's voices echoed in the background. To my regret, I overrode her arguments about not being able to "afford anything new for the children at this time" by some specious nonsense, probably like the classic, "But when you examine this service, you'll see that you can't really afford *not* to take advantage of it." This phony "corporation" had learned well the dialectics of the humbug world of advertising, and learned them without the surface veneer of respectability.

I was a bit slow in my rationalizing about eating—I lasted a week in this nightmare of lickspittle and sham. I had contributed my bit to the grand total of pain and superfluity and money slavery to the tune of thirty-five dollars. Needless to say, it was the cheat's way to solvency, but I belonged to a society that had joined hands with posture and pretense. I had to learn the "heart" way.

Peter Maurin Farm

(From the regular column)

DEANE MOWRER

THE DAY of the great Staten Island fire—the worst in the history of New York—was Agnes' birthday, a day that she and we are not likely to forget. The winds were blowing with such impetuous ferociousness that morning that I felt apprehensive and worried, knowing how tinder-dry the woods, fields, and buildings were, and how April, that "cruelest month," has brought us not much-needed, seed-nourishing rain, but wild, windy weather that might have come right out of the March lion's mouth. As a consequence, a rash of brush fires had kept the fire engines clanging up and down our roads almost every day. I suggested to Charles as we drove to Mass that we say a litany novena for rain and he agreed. Shortly after our return from church I heard the first fire engine go by, and someone said the fire did not seem to be too near. The winds swirled and screeched like demons at play so that the flames leapt from place to place with no perceptible pattern. More fire engines went clanging by. Finally I braved the winds to go to the chapel and pray. After a bit Charles came in and said he thought we should start the litany now. We said a litany of Our Lady. Then Charles went out to help the other men take what measures they could against the fiery enemy.

When the dinner bell rang, I walked out into winds that were even more angrily berserk. The air had filled with the acrid smell of smoke. Most of us did not feel much like eating; Agnes did not eat at all. Stanley tried to relieve tensions with a few jokes, but they sounded more like whistling in the dark. I wondered why so many firemen with so much equipment had not been able to stem the fires that were now threatening to encircle us. Then Charles told me there was no water. Not one drop in the taps in our house. Not one drop in the hydrants in our vicinity. Charles said that Agnes and I should stay downstairs and be ready to go at any moment. Neither of us wanted to go, but we knew we could be of little use in fire-fighting. Agnes is old and I am blind. As I walked out of the house toward the car in the driveway I felt the full demonic fury of the wind, blowing with such scorching impact that I had an immediate visual impression of that hot, heavy, spark-filled smoke mass, like an amorphous dragon spewing fiery deluge on all in its path.

Charles drove to Pleasant Plains and left us sitting in the car in front of Levinson's fruit and vegetable store. The talk from passers-by floated in to us, talk that became more excited, more filled with facts and rumors of disaster as the afternoon wore on. We learned that there were fires in other areas of Staten Island. Someone said that all of Tottenville was ablaze. Another that there were big fires in Huguenot and Annadale. I began to worry about Marge Hughes and her family and our houses on the Anna-dale beach. Someone said that Mount Loretto Orphanage was in danger; another that they were evacuating everyone from the hill. The hill would include Peter Maurin Farm. I wondered where the others were being taken. We sat in the car and waited. I said another prayer while the talk about me seemed louder and louder, like headlines of a disaster.

Meanwhile at the farm, as I learned later, the men kept strug-gling valiantly to beat out the flames springing up in nearby brush and grasses. Buckets of water were carried from our little pond and the roofs of the men's cottages moistened; tubfuls of water were placed at strategic points, and all the fire extinguishers placed in readiness. Charles offered the water from our pond to the fire-men, but they said their engines could never get down to the pond and went clanging dolefully away, leaving our neighbors' houses blazing in the April afternoon without a fireman's nozzle lifted in protest. The police evacuated the others from the farm, some to St. Louis Academy, others to Red Cross and Salvation Army stations.

There is no doubt that the special Providence of God was with us that day, but I think He made use of the strange caprice of those tempestuous winds which blew where they listed, and of the unflagging vigilance and efforts of all those men, the men, not the firemen, but the men of Peter Maurin Farm who battled the flames that fiery Saturday of Easter Week.

By the time Charles finally came for us I felt I had learned a little of what it is like to be a refugee. We had to return by back roads. Charles and the others exclaimed about house after house that had burned completely down leaving only charred debris or a chimney standing alone amid the ashen ruins of a home. Around about us were scorched fields and fire-ruined woodlands. I felt as though I were passing through a war-devastated area. I was deeply grieved for those who had suffered such losses, and indignation rose in me at the thought of the criminal negligence of those responsible for the lack of water pressure in this area, that precious water that might have saved some of these homes. I wondered too why chemical fire-fighting equipment had not been used. But there was no salve for my indignation, only the harsh acrid smoke that rasped in my throat and nostrils.

Larry Doyle managed to prepare supper. Afterward Charles and Lucille put candles on a birthday cake, which Lucille had baked the night before, and there was a small procession to Agnes' room and a happy birthday song. Whatever Agnes may have thought of this particular birthday, her eighty-second, there is no doubt that it was for us all unforgettable.

The thing that struck me the most next morning was the absence of birdsong. I heard a lone robin singing, with a kind of cheerless bewilderment, his familiar cheer-up cadences. When I went downstairs to Mass, Andy told me that just before dawn he had heard a whippoorwill, lonely, with sad song grieving over the desolate embers of his woodland home.

In contrast to this fiery Saturday, the day of the funeral of Tom Cain and Molly Powers was like one stolen from a pastoral idyll. It was Thursday of Easter week, only two days after the fire, a day softly warm and beautiful, fragrant with cherry blossoms, sweet with birdsong, just such a day as Tom and Molly would have loved. As we stood there beside the graves of the Catholic

Worker plot in St. Joseph's cemetery I could hear birds singing not far away. I thought that, though we did not have a high Mass, these were the very choristers that Tom and Molly would have chosen to sing them into Paradise.

I had often heard Molly tell of how she first came to the Catholic Worker. It was a cold day and she was cold and hungry. She walked into the Mott Street house, walked up to the stove and asked if she could warm herself. Tom Sullivan, who was then in charge, welcomed her with his accustomed warmth and love. Since that day Molly was very much part of the CW family. She had many ailments and was in consequence sometimes irritable and quick of temper. She was deeply affectionate by nature, loved life, good food, laughter, Irish melodies, young people, and children. She was a woman who had suffered much but had worked hard all her life. As long as she was able she always tried to do her share of the work at the farm. She died on Holy Saturday night, ready to share in the Easter Resurrection of Our Lord.

Tom Cain was a scholarly man, with much learning in many fields. He was a naturalist and knew the flora and fauna of our region intimately, and kept me informed about any interesting developments. He was also an amateur astronomer, and many of our visitors enjoyed looking through Tom's telescope and hearing him talk about the stars. He was first of all a fervent Catholic, and when he was young attended a minor seminary. He acted as our sacristan and usually served Mass in our chapel. He also worked in the parish, attending Holy Name Society meetings and helping with the choir at St. Joseph's as long as he was able. He was a man of strong and resolute will, and although tubercular resisted to the end any suggestion of hospitalization or medical treatment. Moreover, though he favored the strictest observance in matters liturgical, he cared little for conventional usage in matters of personal hygiene and cleanliness, and preferred to live in a room that was a shambles. But he was faithful to rosary and compline even in his last illness. He died early Tuesday morning, where he would have preferred to die, in his own room, above the chapel, at the beginning of Easter week, the week of Resurrection.

From Rome

DOROTHY DAY

MONDAY, JUNE THIRD, I landed from the *Vulcania*, an Italian Line ship at Forty-fifth Street in New York, at eight o'clock in the morning. Pope John was still alive. (On board ship we had been getting only the most meager reports as to the Pope's health. Each morning at Mass the chaplain had asked our prayers for the Holy Father, and each afternoon at Benediction we had repeated those prayers.)

At three o'clock that afternoon we were still sitting at our lunch with people coming and going in the little apartment on Kenmare Street when someone came in with news of the Pope's death. It had been a long agony and daily I had prayed the Eastern Rite prayer for "a death without pain" for this most beloved Father to all the world. But I am afraid he left us with the suffering which is an inevitable part of love, and he left us with fear, too, if the reports of his last words are correct, fear that his children, as he called all of us in the world, were not listening to his cries for *pacem in terris*. He was offering his sufferings, he had said before his death, for the continuing Council in September, and for peace in the world. But he had said, almost cheerfully, that his bags were packed, that he was ready to go, and that after all death was the beginning of a new life. "Life is changed, not taken away," as the Preface in the Mass for the dead has it. And just as Thérèse of Lisieux said that she would spend her heaven doing good upon earth, so in his love, John XXIII will be watching over us.

It was on the day before I sailed for New York, May 22, Wednesday, that I had the tremendous privilege of being present at his last public appearance. He stood in his window looking out over the crowd in front of St. Peter's. An audience had been scheduled as usual for that Wednesday at ten-thirty, and the great Basilica was crowded to the doors when the announcement was made that the Pope had been too ill the night before to make an appearance that day but that he would come to the window and bless the crowd, as he was accustomed to do each Sunday noon.

I had had an appointment that morning for ten-thirty at the office of Cardinal Bea, to see his secretary, Father Stransky, the Paulist, about a meeting I was to have with the Cardinal that night and was leaving the Number 64 bus at the colonnade to the left of St. Peter's. I noticed that the people leaving the bus were hastening to the square. Word gets around Rome quickly and when I inquired I was told that the Holy Father would be at the window in a moment. I hastened to a good position in the square and was there in time to see the curtains stir and the Pope appear. I had not realized how tremendous that square was until I saw how tiny the Pope's figure seemed, up at that window of the apartment under the roof. Those rooms used to be servants' quarters and had been occupied by the Popes since Pius X.

The voice of the Holy Father came through a loudspeaker, of course, and seemed strong. He said the Angelus (which we say before meals at the Peter Maurin Farm) then the prayers to the guardian angels and ended with a requiem prayer for the dead.

It was the last time the public saw his face. (Many of the crowd had opera glasses, so one can use that expression.) Questioning those at the little convent where I had been staying in Rome the last week, I learned the subject of the Pope's last talk, at his last Wednesday audience. He had urged all to read and study his last encyclicals, the call to the Council, *Mater and Magistra* and *Pacem in Terris*. He had said all he had to say; this was the message he left to the world:

> There is an immense task incumbent on all men of good will, namely the task of restoring the relations of the human family in truth, in justice, in love and in freedom; the relations between individual human beings; between citizens and their respective communities; between political communities themselves; between individuals, families, intermediate associations

and political communities on the one hand and the world community on the other. This is a most exalted task, for it is the task of bringing about true peace in the order established by God.

Admittedly, those who are endeavoring to restore the relations of social life according to the criteria mentioned above, are not many; to them We express Our paternal appreciation, and We earnestly invite them to persevere in this work with greater zeal. And We are comforted by the hope that their number will increase especially among those who believe. For it is an imperative of duty, it is a requirement of Love.

Yes, we will meditate on his words to us all, because he said he was addressing *all men of good will*, and we will know too, as we have known in the past, how difficult it is to apply these words to individual situations. We need all the gifts of the Holy Spirit for our work; we need all the help of our guardian angels; and to make our non-Catholic and non-believing readers know what these words mean, we are printing together with this usual column of pilgrimage, definitions of the gifts of the Holy Spirit, as well as what the guardian angels mean to us who believe. And not to know these things, for those of us who do believe, means not to know the treasure we have, the resources we have to draw upon.

To report further about the trip to Rome: it came about because a group of women, mostly of other faiths, and including those who did not believe, had called for this attempt to reach the Holy Father with a plea for a condemnation of nuclear war, and a development of the ideas of nonviolent resistance. This very attempt brought out clearly how difficult are these attempts at unity and coexistence.

It is no easier to receive a hearing with Princes of the Church than it is to receive one from the princes of this world. There is protocol; there is hierarchy and blocs of one kind or another; there is diplomacy in what we generally consider to be the realm of the spirit.

The day of the audience arrived and the big busses came to the door, and it did not seem that we were being treated as of any more importance than the bus loads of school children who were coming from all over Europe during their Easter holiday to see Rome and attend the large general audience which took place each Wednesday at St. Peter's.

We waited, as everyone else waited, outside in the square, two of our members in wheelchairs. We passed through the gates showing our unprivileged tickets, and back past the bureau of excavations and through one of the side doors and around into a section already packed with people.

It was long to wait. Probably people were standing two hours, and it was not until twelve-twenty that finally there was a surge in that vast mob and a sudden silence followed by almost a roar of greeting. Borne aloft on his chair (and how could any have seen him if he were not conducted in this way), the procession proceeded around the columns and then the Pope, blessing all, was conducted up to his throne where he sat while a list of all the groups of pilgrims was read aloud. As the names of the villages of Italy, and the schools on the Continent, and of England and the United States were read out, applause came from various parts of this vast group. And our pilgrimage was not mentioned!

But then the Pope began to speak and the words that fell from his lips seemed to be directed to us, to our group, speaking as he did about the "Pilgrims for Peace" who came to him, and his gratitude for their gratitude and encouragement. The young woman who had helped us find our places was translating his words as fast as he spoke them and writing them down while two of us read over her shoulder. She kept beaming at us, and all those around us, seeing our buttons, large almost as saucers, bright blue and bearing the legend "Mothers for Peace" in Italian; she also smiled and indicating the Holy Father and us in turn, seemed to be letting us know that he was speaking to us especially.

It seemed too good to be true and if all those around us had not kept assuring us he was speaking to us, I would have considered it but a coincidence. Our messages had reached him we felt, impossible though it had seemed they would.

Such a River

DENIS KNIGHT

"I find . . . London to be a Town so nobly Situated, and upon such a River, as Europe certainly shows not a more useful and agreeable."
—*John Evelyn, 1659*

By BLACKWELL TUNNEL are the Metropolitan Gas Works. There seemed no access to the River. I got into a timber yard and a Negro workman showed me a hole in the river-side fence wide enough to climb through. He pointed east and west, proprietorially, smiling: "London's that-a-way!" It was eight o'clock on Saturday morning, one of those fresh October mornings, mist rising but cloudless, with the sun rising up bright but powerless out of the sopping dews.

On this side of the fence, right by the water's edge, ran a tow-path paved with bricks stamped with diamond markings, and I was to find that this tow-path, with interruptions, runs as far as the Surrey Docks, at Rotherhithe. On the far, north side of the Thames stretched the massed cranes of the East India and West India docks. I started walking west, toward the city.

Barges stacked with timber had nice names: *Ringdove, Whitehorse, Maine, Romani.* Hardly anyone was about, only two men craning up the long timbers from the barge to the stacking-point on the timber yard. The tide was out and the river so low that the black, grimy beach was visible, with an ebb-mark of forlorn sea-shells. Still, each dirty little shell looked in its right place. I wrote three lines of bad poetry about them.

At half past nine, I came upon the Cutty Sark Tavern, a Free House not yet vanquished by the brewery combinations, but selling draught Worthington, draught Guinness, draught Bass, and

Burton bitter ale. Ten minutes further up the river stands the old Trinity Hospital, now an old people's home, as a foreign lady there told me. Above a well-proportioned doorway runs the inscription: "Hospitale Sanctae et Individuae Trinitatis Grenwichi sit gloria. 1616."

Does anyone want a boat built? At Number 19 Crane Street, S.E. 10, are Corbett & Son, Boatbuilders. The Yacht Inn, just beyond, sells Watney's draught Red Barrel ale, and has a garden and terrace overlooking the river. The Curlew Rowing Club next door, founded 1866, looks as if it expired in the same year, broken-backed behind dust and shutters.

At ten o'clock, the sun a bit warmer, the Royal Naval College hove into view, overwhelming a couple of hundred yards of riverbank with its two huge domes, large gates with anchors and tridents wrought, and bare formal lawns. Tugs made a fruity noise, warm and jovial by comparison, going up and down all the time, singly or hauling barges. Here's one with five coal barges.

Bright sun on Greenwich Pier and, startlingly, *Cutty Sark* close at hand, with her smart white masts, trim black shrouds, and eager-bosomed matron at the prow. A lovely race of flying ships, adventurers, sea-sharers with porpoises and whales. No more.

Greenwich Tunnel, opened in 1902, displays an alarming list of by-laws. The riverbank must be the best place in London for boys making bonfires. There are scatterings everywhere at ebb-tide of planks and river wood. All being gotten ready for Guy Fawkes night.

Crossing Creekside by the Creek Bridge, had a hot bacon sandwich and a large cup of strong tea at a docker's cafe on McMillan Street (Deptford) near the old church of St. Nicholas with Christ. Taking a short cut behind the Surrey Commercial Docks I got into Rotherhithe through Southwark Park, where each bench is a beach for a storm-tossed Odysseus, retired, cap on head, newspaper neatly folded. And we talk about the unity of mankind. Each like a sad Napoleon, sick with his own rectitude, or loneliness.

Trying to get back to the river, at the Port of London Authority gate, west of the Surrey Docks, a policeman hauled me out: "It's an enclosed area; you can't get through this way!" I went back past St. Olave's Hospital, which I believe used to be a seamen's hospital, and has a fig tree growing in the courtyard; past the Adam and Eve in Brunel Street; and so to the hidden-away little Mayflower, loveliest of London pubs, hanging over the water, with a veranda, and a curious mile-stone acting as cornerstone which reads: "LONDON BRIDGE TWO MILES," as plain as Dick Whittington. Here by the blackish steps of blackish Thames I indeed sat down and wept at the unpredicted beauty of birds on coal barges, and the human smile of tender London docks. It was here I met, in a curiously entranced moment, Enrico Boggione, landscape painter from Torino, with no word of English, but childlike eyes and visionary fingers. "*Signore, arriverderla!*"

At one o'clock arrived at the Angel, famous on the waterfront, and King's Stair Gardens. Carried out a glass of bitter to the veranda above the beach, and ate my hard-boiled egg and an apple. Much encouraged, I made for the Bermondsey Wall, East, where a right of way begins. This "wall" is a narrow road, mostly deserted, which runs as far as the creek by Shad Thames. The sun was warm and the air motionless (vibrant, very pure and sweet). Aromas alternately of flour, bran, pine resin and Turkish Delight drifting between tall, shadowy warehouses, under ancient doors with huge padlocks, through broken and barren windows.

At half past one I arrived at Mill Street, where the Bermondsey Wall, West, begins. Here walls were smothered in white flour, and cocoa-coloured bran. Curry odors were intoxicating on Shad Thames Street, depository of teas, seeds, grain and feeding-stuffs. On to Boss Street. Why "Boss Street"? That people should live on Boss Street! And never in More's *Utopia*, though he lived and died quite near. Shad Thames Street leads up stone steps on to Tower Bridge, stuck over with bits of Victoriana like Windsor Castle. Over the river at last, and down past the old cannons in front of the Tower. By the Monument, a very strong fishy smell. Now Pudding Lane, and Fish Street Hill beside it, with a couple of Jamaicans briskly sweeping up fish heads and tails. The Parish

Church of St. Magnus the Martyr. Lower Thames Street, and Upper Thames Street (the Fishmongers' Company inhabit here) which houses the extraordinary, brand-new Corporation of London car-park in six tiers, by Duck's Foot Lane.

Sad, lovely stones remain tumbled on the site of All Hallows the Less destroyed in the fire of 1666. Bitter irony, that the very limestone slab commemorating this catastrophe should itself be split in two by a bomb from the twentieth century.

Turned riverward down All Hallows Lane, dark and inexplicably derelict between towering warehouse walls, past Number 2, the Trident Press, and Dolphin's Press doorways, now abandoned to the birds and sky-longing weeds shooting from hedges. With no warning the lane ends in a sheer drop thirty feet to the slimy river beach, right under Cannon Street Railway Bridge. So back to Cannon Street, and through Ludgate Circus, and then St. Paul's in the sunlight, the west front gleaming white under the stonemasons' hands. And on the east side, there is such a quiet little tree-espaliered courtyard, with bright green sunken lawn, and three streams of water out of lions' mouths.

Along Fleet Street, still with the shining front of St. Paul's in view, and up the narrow alley of Hind Court, leading to Gough Square and Samuel Johnson's house in Bolt-court, where Miss Eliot, the new Curator (the legendary Miss Rowell having at last this year retired), guards the Folio Edition of the great Dictionary, Tetty's teacups, and the friendly ghosts that still converse there in indignation, laughter, high sentences, much kindliness and wit.

Josephine, R.I.P.

JEAN FOREST

THE FIRST TIME I came across Josephine at *The Catholic Worker* was during one of her appearances at a Friday night meeting. She was wearing a low-cut, yellow evening dress which she told us she wore especially for weekends. I couldn't believe my eyes— she looked like a grotesque, aged Ophelia or a caricature of a fairy queen. She was eventually shuffled from the meeting after causing some disturbance. Our next encounter was in the clothing room where I distributed clothes. Each week she would appear with a different and imaginative tale of what happened to the clothes we had given her the last week. Very often, it was the tale of some interesting thief she had "entrusted" them with. It didn't matter for I could never refuse her. I found, quite to my amazement, that I really liked and enjoyed her stories.

One can get "impersonal" to the people one serves. It's the easiest way out on the nerves. Josephine never allowed anyone to treat her "impersonally." With her it wasn't "business" or a "hand-out"; it was a person-to-person encounter. She worked on you until you had to "respond" positively or negatively. When she asked you for a bandage (she was usually bruised either from falls or beatings), you knew better than to procrastinate for a minute. Her needs were "immediate" and she'd tolerate no delay. Not that she was a nag. It was never that way because of her fantastic sense of humor. Fantastic, in the face of living on the streets (she preferred their freedom and excitement). She was an alcoholic with an ailing liver, always bruised and abused, begging for the next meal and drink. How did she escape despair? The answer may be in the mystery of her humor. When feeling especially exuberant she serenaded the kitchen and office with her most prized possession, a harmonica. The Bowery was a way of life which she accepted and, you might say, made the most of. She would tell a variety of stories of how she got here. She claimed to have become an alcoholic while a nurse. She said she had a husband somewhere and a child. She could have been any age from fifty to eighty.

Her last years were spent as music-maker and clown—harming no one and bringing laughter to some. She died in the hospital ward of the poor. It was a hard life which she managed to transcend—as though by magic.

OCTOBER 1964

 ## Project Loaves and Fishes

DAVID MASON

IN LAST MONTH'S ISSUE of *The Catholic Worker* I called attention to the need for non-profit restaurants for many Social Security pensioners who must live in rented rooms without cooking facilities and cannot afford to eat in commercial restaurants. Agreement with the idea, as expressed in letters and phone calls, has been gratifying. Philadelphia city officials are still working on plans for meetings with persons interested in organizing a pilot project. A meeting, which should result in definite action, is to be held on Friday, October 16.

Correspondents have asked for more definite information on the plan. Miss Caroline A. Bublic, of Pittsburgh, wrote to Mayor Joseph M. Barr, calling his attention to the article. She wrote, in part: "In doing just a tiny bit of parish apostolic work I have felt the tremendous need for just exactly that as described in the attached. I personally know three fine men that could use what is recommended by Mr. Mason. I frankly don't understand at all the operations of the attached, only recognize the need, and thought perhaps Mr. Mason could fill you in with details."

For the information of all who are interested, I will try to summarize the plan as clearly and briefly as possible.

One restaurant should be started in each city as a pilot project by a community organization. The Domestic Peace Corps might be an ideal organization for this job. Government aid is available, under the War on Poverty program, for initial cost, such as purchase of equipment.

The restaurant should be located in a neighborhood where there are sufficient numbers of pensioners living within walking distance. The building should not be in a high-rent location. Commercial restaurants must pay high rentals for locations where there is heavy traffic, but the pensioners can avoid that expense. The number of persons to be served will have to be determined by need and experience. I think that three hundred to five hundred might be a good number initially. With five hundred members, a building renting for five hundred dollars a month would cost each member only one dollar.

All expenses of the restaurant would be paid by the members. They would purchase weekly or monthly meal tickets (preferably monthly, since they receive monthly checks and would be assured of having their meals paid for a month in advance). This would simplify bookkeeping and no money would be handled in the restaurant. The meal ticket would be priced to cover all costs of operation. It would be a punch card bearing the Social Security number of the holder and could be used only by him.

Social Security pensioners with low incomes are entitled to receive government surplus food. Under present conditions many do not accept such food because they are unable to cook it. The non-profit restaurant could make good use of this surplus, thereby effecting a substantial saving. When food stamps replace the surplus-food program, they too could be used.

Two meals a day might be sufficient service, to hold down operating costs, with provision for take-out food, such as sandwiches, pastry and milk. The menu should be *table d'hote*, rather than *à la carte*, which is far more expensive to maintain.

Restaurant management and administration should be in the hands of men experienced in this work. Such men could be found in the ranks of the pensioners. The restaurant would not need the high-pressure, high-salaried executive type, but efficient men with good practical experience. Restaurant earnings would be sufficient to allow for payment of necessary salaries. Over-all democratic control should be exercised by the pensioners, acting through an elected committee. Men with trade-union experience would be especially useful in this phase of the project. Cooperation could be arranged with vocational-training programs for the assistance of trainees in restaurant work.

An important feature of the cooperative restaurant would be its social aspect. It would be a meeting place for men and women who might otherwise have to remain in drab, lonely rooms.

Regarding the number of men and women who would benefit by this plan, I have no figures, but here is a very rough calculation of possible numbers. The Social Security office in Philadelphia has approximately two hundred and twenty-three thousand beneficiaries on its rolls. If only one in fifty needs the cooperative restaurant, the number would be close to five thousand, who would require ten restaurants, each serving five hundred persons. I think that five thousand is a low estimate. This aid is needed not only by aged single persons living in rented rooms, but also by old couples who are too feeble or ill to prepare adequate meals.

The relationship between nutrition and health has been thoroughly established. I believe that if aged persons could have the adequate diet which the cooperative restaurant could provide they would have less need of medical attention.

Anyone interested in this plan should bring it to the attention of agencies and organizations which might be interested in doing something about it. It will require a great deal of work and dedication, but I believe that it will be worth all the effort it will cost.

When Peter Maurin began to talk about Houses of Hospitality for the poor and the homeless way back in the dark days of the depression, no one knew exactly what he was proposing, but soon some caught on and groups of Peter's disciples began to open Houses of Hospitality all over the country. It was a new experience for the men and women who undertook the work, and many did very well at it. Now there is a new need, or perhaps I should say an old need in a new guise. The men and women who need our help today have money to subsist on, in the form of Social Security pensions. Industry no longer has need of them. They could live comfortably (if not luxuriously) if the operation of the free-enterprise system made provision for persons in the low-income bracket. Unfortunately, it does not. It is up to those of us who are concerned with their problems to make it possible for the pensioners to enjoy the ease they have earned and still retain their self-respect.

I wish it were possible to present an exposition of this plan in a beautiful four-color brochure, with charts and diagrams, financial analyses and commendations by prominent persons, but it is not. I myself am a Social Security pensioner, and this comes from Madison Street, Philadelphia—not Madison Avenue, New York.

I will be happy to receive all suggestions and criticisms relative to this plan.

ED. NOTE: *Within a year after the above was published, Mr. Mason was elected to the Community Action Council in his area, one of the twelve designated "pockets of poverty" in Philadelphia. He presented a formal statement of the project to the central body, the Philadelphia Anti-Poverty Action Committee (P.A.A.C.), the next step being its presentation to the Office of Economic Opportunity in Washington.*

Red Roses for Her

(In Memoriam: Elizabeth Gurley Flynn)

DOROTHY DAY

I DREAMED of Gurley Flynn last night, and woke up thinking of how on Christmas Eve in 1957, Ammon Hennacy and I had gone to her apartment just off Second Avenue, which she shared with her sister. Not long before, she had been released from the Women's Federal Reformatory, at Alderson, West Virginia. Ammon and I had just come from the Women's House of Detention, over in Greenwich Village, outside of which we had been singing Christmas carols with a group of about fifty young people, a custom we had started the year before after the first of four brief sentences a number of us served for breaking the State Civil Defense Law by refusing to take shelter during the air-raid drills.

I had served a sentence of thirty days. But Gurley Flynn had spent twenty-eight months in a jail (I hate to call them "reformatories") far away from home and friends. Her sister had faithfully visited her each month. Ammon had brought a red rose for each of them, but it was really to Elizabeth Gurley Flynn that he was paying tribute. First of all, because she had valiantly endured jail many times; she had laid down her life for her brothers in this way. Certainly going to jail is dying to oneself, and living according to the great commandment of Jesus, who went beyond the Old Testament when he said: "A new commandment I give you." (Not only loving your neighbor as yourself, but loving him enough to lay down your life for him.)

In my dream I was there again with Ammon and Gurley Flynn, experiencing again her warmth, her equanimity, her humor, and above all, the *purpose* of her life. Her aim to help bring

243

about the kind of society where each would work according to his ability and receive according to his needs, truly one of the noblest possible aims in life.

I had first met her when I was eighteen and she was lecturing at some workers' hall in Brooklyn. I was a reporter on the New York *Call*, which boasted a staff of socialist, anarchist, and Wobbly reporters, in addition to trade–unionists who divided their allegiance between the American Federation of Labor and the Amalgamated Clothing Workers, who had stayed outside the Federation. She was a member of the I.W.W. (Industrial Workers of the World), that truly indigenous form of unionism and radicalism. There had been no revolution in Russia as yet, and the I.W.W. was fought as bitterly as the Communists are today. In fact, it seems to me that anything that threatens money or property, anything that aims at a more equitable distribution of this world's goods, has always been called Communism. I like the word myself; it makes me think of the Communism of the religious orders. In fact, the success and prosperity of religious orders shows how beneficial Communism could be if it were practiced for all, rather than for only those professed religious who give up family, marriage and personal belongings to devote themselves to the problems of poverty. But, as the Ecumenical Council has stressed, this is the age of the laity, and the laity comprises all those who are not monks, priests, or nuns, but just ordinary brothers and sisters, in the widest sense of the word. Gurley Flynn was of the laity, and she was also my sister in this deep sense of the word. She always did what the laity is nowadays urged to do. She felt a responsibility to do all in her power in defense of the poor, to protect them against injustice and destitution.

On that night I first met her, she was speaking in behalf of the Mesabi iron miners of Minnesota, who were on strike at the time, and her words moved the large audience to tears. She charmed us out of our meager money; people emptied their pockets when the collection was taken for the strikers. I forsook all prudence and emptied my purse, not even leaving myself carfare to get back to the office. (My salary at the time was not more than ten dollars a week.) In this way she aided countless workers–miners throughout the far west, workers in wheat, lumber, textiles, all have benefited from her early work. If there had not been an I.W.W., there would have been no CIO.

You must forgive me if my emphasis is religious. Whenever Jesus spoke about the attitude man ought to have towards his brother, He always emphasized the problems of wealth and poverty. He told the story of the rich man who burned in hell while the poor man who had sat at his gate, sick and unemployed, was taken up into Abraham's bosom. (How loving a phrase that is!) He told the story of how the men who came to work at the end of the day got paid as much as those who had worked since early morning. How different from the attitude of the associated farmers of California, who consider themselves Christians! And when people asked Jesus, "When did we see you hungry or homeless, or in jail or sick, and did not visit you?" He answered them: "In so far as you did not do it to the least of these my brothers, you did not do it to me."

The great English writer George Orwell once said that one of the greatest tragedies of our age has been the loss of a sense of personal immortality. It may sound exaggerated to say that Gurley Flynn's *name* will be immortal in the labor and radical movements, but it brings out the point I wish to make. Orwell spoke of *personal* immortality, and that is the kind people who have a religious faith believe in, because it is clearly taught in the New Testament. "If we did not believe this, how vain our faith would be," St. Paul wrote. It is the core of our faith.

I don't think anyone really wants to die. Unless, of course, he is in such pain that he seeks death as a relief. But not a person as vital as Gurley Flynn, who enjoyed life so much, found so much to do, lived so keen an intellectual life (not in a philosophical sense, but rather in a "sociological" sense), who loved so ardently—no, I do not think that she wished to die, to go into oblivion, personally, she herself.

She has long been in my prayers, and I really believe that one's prayer is always answered. "Ask, and you shall receive," Jesus said, and He also said that God wills that *all* men be saved. I was once told by a good priest, and have often read it since, that there is no *time* with God. That is a difficult concept, philosophically and theologically. But it means that in this particular case all the prayers I have said, and will say in the future, will have meant that Gurley Flynn held out her arms to God (and the word God itself means Good, Truth, Love, all that is most beautiful) at the moment of her death, and was received by Him. And she will be judged by the love that is in her heart.

ED. NOTE: *Elizabeth Gurley Flynn, Secretary of the Communist Party of the United States, died in Moscow on September 5, 1964, at the age of seventy-two. Dorothy Day, invited to speak at the memorial meeting held for her in Community Church, New York City, in October, was in Vermont and unable to attend. However, she sent a message to the meeting, which was read aloud by Associate Editor Tom Cornell. Above is the substance of her remarks.*

OCTOBER 1965

 ## Chrystie Street

NICOLE D'ENTREMONT

EVERY DAY a little brown packet comes in the mail to 175 Chrystie Street. Inside there is usually a carefully wrapped sliver of soap or a half-roll of toilet paper or an envelope of sugar like the ones you find in restaurants. No one is quite sure who sends them. Bob Stewart tells me he remembers them coming when the CW was at Spring Street, a good five years ago. In any event the little packets continue to come and Walter files them in a basket on his desk. In moments of whimsy I often transplant the whole scene downtown to Merrill Lynch, Pierce, Fenner and Smith. I see visions of a three-buttoned, angular executive snapping the command, "Fisby, would you place these little packets in my basket?" The incongruity of the scene always amuses me. In fact, if a definition were ever attempted of our house on Chrystie Street I think it would have to symbolically include these little packets, since one of the facts of our community is that each person contributes what he can, with no thought as to whether the gift contributes to material gain. I wonder if Merrill Lynch, Pierce, Fenner and Smith could ever run that way.

There is a difference, of course, between profit and subsistence, and it looks as if we're in for a lean year of subsistence on Chrystie Street. The car is now running on two cylinders out of six and although Chris Kearns is a good mechanic, he's not a magician. A working car is a necessity for our house, since we have to pick up vegetables twice a week and run errands around the city. As it is, it's only a wish and a prayer and an expert kick from Chris that gets it going when we need it. Rents keep piling up, both on the Chrystie Street house and the apartments, and with winter on our heels the gas bills will soon rival the rent. Even Charlie's soup bones cost money, and lately these have been dwindling. Dorothy says that it's expensive to be poor and the truth of that statement is continually confirmed in any tenement community.

Even though the wolf's at the door, there is a lot of activity in the house with people working to mail out both the appeal and this issue of the paper. Quite a few new people have arrived since the summer. Terry Sullivan, fresh from Ammon Hennacy's house in Salt Lake City and enthused by the Peacemaker conference in Tivoli, has set up a program of traveling peace teams to go around and visit Catholic high schools and colleges, speaking on Vietnam, alternatives to the draft, and Christian pacifism. Three weeks ago we visited LaSalle College in Philadelphia, showed a film on Franz Jagerstatter, the Austrian peasant who refused Hitler's draft and was beheaded, set up a table in the Student Union with literature, and tried to talk with the students on a personal basis. It's hard to talk with students who have, for the most part, been systematically conditioned by both Church and state to reject pacifism. Almost every student I spoke to said that we must stop Communism now, and most, when pressed to suggest how, unhesitatingly answered that we should bomb China. Usually when speaking with students about the war in Vietnam you have several options. You can speak the language of logistics, suggesting that land war in Southeast Asia is doomed to a fruitless stalemate; you can speak historically, pointing out the United States prevented free elections in accord with the Geneva Agreement; or you can speak of the witness of Christ. We found that the third option is irrelevant to most Catholic students, who have yet to realize that religion is a way of life and not only a cult of worship. Jim Wilson, a young draft refuser now at *The Catholic Worker*, has recently written a pamphlet on a Christian approach to peace in which he speaks unequivocally on war, the Church and Communism. In it he says:

> Most of us feel that we must fight or kill in order to defend something; a way of life, freedom, religion or Christ Himself. Many ask what would become of Christendom if Communism were allowed to spread. We cannot use Christ as an excuse for killing. We don't have to defend Christ or the Catholic Church by taking up arms. This was Peter's reason for raising his sword, to defend Christ from the mob that had come to crucify Him, and he was told by Christ Himself to put up his sword. We are being told today to put up our bombs, and not to defend Christ with violence but with love. This is not a defeatist attitude of "better red than dead." You must be ready to die if you are going to make a commitment to Christ. Anyone who states that he will not be able to remain a Christian under the Communist way of life, cannot really believe that he is a Christian now.

Terry, Paul Mann, Jim Wilson, Cathy Swann, Dave Miller and myself plan to leave tomorrow for New Hampshire to speak at St. Anselm's College, and then go on to Connecticut to speak at Albertus Magnus and St. Joseph's College. We are not so naive as to think we will convert people to pacifism because of a one-day or two-day stay on campus; what we hope to do is to challenge concepts of war and peace that need drastic rethinking in the twentieth century.

Paul, Jim and Dave are what is known in the unprejudiced argot of the press as "draft dodgers." Dave, now working for *The Catholic Worker* and a recent graduate of Le Moyne College, is one of the sanest and most temperate individuals I've ever known. Yesterday, at the Whitehall Street Induction Center in New York, he publicly burned his draft card while Federal agents and the press looked on. Such symbolic disobedience is not the action of a man out to dodge the draft but the action of a man who wishes to confront the system he opposes. The young men working at *The Catholic Worker* are conscientiously opposed to war. Perhaps after having seen the victims of the class war here in this country sleeping forgotten on the Bowery, running up and down the steps of crumbling tenements, or staring wide-eyed and alone in state mental hospitals, they do not want to fight for a materialistic system that cripples so many of its citizens. These are young men committed to the nonviolent revolution of our time. They are not the doctrinaire Marxists whom many of our right-wing friends oddly resemble, with their belief in the inevitability of a bloody conflict between East and West. These are young men who have learned well one historical fact, and that is that you can never win over an ideology by killing the men who have the idea. The job of the twentieth century Christian is that of a peacemaker performing the works of mercy, not the works of war. Are such young men dodging or are they confronting reality?

Random Reflections on Poverty and
Selling *Catholic Workers*

THOMAS P. MURRAY

THE CUSTOM of selling *The Catholic Worker* on the street began with Volume One, Number One, when Dorothy Day and Peter Maurin distributed the paper at the May Day celebration of 1933 at Union Square. Since then, many people have gone out to sell papers on the streets of New York. Ammon Hennacy has a regular schedule for paper sales in various locations, and sometimes I looked up his schedule in his book, *The Book of Ammon*. I would try to follow his schedule because the locations and times were well tested and productive, and many of his old friends still came by these places.

Several months ago, money being especially hard to come by, I began to sell papers in order to get carfare to get around the city. I would leave my place on Avenue A and 14th Street and walk over to Broadway and 14th Street, where I would sell papers until I had fifteen cents for a subway token. On my way back from wherever I had gone, I would sell fifteen cents worth of papers to get back.

One day I decided to walk through the cars of the subway train and sell papers. I had always enjoyed selling papers on the street, with people whizzing by. I would watch all of their re- actions—ignoring my outstretched copy of the paper, pausing and deciding if they wanted it, telling me they already had it at home, asking me what the paper had to say to Jewish workers, telling me in no uncertain terms that the paper wasn't Catholic and that if I was a worker I'd be out working instead of stand- ing on a street corner doing nothing.

The subway was different. I am not sure I can explain completely how, but it was. On the streets people are in too much of a hurry to let a "newsboy" attract any more of their attention than is comfortable for them. On the subway they are trapped —they have to notice you. On the street I am reminded of the self-sufficient CW "salesmen" like Ammon and Jim Forest, but in the subway I am constantly aware that the looks I get from people are the same ones I notice when a blind or halt beggar moves through the car.

Perhaps that is the essential difference. On the subway I am a beggar. There is no getting around it, no losing sight of it. Sure, I am giving people something worth much more than the penny it costs. I am still begging. I am taking nickels, dimes and quarters because I need them. I am thrown upon these people. I am reduced to asking them to give—not in the impersonal exchange of a business transaction, or the friendly banter of the street, but in the bare reality of my need and my imposition of that need on largely unwilling and captive eyes and ears. Before I could analyze it or understand the dynamic of it I found myself, for a time, unable emotionally to bring myself to that first "*Catholic Worker*—only a penny—the Catholic anti-war paper—only a penny." I would stand mutely as station after station went by, trying to bring myself to speak up and at the same time trying to define whatever it was that was keeping me silent. I am only now beginning to realize what my feelings were and what their genesis was.

Voluntary poverty is hard to come by, and most often we really don't work as hard as we should to understand and practice it. Living in community helps somewhat, because you learn to accept the disappearance of your personal property into the community to meet the needs of others; but even this can happen without that stripping of self which poverty demands ever taking place. Voluntary poverty has to be a sharing in the lot of the poor. A great part of that poverty is the realization that *you* are poor, that is you are dependent upon the giving of others. If you are poor, *you* become the beggar—not in enjoying the fruits of others' begging, but in the humiliating stares of people on the subway. What the subways had that frightened me was the stark confrontation with the fact that I was a beggar—not for others who were in need but for myself. The people sitting there didn't see a soup line or a clothing room, they saw *me,* were forced by my imposing chant to see *my* need. One of the things which brought me to see the personal nature of my fear was an encounter with a young college girl. We were standing on the BMT platform at Times Square, and I was churning inside at the prospect of selling papers on the train. As it pulled into the station this girl saw my papers and asked if I was selling the current issue. When she bought the paper I wasn't as clearly—in my own mind—the blind beggar, but the bearer of good news once again, and this gave me strength to sell papers after we got on the train.

Now I like to sell papers on the subway. It is still hard, but now I understand it and it helps to remind me of who I am and what my poverty is. It helps me to gain more understanding of my relationship both to those upon whom I am imposing my need and to those others who are brought to impose their need. I have got to let this teach me the necessity of letting others see my need and of letting them give. It is so easy to hide our need, to disguise it—to ourselves as well as to others.

This concept of letting other people give is also a "hard saying." It is really a part of our poverty. One night, during a snowstorm, my wife Jan and I decided to take a cab home from downtown. It was a bitter cold night, the snow was deep on the ground and heavy in the air. It was late, with no bus in sight. Our driver was a man with a full black beard, and he had a Bible on the dashboard. I assumed that he was an orthodox Jew, but he told us he was a Jehovah's Witness. As the cab came along the Bowery to Houston Street we saw a man lying across the traffic island in the middle of the street. He was struggling to get up but each time was thwarted by the snowy slush and his own inebriation. I asked the cab driver to pull over and went over to help the man across the street to the sidewalk. He was very drunk and had no home. He said that he had been staying at a flophouse nearby but had no money to stay there that night. I helped him upstairs and paid him in for the night.

The night clerk knew him and gave him the room he had had the night before.

After the man was registered I went back to the cab. The driver asked if I knew him. I told him that I didn't but that the group I belonged to regularly paid men into the hotels on the Bowery when they had no place to go. When we got to the end of our trip, and I paid the driver, he asked me how much the flop had cost and offered me fifty-five cents, to pay half the cost. I started to refuse it, explaining that the *Worker* had a fund for this purpose and that I would be reimbursed, but he insisted that I had to let him share in my giving to the man on the Bowery. He was right. I had been all set to deny this man the joy of giving, the satisfaction of being a part of this act. Why? Because of the same image of self-sufficiency which made selling papers in the subway so hard. I didn't need his help to give. I could do it by myself—I could give without needing to take in this very personal way. I could not admit that I was as dependent upon the cab driver as the man on the Bowery was upon me— in fact, we were all equally dependent upon each other.

Jan tells another story which brings this home. During the subway strike, while she was walking uptown, she was approached by an elderly lady who asked if Jan would take her arm for the remaining two blocks. The woman only lived a block out of the way Jan was going, so Jan took her to her destination—a cheap hotel. While they walked Jan mentioned that she was on the way to buy a link for her bicycle chain. When they reached the hotel the woman reached into her handbag and took out some change. She offered it to Jan to buy the link—two quarters, a nickel and a penny. Jan could tell that the woman didn't have much, she was not richly dressed and the hotel she was living in was not an expensive one, and she didn't want to take the money. Then she realized that she had to take something. Even though the woman didn't have much, Jan couldn't refuse or just take a nickel as a token gesture. She had to take enough for the bicycle link—one of the quarters—because she couldn't refuse the woman the dignity and joy of giving. Even though the woman couldn't afford the quarter, she could even less afford to lose the opportunity to give.

This is a real truth about our voluntary poverty. We must constantly allow ourselves to see that we are beggars, that our poverty is a calling to allow others to give, not to take pride in our own giving. We all must be humble takers so that our giving will be real instead of self-serving. There is a Shaker hymn that Ed McCurdy sings:

> 'Tis a gift to be simple, 'tis a gift to be free,
> 'Tis a gift to come down where we ought to be,
> And when we find ourselves in the place just right,
> It will be in the valley of love and delight.
>
> When true simplicity is gained,
> To bow and to bend, we will not be ashamed,
> To turn and to turn will be our delight,
> 'Till by turning, turning we come round right.

I guess the subway was part of the turning which leads to true simplicity. Once it is gained, I guess I won't be ashamed to be the bowing beggar. I guess that is part of what our voluntary poverty is for.

DECEMBER 1966

  Albert Camus and the Church

THOMAS MERTON

> "Why do you call me 'Sir'?" said the prison chaplain, "why don't you call me Father?"
> "You are not my Father," said the condemned prisoner, "you are with the others."

AT THE END of Albert Camus' novel *The Stranger*, there is a long dialogue between priest and condemned prisoner. The chaplain, an average, sincere, zealous and not overbright priest is trying to grapple with the stolid unbelief of a man whom he considers the worst possible type of hardened criminal. He finally drives the man to complete desperation which explodes at last into a curious blend of Zen-Satori and existentialist revolt: the unexpected result of priestly zeal! The prisoner is a single-minded Algerian clerk, Meursault, who in a moment of thoughtlessness shot a man. He felt himself to have been partly irresponsible but failed to realize the importance of defending himself in terms that his society was willing to understand and accept. As a result he got the death penalty when, in fact, there were enough extenuating circumstances to warrant a much lighter sentence.

One of the themes of the novel is the ambiguity and "absurdity" of a justice which, though logical and right in its own terms, is seen to be an elaborate tissue of fictions—a complicated and dishonest social game in which there is no real concern for persons or values. Meursault is condemned, in fact, for not playing that game, as is made abundantly clear when the prosecution proves to the jury's outraged satisfaction that the accused did not weep at his mother's funeral. In the trial the sentimental exploitation of this fact curiously assumes a greater importance than the murder itself. The whole prosecution is sensational, pharisaical and indeed irrelevant to the actual case. All through the trial the accused, though not particularly smart, gradually realizes that society is interested not in what he really did, but only in completely reconstructing his personality and his actions to make him fit its own capricious requirements—its need for the complete evildoer.

And now the prison chaplain, having taken for granted all that has been decided in the courtroom, proceeds to work the prisoner over in the interests of other requirements; the need for a complete penitent. Since to repent one must first believe, the chaplain simply tries to convince Meursault that in his heart of hearts he "really believes" but does not know that he believes. Meursault replies that though he cannot be quite sure what interests him, he is quite certain of what does not interest him; and this includes the whole question of religion. Meursault is right to feel offended by the priest's self-assurance, which simply adds to the affront that the court has visited upon his dignity as a person.

All through the imprisonment and the trial, the prisoner has in fact been treated as if he were not there, as if he were so complete a nonentity that he was not able to think or even experience anything validly for himself. "I am with you," says the chaplain with smug assurance based on perfect moral superiority, "but you cannot realize this since you have a blinded heart." In the end the prisoner reacts with violent indignation against this cumulative refusal of lawyers (his own included), judges, jury, the press, the Church and society at large to accept him as a person. There is considerable bite in the sentence: "I answered that he was not my Father, he was with the others." After all what is a Father whose relation with his "son" is no more than his relation with a chair or a table—and a chair that is about to be thrown out with the rubbish?

Another ironic sentence shows up what Camus thought of the Church, as exemplified at least by this priest: "According to him the justice of men was nothing and the justice of God everything. I remarked that it was the former that had condemned me." The chaplain appears to make a distinction between the justice of man and the justice of God, but in actual fact he has assumed that the justice of man *is* the justice of God and that the truth of the verdict is the truth of God. When *bourgeois* society speaks, God speaks. This is taken so much for granted by him that he does not even think of questioning it.

Another priest, more subtly portrayed by Camus, is the Jesuit Paneloux in *The Plague*. In this novel Camus created a great modern myth in which he described man's condition in this life on earth. It refers more especially to French society. We know that *The Plague* is also about the German occupation of France, and Paneloux represents in some sense the French clergy under the Nazis. But he also represents the Church as she confronts man in his moral and metaphysical estrangement—his "lostness" in an absurd world. What will she offer him? Can she give him anything more than a predigested answer and a consoling rite? Does she ask of him anything more than conformity and resignation? At the outbreak of the plague Paneloux delivers a hell-fire sermon on the Justice of God and the punishment of iniquity, the need for penance and for a return to decent church-going lives. In other words the plague is a punishment. But for what, precisely? Sin! Later he learns, by working with the doctors in the "resistance," that things are not quite so simple as all that and that such a black-and-white interpretation of social or moral crises no longer convinces anyone. He proceeds to a new position which is, however, still unconvincing because no one can make out quite what it is. He now, in fact, demands a wager of blind faith that sounds like fatalism. In the end he lays down his life, but his sacrifice is ambiguous because, for obscure motives of his own, he has refused medical help.

There is in *The Plague* a decisive dialogue between Rieux the doctor and Paneloux the priest after they have witnessed the sufferings and death of a child. Paneloux no longer has any glib explanation, but only suggests that we must love what we cannot understand. Rieux replies, "I have a different conception of love. And I shall refuse to the bitter end to love this scheme of things in which children are tortured." This is a caricature of the theology of evil. Does Christianity demand that one "love a system, an explanation, a scheme of things," which for its coherence demands that people be tortured? Is that what the Gospel and the Cross mean? To some Christians, unfortunately, yes. And it is they who present Camus with an absurdity against which he must revolt. This is not a question of ill-will or culpable scandal—only a tragic misunderstanding. Camus' evaluation of the Church is not unusual and not totally unsympathetic, but it is especially worth attending to, since Camus has retained a kind of moral eminence (which he himself often repudiated) as the conscience of a new generation. By reason of his personal integrity, his genius, his eloquence and his own record in protest and resistance, Camus still speaks to our world with resounding authority. His judgments carry much more conviction than those of Sartre, for example, who has thrown in his lot with Marxist power politics, or those of Marcel and Mounier, who, though respected outside the Church, have exercised their influence mostly inside it.

II

If we as Catholics wish to get some idea of what the secular world thinks of us and expects of us, we can still with profit turn to Camus and question him on the subject. As a matter of fact, shortly after the end of the War the *avant-garde* Dominicans at the publishing house of Le Cerf invited Camus to come and answer this important question. Notes on the talk were preserved. They were very instructive and have lost none of their vitality today.

Camus opened his remarks to the Paris Dominicans with some interesting observations on dialogue. We are by now familiar enough with the fact that dialogue requires openness and honesty, and this supposes first of all that on both sides there is a complete willingness to accept the other as he is. This also presupposes a willingness to be oneself and not pretend to be someone else. On the part of the nonbeliever (Camus courteously begins with the nonbeliever), it is essential to avoid a kind of secular pharisaism (*pharisaisme laique*) which in the name of Christianity demands more of the Christian than the secularist demands of himself. "I certainly believe that the Christian has plenty of obligations," Camus admits, "but the man who himself rejects these obligations has no right to point them out to one who has recognized their existence." This is charitable of him, indeed. Pharisaism works two ways: on one hand the man who thinks that it is enough to *recognize* an obligation by a purely formal and punctilious fulfillment is a pharisee. On the other the man who detects the failure and points to it, without fulfilling an equivalent obligation himself, is also a pharisee. Camus had an exquisite eye for this kind of a thing, as his novels show. (See especially the perfect pharisaism of Clamence in *The Fall*.) According to him, pharisaism is one of the worst plagues of our time. In *The Stranger* the whole trial is an exhibition of the pure pharisaism of French *bourgeois* culture. Camus is no less aware of the pharisaism of Marxists, as we see in the long section devoted to them in *The Rebel.*

If it is not the business of the nonbeliever to judge the Christian's behavior, it is nevertheless essential that the Christian be a Christian if he is going to engage, as Christian, in dialogue with somebody else. Already in those days Camus had run into Catholics who, in their eagerness to be "open," were willing to throw their Catholicism out the window. True, the example he cites is not convincingly scandalous. In a discussion with Marxists at the Sorbonne, a Catholic priest had stood up and exclaimed, "I too am anti-clerical." There are a lot of us who know exactly what he meant and would, by now, be willing to join him in his declaration, if by "anti-clericalism" is meant weariness and exasperation with the seminary veneer of self-assurance, intolerance, expert knowledge of inscrutable sciences, and total moral superiority to the laity. Nevertheless, if one is a priest, one cannot allow oneself the rather indecent luxury of repudiating one's fellow priests *en bloc* in order to indulge one's own vanity or wounded feelings. It is quite true, and we must admit it, that life as a priest in these times of questioning and renewal is neither simple nor easy. One has to live with things that do not seem to be authentic or honest, let alone agreeable. One is likely to be impatient for reforms that are not only long in coming but may never come at all. And one may at the same time be the target of criticism which, though ambiguous, has enough ground in fact to be irritating. A cleric might well be tempted to free himself of these distressing conditions by joining some radical minority and taking up a position from which he can righteously attack his fellow clergy. If what he seeks by this is comfort for his own ego and recognition by an in-group of his own choice, Camus warns him that he is deluding himself.

Nevertheless, we must not take Camus' dislike of "anti-clerical priests" too absolutely. He did not mean to silence all public opinion and self-questioning within the Church. On the contrary, he called for such self-criticism and self-examination and he approved of it when he met it, for example, in his friend the Dominican Père Bruckberger ("Bruck"). Camus' notebooks abound in spiritual nosegays like these, culled from the garden of Bruck's conversation:

"G. has the look of a priest, a sort of episcopal unction. And I can hardly bear it in Bishops."

"Those Christian Democrats give me a pain in the neck."

Camus naively said to Bruck: "As a young man I thought all priests were happy." Bruck replied: "Fear of losing their faith makes them limit their sensitivity. It becomes merely a negative vocation. They don't face up to life." And Camus added: "His dream, a great conquering clergy, but magnificent in its poverty and audacity." Poverty and audacity were two qualities that appealed more and more to Camus. He looked for them, as we shall see, in the Catholic Church but did not always find them.

III

It would unduly complicate this article to go into Camus' difficulties with the Augustinian theology of sin and grace, and the reasons why he took scandal at a certain pessimistic religious approach to the problem of evil. But we recall that at the University of Algiers, Camus wrote the equivalent of an M.A. thesis on "Plotinus and St. Augustine." It is not enough to say, as one recent writer has said, that if Camus had read Teilhard de Chardin instead of Augustine he would have been more likely to become a Christian. Maybe so, maybe not. But he remained more or less impaled on the same dilemma as Ivan Karamazov: if there are evil and suffering in the world, and if God is omnipotent, then the fact that He permits the evil must mean that He is responsible for it. And if the evil has to exist in order somehow to justify the divine omnipotence, then Camus will return his ticket to paradise, he doesn't want to go there if it means admitting that this is "right."

Stated in the terms in which he states it, the problem becomes an esthetic one which cannot really be solved by logic or metaphysics, a question of structure that is unsatisfactory because it lacks harmony and unity—it is in fact to him esthetically and morally absurd. He cannot accept it because it repels his

imagination. It is like a play that falls apart in the third act. To
demand that one simply accept this with resignation and to say
it is "right" (in the sense of satisfactory to man's deepest sense
of fittingness and order) is simply an affront to man, thinks
Camus. And a lot of other people go along with him. We need
not argue the theoretical point here.

What is crucially important in our world is not evil as an
abstract scenario but evil as an existential fact. It is here that
Camus speaks most clearly to the Church. The unbeliever and
the Christian both live in a world in which they confront evil
and the absurd. They have different ways of understanding these
facts, but this does not make too much difference provided they
offer authentic protest and resistance. Camus then raises the
question that recently has been hotly debated as a result of Hoch-
huth's *The Deputy*. Why did not Rome speak out more clearly
and forcefully against the crimes and barbarities of Nazism?

> Why shall I not say this here? For a long time I waited during
> those terrible years, for a strong voice to be lifted up in Rome.
> I an unbeliever? Exactly. For I knew that spirit would be lost
> if it did not raise the cry of condemnation in the presence of
> force. It appears that this voice was raised. But I swear to you
> that millions of men, myself included, never heard it; and that
> there was in the hearts of believers and unbelievers a solitude
> which did not cease to grow as the days went by and the execu-
> tioners multiplied. It was later explained to me that the con-
> demnation had indeed been uttered, but in the language of
> encyclicals, which is not clear. The condemnation had been
> pronounced but it had not been understood. Who cannot see
> in this where the real condemnation lies? Who does not see
> that this example contains within it one of the elements of the
> answer, perhaps the whole answer to the question you have
> asked me? What the world expects of Christians is that Chris-
> tians speak out and utter their condemnation in such a way that
> never a doubt, never a single doubt can arise in the heart of
> even the simplest man. *That Christians get out of their ab-
> stractions and stand face to face with the bloody mess that is
> our history today. The gathering we need today is the gathering
> together of men who are resolved to speak out clearly and pay
> with their own person. When a Spanish bishop blesses political*

> *executions he is no longer a bishop or a Christian or even a*
> *man. . . . We expect and I expect that all those will gather*
> *together who do not want to be dogs and who are determined*
> *to pay the price that has to be paid if man is to be something*
> *more than a dog.*

This is strong meat and it has lost nothing of its strength since 1948. It can be repeated today and perhaps with greater effect than before, since the Vatican Council has so obviously and explicitly told all Catholics to listen to what the world has to say to them. This is it!

Camus' challenge is nothing new. We can say the same thing to ourselves and we do when we are in the mood. And yet there remains always that fatal ambiguity, that confusion, the muddle, the fuss, the hesitation, the withdrawal into obscurity, and finally the negation of what we just said. We give it out with one hand and take it all back with the other. We promise everything and then cancel it all out by promising the opposite to someone else. In a word we have to please everybody. So we are uncertain, dubious, obscure. And finally we just give up and keep our mouths shut.

Fully to understand the implications of Camus' stark demand we have to see it against the background of his thought and not against the background of what has been standard practice in Christian society for centuries. We can accept with great good will Camus' declaration of the necessity to protest against injustice and evil. But when we look a little closer at society the picture is not so simple. It is on the contrary very intricate, and threads work within threads in a complex social tapestry in which, everywhere, are the faces of bishops, of priests and of our fellow Catholics. We are involved everywhere in everything and we have to go easy. . . . Perhaps that is why it is so simple to blast off against Communism. There are no bishops of ours in Russia and we have nothing invested there except hopes. Communism has made it easy for us; by its single-minded hostility to the Church it has become the one force we can always condemn without compromise at any moment—until perhaps we start making deals with Communism too. Then there will be nobody left!

Where we see unavoidable, distressing and yet "normal" complications, Camus sees the "absurd." What we accept and come to terms with, he denounces and resists. The "absurd" of Camus is not the metaphysical absurd and *neant* of Sartre, and his "revolt" is not the Sartrian nausea. The absurd of Camus is the gap between the actual shape of life and intelligent truth. Absurdity is compounded by the ambiguous and false explanations, interpretations, conventions, justifications, legalizations, evasions which infect our struggling civilization with the "plague" and which often bring us most dangerously close to perfect nihilism when they offer a security based on a seemingly rational use of absolute power.

It is here we are forced to confront the presence of "the absurd" in the painful, humiliating contradictions and ambiguities which are constantly and everywhere evident in our behavior as Christians in the world. To mention only one: the scandal of men who claim to believe in a religion of love, mercy, forgiveness and peace, dedicating themselves wholeheartedly and single-mindedly to secular ideologies of hate, cruelty, revenge and war and lending to those ideologies the support of a Christian moral casuistry. And when the Church officially examines her conscience before the world and repudiates this contradiction, many Catholics still find ways of ignoring and evading the consequences of what the Church has said. "The arms race is an utterly treacherous trap for humanity and one which injures the poor to an intolerable degree. . . . Divine Providence urgently demands of us that we free ourselves from the age-old slavery of war. But if we refuse to make this effort . . ." (Vatican Council II, *Gaudium et Spes*, 81.) Who is making a really serious effort? A few of us are perhaps thinking it over! Certainly the Church has spoken without ambiguity though still in official language: but if Christians themselves do not pay attention, or simply shrug the whole thing off, the ambiguity persists, and it is perhaps more disconcerting than it was before. The prisoner in *The Stranger* did not even hope that the chaplain would be any less absurd than the lawyers and the judges. He knew in advance he was "with all the others"!

To really understand what Camus asked of Christians that evening at the Dominican house of Latour-Maubourg, we would have to understand his difficult analysis of two centuries of cultural and political history in *The Rebel*. This book is, admittedly, a failure. But its insights remain nevertheless extremely precious, and they enable us still to see through the specious claims of the power politician (so often accepted without question by Christians both of the right and of the left) and to detect beneath the superficial arguments the absurd void of nihilism and mass murder. At this point we might quote a Catholic thinker, Claude Tresmontant, who restates in purely Catholic terms exactly what Camus means by being a "Rebel" against the "absurd."

> But the child is going to inherit also, and especially by the education he is going to receive from his environment, a set of ready-made ideas, a system of judgments, a scale of values which, as often as not, he will not be able to question or criticize. This system of values, in the aggregate of nations, in large part is criminal. It is the reflection of a criminal world in which man oppresses, massacres, tortures, humiliates and exploits his brother. The child enters into an organized world, on the political, economic, mental, mythological, psychological and other planes. And the structure of this world is penetrated and informed by sin. The child is not born in Paradise. It is born in a criminal humanity. In order to have access to justice, to sanctity, the child, as it grows up, will have to make a personal act of judgment, of refusal, of choice. It will have to make a personal act of opposition to the values of its tribe, of its caste, of its nation or of its race, and of its social class, in order to attain justice. To a certain extent it will have to leave its tribe, its nation, its care, its class, its race, as Abraham, the father of the faithful did, who left Ur of the Chaldees to go into a country that he did not know. Holiness begins with a breach. Nothing can dispense this child from breaking with "the world." In order to enter into Christianity, the child will have to choose between the values of the world, the values of the tribe, its nation or its social class, and the values of the Gospel. It must renew its scale of values. It must, as it were, be born

anew from the spiritual point of view: it must become a new creature. Tertullian said one is not born a Christian. One becomes a Christian. The access to Christianity represents a new birth. One can then legitimately distinguish between the state which precedes this new birth and the state which follows it. The state which precedes this new birth is the state which the Church calls "original sin."

(Christian Metaphysics)

But does the Catholic Church clearly and always define the relation of the Christian to secular society in these terms? Does it not, in fact, like the chaplain in *The Stranger*, identify itself at times with this society?

For Camus it is clear that a certain type of thinking and talking, a certain type of mental attitude, even though it may be vested in the most edifying clichés, betrays a firm commitment to economic and political interests which are incompatible in the long run with the message of the Gospel, the true teaching of the Church and the Christian mission in the world. It is the commitment that speaks louder than any words. It manifests itself in the peculiar absurdity of official double-talk, the language of bureaucratic evasion, which, while nodding politely to Christian principles, effectively comes out in full support of wealth, injustice and brute power. For Camus it is axiomatic that any ideology, any program, whether of the right or the left, which leads to mass murder and concentration camps as a direct consequence is to be revolted against, no matter how "reasonable" and "right" it is made to appear.

Speaking in an interview in São Paulo, Brazil in 1949, Camus said: "Only the friends of dictatorships, the people who set up concentration camps, can be in favor of war. It is the duty of writers to sound the alarm and to fight against every form of slavery. That is our job."

The Camusian "Rebel" fulfills the role of the prophet in modern society, and it is to the writer and the artist that Camus looks above all to carry out this essential task. Nowhere in his work do we find him expressing any real hope of this prophetic voice being in the pulpit or in the documents of the Church, though as we have seen, he still says it is the Church's job to speak out also. He no longer looks to her for guidance—but he does at least hope for a little support. If she cannot lead, she can at least follow!

In the same interview, speaking of the poet René Char, "the biggest event in French poetry since Rimbaud," he says he expects far more from poets than from moralists: "When you say 'poetry' you are close to love, that great force which one cannot replace with money, which is vile, nor with that pitiable thing they call 'La Morale'." (Note that in French primary schools there is—or was—a weekly class in "La Morale" in which the children memorize the most appalling platitudes. One wonders if our catechism is much better.)

It was said above that *The Rebel* is not a fully successful thesis on revolt. In spite of some acute and detailed analysis and diagnosis nothing is very positively prescribed. But there remains a basic ambiguity in the book. In his study of modern revolutionary violence and his analysis of its inevitable trend toward tyranny and mass murder, Camus attributes this to the godlessness of modern revolutionaries. At the same time he admits that without God there can be no rational philosophy and practice of nonviolence. Yet he still cannot make the Pascalian wager of faith (by which he seems at times to be tempted). If there is to be a choice between faith and the absurd, his stoic conscience will, in the end, dictate the choice of the absurd. And the "absurd man" of Camus remains strangely isolated, even though, if he is consistently faithful to his steady view of the absurd, he should proceed to a revolt that joins him in solidarity with other men of his own kind. But this solidarity lacks human validity unless it is in the service of life and humanity. In other words, revolt is legitimate only if it refuses all complicity with mass murder and totalitarianism of whatever kind, whether of the right or of the left.

"There is one problem only today," said Camus in a statement of 1946, "and that is the problem of murder. All our disputes are vain. One thing alone matters, and that is peace."

However, Camus was never an out-and-out pacifist. He always admitted the possibility of a strictly limited use of force. He had various reasons for this, besides the rather complex one of his rejection of faith in God, which at the same time implied the impossibility, for him, of consistent nonviolence and pacifism. Since many can attain only an "approximation of justice" then it is futile for him to hope to avoid all use of force, but he must restrain himself and exercise full, indeed heroic responsibility in keeping the use of force down to the minimum, where it is always provisional and limited and never in favor of a cause that consecrates and codifies violence as a permanent factor in its policies.

The peculiar isolation of Camus' position comes from his inability to cope with the idea of God and of faith to which his sense of justice and his instinctive nonviolence nevertheless enticed him. In the same way, he was led up to the "silence of God" by his interest in the studies on phenomenology of language written by his friend, Brice Parain, an existentialist who became a Catholic in the late forties, when he was closely associated with Camus. In fact we cannot do full justice to Camus' relations with the Church without taking into consideration his interest in the ideas of Parain. It is here that Camus' dialogue with Catholicism developed on the most intimate and profound level.

In an age of highly academic linguistic analysis, Camus appreciated the courage of Parain, who sees the problem of language as ultimately a *metaphysical* problem. The questioning of meaning raises the whole question of reality itself and in the end Parain is asking one thing above all: can language make sense if there is no God? In other words, what is the point of talking about truth and falsity if there is no God? Is not man, in that case, reduced to putting together a series of more or less arbitrary noises in the solitude of a mute world? Are these noises anything more than the signals of animals and birds? True, our noises exist in a very complex on-going context of development and are richly associated with one another and with other cultural phenomena: but can they be true? And does this matter? Or are they merely incidents in a developing adventure that will one day end in some kind of meaning but which, for the time being, has none?

Parain rejects this post-Hegelian position and returns to the classical ideas of language as able to provide grounds for at least elementary certitude. If language has no meaning then nothing has any meaning. Language has enough meaning, at least, to reassure us that we are not floating in a pure void. In other words, communication becomes possible, and with it community, once it is admitted that our words are capable of being true or false and that the decision is largely up to us. "To name a thing wrong is to add to the miseries of the world." We are thus called to take care of our language, and use it clearly. "The great task of man is not to serve the lie." These words of Parain might have been uttered—and have been uttered equivalently, many times—by Camus. And so Camus says in a review-article of Parain's books: "It is not altogether certain that our epoch has lacked gods: it seems on the contrary that what we need is a dictionary."

It is certainly true that the twentieth century has been distinguished for its single-minded adoration of political and cultural idols rather than for the clarity and honesty of its official speech. The sheer quantity of printed and broadcasted doubletalk overwhelms the lucid utterances of a few men like Camus.

But once again, Camus remains sober and un-idealistic. Our task is not suddenly to burst out into the dazzle of utter unadulterated truth but laboriously to reshape an accurate and honest language that will permit communication between men on all social and intellectual levels, instead of multiplying a Babel of esoteric and technical tongues which isolate men in their specialities.

> What characterizes our century is not so much that we have to rebuild our world as that we have to rethink it. This amounts to saying that we have to give it back its language. . . . The vocabularies that are proposed to us are of no use to us . . . and there is no point in a Byzantine exercise upon themes of grammar. We need a profound questioning which will not separate us from the sufferings of men. . . .

It is unfortunately true that the "Byzantine exercises" not only of logical positivism (which nevertheless has a certain limited value) but of all kinds of technical and specialized thinking, tend to remove us from the world in which others, and we ourselves, are plunged in the dangers and the sufferings of an increasingly absurd and unmanageable social situation. As Camus and Parain have seen, we have to *rethink* that whole situation and we no longer possess the language with which to do it.

Such a language will necessarily confine itself at first to formulating what is accessible to all men. But it will not talk down to them or cajole them. It will enable them to lift themselves up. Yet if the artist, the peasant, the scientist and the workman are all going to communicate together, their language will have to have a certain simplicity and austerity in order to be clear to them all without degrading thought. This means not the attainment of a pure classic prose (though Camus admits he thinks of a "new Classicism") but rather of a kind of "superior banality" which will consist in "returning to the words of everybody, but bringing to them the honesty that *is required for them to be purified of lies and hatred.*"

It is at this point that we can see what Camus is asking not only of intellectuals but also of the Church: this *purification and restitution of language so that the truth may become once again unambiguous and fully accessible to all men, especially when they need to know what to do.*

I think that everybody will readily admit that the language of the Church is distinguished by a "superior banality," but this is not the kind that Camus was talking about. We can certainly say that the Church speaks without hatred and that she does not lie. On the other hand, as we saw, it is quite possible for her to speak in such complex, unclear, evasive and bureaucratic language that her message is simply inaccessible even to a reader of some education and average patience. With a few outstanding exceptions, the clergy, Catholic thinkers, teachers, writers, too often speak so confusedly, so timidly, so obscurely, that even when they are telling the truth they manage to keep it out of circulation. In fact one sometimes wonders if some of the writers of official documents have not trained themselves to tell the truth in such a way that it will have no visible effect. Then one can say indeed that one has "told the truth" but nobody will have gotten excited or done anything about it!

After all, it was not Camus who said to the Church: "Go, teach all nations." And the teaching of the nations is not to be accomplished by the triumphant utterance of totally obscure generalities. It is not enough for us to be at once meticulously correct and absolutely uninteresting and unclear. Nor, when we have clarified our speech and livened it up a bit, can we be content that we have merely *declared* the truth, made it public, announced it to the world. Are we concerned merely to get others to *hear* us? We have a hearing. But how many of those that hear us, and understand what we are saying, are convinced? Perhaps we are satisfied with proving to them (and thereby to ourselves) that we are convinced. But the kind of rethinking that Camus— and the world—calls for demands not only the publication of official statements but the *common effort to arrive at new aspects of the truth,* in other words dialogue, community, not only among believers but between believers and unbelievers as well.

The whole truth of Albert Camus is centered upon the idea of *telling the truth.* The relation of words to the inscrutable presence of what he called the power of words to identify the absurd as such. The function of words in establishing community among men engaged in resisting and overcoming the absurd. The power of words to lead revolt in a creative and life-affirming direction. The power of words against murder, violence, tyranny, injustice, death. The novels, stories and essays of Camus explore this question from many angles, and everywhere they reach the conclusion: we live in a world of lies, which is therefore a world of violence and murder. We need to rebuild a world of peace. We cannot do this unless we can recover the language and think of peace.

The tragedy that is latent behind the fair and true declarations of the Church on peace, justice, renewal and all the rest is that these words of truth and hope are being devoured and swallowed up in the massive confusion and indifference of a *world that does not know how to think in terms of peace and justice because in practice the word peace means nothing but war and the word justice means nothing but trickery, bribery and oppression.*

Anything the Church may say to such a world is immediately translated into its opposite—if indeed the Churchmen themselves are not already beguiled by the same doubletalk as the world in which they live. To all of us, Camus is saying: "Not lying is more than just not dissimulating one's acts and intentions. *It is carrying them out and speaking them out in truth.*"